GRACE
PALEY

A Study of the Short Fiction

Twayne's Studies in Short Fiction

Gordon Weaver, General Editor
Oklahoma State University

In a women's Wall Street action, in 1984, Grace Paley's presence and words tell a succinct story for all who would or could hear.
Photograph by Dorothy Marder.

GRACE
PALEY

—————— *A Study of the Short Fiction* —

Neil D. Isaacs
University of Maryland

TWAYNE PUBLISHERS • BOSTON
A Division of G. K. Hall & Co.

Copyright 1990 by G. K. Hall & Co.
All rights reserved.
Published by Twayne Publishers
A Division of G. K. Hall & Co.
70 Lincoln Street, Boston, Massachusetts 02111

Twayne's Studies in Short Fiction Series, no. 13

Copyediting supervised by Barbara Sutton.
Book design and production by Janet Z. Reynolds.
Typeset in 10/12 Caslon by Compset, Inc.

Printed on permanent/durable acid-free paper
and bound in the United States of America.

First published 1990.
10 9 8 7 6 5 4 3 2 1

Library of Congress Cataloging-in-Publication Data

Isaacs, Neil David, 1931–
    Grace Paley : a study of the short fiction / Neil D. Isaacs.
        p.   cm.—(Twayne's studies in short fiction ; no. 13)
    Includes bibliographical references.
    ISBN 0-8057-8324-5 (alk. paper)
    1. Paley, Grace—Criticism and interpretation.   2. Short story.
I. Title. II. Series.
PS3566.A46Z7   1990
813'.54—dc20   89-77341
                                                                  CIP

Ellen, my love,
for all you are and do,
this book's for you.

Contents

Preface

That this book has been a labor of love will be clear throughout the pages that follow. Grace Paley's stories, from their first appearance through the most recent work, have aroused the affection of many readers and the admiration of many of Paley's fellow writers. I have been teaching Grace Paley's stories in short story courses for a quarter-century, and I take some delight in writing about stories I have never tired of reading and sharing with others. As a viewer of the contemporary scene from the perspective of cultural history and also as a person actively concerned about danger and disaster from neighborhood to planet, I admire the way Grace Paley's stories reflect her commitment to activism. And as a clinical social worker, I believe that I have grown to share the humanistic values her life and work enact. Other, less personal reasons for this undertaking may be inferred from the following commentary on the stories.

What Nabokov has called combinational magic and Henry James once diagnosed as the madness of art becomes in Paley's stories a gift, a benediction, of integrity. And it all seems so natural, this wholeness, this seamless entity of her writing, her private life, and her public life, with all the perpetuating commitments it entails. Her distinctive voice, almost always on the edge of laughter, may as easily bespeak an intimacy between grandmother and granddaughter as comment on a policy of international cultural revolution. She is the canny veteran of ironic experience and the wide-eyed discoverer of innocent wonderment. Yet the very naturalness is a product of slow, painstaking, meticulous craftwork. The commentator, then, is called on to relate both individual touches of her craft and characteristic touchstones of her art to the integrity of the whole. Ostensibly about her published stories, this book cannot help being about Grace Paley herself, the storytelling story hearer.

A primary incentive for this project is the fact that no thorough study of Paley's stories antedates it, and that element has significantly determined several aspects of my approach. Part 2, for example, assembles remarks made by Paley over a twenty-year period. The consistency of her vision of the nature and function of her writing, along with her appreciation of its place in her life and the world, is here demonstrated by the coherence and cohesion of these samples. In Part 3 I have undertaken to present a comprehensive account of the critical reception and treatment of her work so far. The survey is, I believe, complete; it is selective only in terms of emphasis.

Because no useful bibliography is available anywhere at this writing, I offer here a comprehensive listing, organized in such a way as to facilitate further study, according to the following scheme. First there is a publication history of the stories, arranged by collection in the order of their respective contents and including selected reprintings. A chronological listing of Paley's other writing follows. Then comes a list of published interviews. Selected reviews of each collection are grouped together, followed by a listing of review essays that include Paley. The critical commentary on Paley includes both exclusive studies and studies that group or pair her with others.

The main body of this study, in particular, has been determined by the nature of its subject. The stories themselves have dictated my treatment of them. Though Grace Paley's stories are occasionally meta-fictional, stories explicitly concerned with the subject of telling stories, the reader will find no "metacriticism" here. There is not even a consistency of critical approach, since the imposition of any one method could not grant equal consideration to each variety of her storytelling forms, not to mention the idiosyncratic nature of each story.

What I have done, then, is present a reading of Grace Paley's stories, all of them, one at a time. I have tried to locate each one in larger contexts of groups of stories, collections, and the whole corpus, but those connections are designed primarily to illuminate the workings of the story at hand. I have also tried to identify those common elements of subject and attitude, theme and motif, and device and image which make her storytelling voice unmistakably hers.

The mission may well be impossible—to account for a taste. But essentially that is the goal: to describe the stories in such a way as to account for how they achieve their effects, to identify what there is in a Grace Paley story that makes a devoted reader laugh or smile or recognize a truth, that causes a thump of the heart or a catch in the throat, that grants the thrill of epiphany or the pleasure of recognizing the familiar. There may be something grim or painful in associations with the beloved, but they are no less to be treasured.

Preface

Many people helped me with this project. I am grateful to Karl Bis-singer, Sheila Gilooly, Susan Gleason, Anne Isaacs, Philip Isaacs, Syl-via Lichtman, Alice Overton, Paula Roper, and George T. Wright for helping me track down certain elusive material. Geri Thoma of the Elaine Markson Agency was also helpful, and I thank her. Thanks, too, to Henry B. and Carolyn Parks for professionally monitoring my French. I am grateful to Anne Jones for her initial approval, to Liz Traynor Fowler for seeing the project through with her insightful dili-gence, and to Gordon Weaver for his invitation, his unfailingly con-structive criticism, and his good judgment.

Among people who have worked on Paley are several who gener-ously shared their time and efforts with me: Thank you, Judith Arcana, E. M. Broner, Marianne DeKoven, Frieda Gardner, Kathleen Hulley, Ruth Perry, Audrey Roberts, Thelma Shinn, and Jacqueline Taylor. It is unusual in my experience for a genuine community of scholars to emerge in a world where academic careerism inhibits cooperation; it is as if those who have studied Paley's work have identified with her values. For this and for many other blessings and kindnesses, I am very grateful to Grace herself.

The dedication barely suggests an enormous debt of lasting moment in my life. It seems appropriate here also to thank our children, Josh and Emmi, for their patience and consideration—especially measured in computer time—during these hectic months.

Neil D. Isaacs

University of Maryland

Acknowledgments

Excerpts from "Faith, Grace, and Love" by Clara Claiborne Park reprinted by permission from the *Hudson Review* 38, no. 3 (Autumn 1985): 482, 488. © 1985 by The Hudson Review, Inc.

Excerpts from "Fooling Around and Serious Business" by Roger Sale reprinted by permission from the *Hudson Review* 27, no. 4 (Winter 1974–75): 629–30, 635. © 1974 by The Hudson Review, Inc.

Excerpts from *Women Writers Talking*, ed. Janet Todd (New York: Holmes & Meier, 1983), 35–56, reprinted by permission of Holmes & Meier Publishers, Inc. © 1983 by Holmes & Meier.

Excerpts from "Chronicles and Chroniclers" by Blanche Gelfant reprinted by permission from the *Massachusetts Review* 16 (Winter 1975): 127–43. © 1975 The Massachusetts Review, Inc.

Permission is granted by Daniel Walden, editor, and Kent State University Press, for Dena Mandel, for reprinting excerpts from "Keeping Up with Faith: Grace Paley's Sturdy American Jewess," by Dena Mandel, *Studies in American Jewish Literature* 3 (1981): 85–98.

Excerpts from "To Aggravate the Conscience: Grace Paley's Loud Voice" by Rose Kamel reprinted by permission of the *Journal of Ethnic Studies* 11:3 (Fall 1983): 29–49.

Excerpts from Joan Lidoff, "Clearing Her Throat: An Interview with Grace Paley," *Shenandoah* 32, no. 2 (1981): 3–26, and from "A Symposium on Fiction," *Shenandoah* 27, no. 2 (1976): 3–31, reprinted from *Shenandoah*, the Washington and Lee University Review, with the permission of the editor. © 1981/1984 by Washington and Lee University.

Permission to quote from *Reaching Out: Sensitivity and Order in Recent American Fiction by Women* by Anne Z. Mickelson granted by Albert W. Daub, President of Scarecrow Press, Inc., on behalf of the late Anne Z. Mickelson.

Copyright © 1987 by Martha Satz. "Looking at Disparities: An Interview with Grace Paley" by Martha Satz excerpted by permission from *Southwest Review* 72 (1987): 478–89.

Excerpts from "Conversation with Grace Paley" by Leonard Michaels reprinted by permission from the *Threepenny Review*, no. 3 (Fall 1980): 4–6.

Excerpts from "An Interview with Grace Paley" by Maya Friedler reprinted by permission from *Story Quarterly* 13 (1981): 32–39.

Excerpts from "The Dirty Ladies: Earthy Writings of Contemporary American Women—Paley, Jong, Schor, and Lerman" by E. M. Broner reprinted from *Regionalism and the Female Imagination* 4 (Winter 1979): 34, 41, by permission of Susan Toth and E. M. Broner.

Excerpts from John Hawkes, "The Voice Project," and Grace Paley, "Some Notes on Teaching: Probably Spoken," in *Writers as Teachers/ Teachers as Writers* (New York: Holt, Rinehart & Winston, 1970) reprinted by permission of Jonathan Baumbach.

Excerpts from Jonathan Baumbach's "Life-Size" in the *Partisan Review* 42, no. 2 (1975): 303–6, and Marianne DeKoven's "Mrs. Hegel-Shtein's Tears" in the *Partisan Review* 48, no. 2 (1981): 217–23, are reprinted by permission of the *Partisan Review*. Permission also extended by Jonathan Baumbach and Marianne DeKoven.

Excerpts from "Grace Paley: Fragments for a Portrait in Collage" in *Women Writing in America: Voices in Collage* by Blanche H. Gelfant reprinted by permission of University Press of New England. © 1984 by Trustees of Dartmouth College.

Excerpts from "An Interview with Grace Paley" by Kathleen Hulley (*Delta* no. 14, May 1982) reprinted by permission of Kathleen Hulley.

Grateful acknowledgment is made to Grace Paley for permission to quote from her published works and interviews.

Part 1

THE SHORT FICTION

Introduction

Mr. Bons, a character in E. M. Forster's "Celestial Omnibus," says, "I believe we have seven Shelleys." A student of Grace Paley might go him at least two better. Nine biographies could treat her lives:[1] as mother, wife, daughter, sister, that is, as family person intimately involved within and across generations; as poet; as antiwar activist; as short story writer; as antinuclear activist and environmentalist; as teacher; as neighborhood organizer and agitator; as feminist; and as friend to those whose lives interact with hers in these several spheres. Because she is no common cat, I would add a tenth life—a shadowy one as a subject of an FBI file.[2]

Perhaps the greatest accomplishment of Paley the writer is that her stories, taken as a whole, encompass all those lives. Her corpus presents the substance of her worlds and the values of her worldview. And it is all woven seamlessly together, offered up with a generosity of spirit that mocks its modest packaging, wryly sentimental, compassionate and unforgiving, ironic and idealistic, satiric and hopeful, open-ended and etched-in-stone, traditional and experimental, funny and profound.

Almost all of Paley's fiction[3] has been collected in three volumes: *The Little Disturbances of Man* (1959), *Enormous Changes at the Last Minute* (1974), and *Later the Same Day* (1985).[4] The titles themselves are instructive, indicating not so much three "periods" in an artist's development as a shifting degree of emphasis on three elements that are constants in her work. The first title is ironic. The "little disturbances" are the major stressors in contemporary lives. In addition, since this collection addresses primarily the issues of women in their status of second-class citizenship, the "of man" cuts two ways: how little are men disturbed by sexist patterns of society and how little are women essentially diminished despite being much put upon.[5] The title focuses attention, then, on the *tonal* achievement of the collection.

The second title plays off the first, the word *enormous* ironically inverting *little*. But more significantly, the whole title draws attention to views of the world and of literature. The emphasis has become the-

3

matic, not in the sense of statements—political, philosophical, ethical—but in the dramatic play and interplay of ideas, of intellectual attitudes, in the stories. It is almost as if the characteristic tones had become a given of Paley's work so that awareness of characteristic topics, motifs, and the like—the very substance of the matters at hand— might emerge with greater clarity.

The third title, a cliché of narrative transition in which a thematic statement is embedded, draws immediate attention to technique, to craft, to tactics. The reference to a traditional device of structure is inherently ironic because Paley eschews all that, but her primary point is to redirect attention to the storytelling itself. From emphasis on a strategy of tone (*LDM*) or a rhetoric of substance (*ECLM*), the third collection moves to focus on the tactics of transmission.

Another way of looking at the progression through the three collections is to chart the evolution of self-reflexivity in Paley's work. This process seems doubly paradoxical. In one way, we may see a degree of self-consciousness in the self-effacement of the early stories' technique giving way to a self-assured openness in acknowledging the storytelling self's presence in the more recent work. In another way, the emergence of the "self," the narrator-persona who progressively pulls together more and more of the stories, is seen with increasing clarity as an imagined consciousness. The more the whole of Paley's experience and worldview are found in the stories, the less we can comfortably identify *her* as a *character* moving in that world. More biographically related fragments can perhaps be identified or inferred, but they are diffused among several characters and across a familiar yet wholly imagined terrain.

Faith, a character who appears in one way or another in roughly half of Paley's stories, is a key to understanding this process. It is both very easy and very wrong to identify Faith Asbury with Grace Paley. The character is based first on a particular friend of the writer and then on facets of several other friends, not to mention invented characteristics and experiences. Because many details relating to Faith come from Grace Paley's life and world, there are *similarities* between creating person and created persona, but Paley has always been careful to hint at or spell out the differences. Nevertheless, commentators frequently assume an identity, whether Faith in any given story is storyteller, story hearer, or bit player. As Faith has grown in importance in Paley's created world, the presumption of her identity with her author has also grown, and this factor has increasingly distorted some interpretations of the stories. Paley is keenly aware of the dangers, for reader and writer alike, of this confusion. Her remedy has been to expand the roles of others in Faith's world, especially Faith's friend Ruthy. Readers no doubt will continue to find Grace in Faith, but except in the sense that every character is derived from or part of the creator (just as every dreamed figure is the product of the dreamer), they do so at mortal risk of proper understanding.

Parts 2 and 3 of this study will show how interviewers, reviewers, critics, and commentators have generally approached Paley's work from one of a half-dozen perspectives: by way of her politics, her feminism, her social conscience (what I call a social-work perspective), her "poetics," her humor, her ethnic or regional focus. Each of these approaches has an intrinsic validity based on the presence of appropriate elements in individual stories.

The validity of approaching the work as a whole by adopting a consistent critical stance could also be argued, though the justification there is found more in the *reading* than in what is being *read*. My approach will be to allow the stories to dictate the shape of the commentary. While I will be concerned to observe contributions of individual pieces to the whole body of work, I hope always to respect the integrity of the stories, subordinating critical predilections to whatever seems useful on a case-by-case basis. In this way, it seems to me, my attitude toward criticism mirrors my subject's social-work perspective.

Issues of poetics—form, language, style, technical devices, and the like—are subordinated to my focus on Paley's often admired, occasionally described, but rarely analyzed use of language to achieve a genuinely original authorial voice. That idiosyncratic voice is more than a matter of distinctive style. I am reminded of what Whitney Balliett has said about George Shearing: "He does not have a style in the conventional sense. He has perfected a unique *sound*, a kind of handsome aural presence." Balliett goes on to delineate the elements of that sound—airborne tone, wit, harmonic sense, and rejection of clichés— and his description of Shearing may be aptly applied to Paley to suggest that as a literary performer she is no less than a great jazz artist, though in another context I have likened her to a great stand-up comedian.[6]

The concept of voice in literature subsumes such properties as cadence, tone, intonation, register, lilt, rhythm, pacing, timbre, resonance, volume, dialect, and diction. Since Paley's voice is unmistakable to so many readers, perhaps "voice" may be used to mark her achievement. John Hawkes, whose own literary voice has also often been identified as unique and distinctive, found it a constructive concept in the teaching of writing in "The Voice Project," to which he brought his experience not only as a writer but also as a student of acting and of criticism. Aside from being "the instrument of speech [voice] may be taken to mean the summation of style; but also in writing it may be taken to mean the whole presence of the writer-as-writer rather than the writer-as-man." It was hoped that students in the project would learn

> that the sound of [their] voice conveys something of [their] personality; that this personal intonation might well relate to the diction and rhythms of [their] writing; that a professional writer has a kind of total presence that can be perceived and responded to as authorial "voice"; that there is a difference between "voice" and style; that reading aloud is a way to achieve dramatic comprehension of literature as well as a better understanding of what may be happening in a student's own writing. To us, then, "voice" meant (1) personality as heard in speech, (2) the kind of understanding we are able to "hear" in the voice of someone reading aloud, (3) the author's presence that we "hear" when we read silently, and (4) the various roles we sometimes assume in writing.[7]

The experiences of reading Paley and hearing her read, it seems to me, would be ideal examples of these principles at work.[8]

Paley herself has acknowledged the significance of voice in her development as a storyteller. Until she could really hear the voices of others, she has often said, she could not tell stories, because storytellers must be story hearers first. A related observation she has frequently made is that her stories are the sounds she hears when two things (ideas, incidents, characters) bump into each other. Neither remark should be taken as equivalent to Flannery O'Connor's notion that "Actually, there is no such thing as the short-story form. A nutty phrase."[9] But Paley has gone on to say that she might have "the story of a story" in her head for a long time and might tell it over and over to friends before discovering a form (or having it revealed to her) to set it down as a "hard-written" story.

It is a matter, then, of finding *the* form for the story (a caseworker's eclecticism, again). In many cases, that discovery entails the bumping together of storyteller and story hearer, with the reverberations rippling outward to audience from the centered performer. The growing emphasis on self-reflexivity in Paley's work includes both explicit and implicit attention to that process, what we might call "technique as discovery of technique," if Mark Schorer hadn't preempted the phrase for a different process. Grace Paley's readers must make their own analogous discoveries, namely that comfortable assumptions—about form and format, structure and texture, narrator and persona—cannot be carried over from story to story with any confidence. In our own role as story hearers we must listen anew to every individual telling.

One other frequent remark of Paley's might helpfully guide our listening to her stories: "I went to school on poetry." What this reader hears most often, as the following commentary will point out, are echoes of the poetry of High Romanticism, especially of Keats and Shelley—ideas and attitudes as well as language and imagery. And the ability to effect a synthesis between that literary teaching/language and the spoken teaching/language of New York–American ethnics is another measure of Paley's extraordinary success as storytelling story hearer.

Finally, Paley has presented the student with a valuable guide that goes beyond her own spoken, written, quoted, or interpreted commentary: the evidence of the stories themselves, moving through their originally published versions in magazines to their collected presence in the books. I say "finally," but the process goes on, since Paley will often tinker with the "final" version for the purposes of subsequent readings. In any case, I have found it instructive to compare versions in order to draw inferences about the directions and redirections of particular stories.

The Little Disturbances of Man

In "Goodbye and Good Luck," Grace Paley's first published story and the one subsequently given primacy in *The Little Disturbances of Man*, her distinctive voice was first heard and her capacity for performance clearly established. By *performance*, I mean a particular type of short story, one that I have defined elsewhere: "The author adopts a character clearly removed, if not remote, from her own and delivers the entire presentation from that point of view, usually in the first person. As with the dramatic monologue perfected by Robert Browning, this technique in the short story requires a gift for consistent projection of attitudes and consistently appropriate language, and thus is frequently described as a tour de force."

One of the best-known and most admired stories of this type is Eudora Welty's "Why I Live at the P.O.," in which "it is the *sounds* that largely inform the story, especially those sounds that derive from speech patterns, regional idiom, and intonation. Speaking to an immediate audience, as in a dramatic monologue, Sister accounts for herself and, inadvertently, betrays herself. . . . The situation of the story is externalized and dramatized when the character delivers a kind of oral mime, acting out her situation in the telling of it."[10]

"Goodbye and Good Luck" seems not only to satisfy the terms of that definition but also to live up to the highest standards of that model. The narrator is Aunt Rose, her immediate audience is her niece Lillie, and the situation is her announcement that after a thirty-year affair she is finally going to marry Volodya Vlashkin, once known as "the Valentino of Second Avenue" (10).

Several times Rose addresses Lillie directly, at least twice responding to implied reactions on the part of her audience: "Don't laugh, you ignorant girl" (13) and "Nowadays I suppose it is easier, Lillie? My goodness, I ain't asking you nothing—touchy, touchy" (16). Beyond the audience of one stands another, her "little sister" (9), Lillie's mother, to whom she wants Lillie to report the happy and triumphant ending to her story. But it is equally clear that the real audience is both herself and the world at large to whom she intends to justify her life-

8

style and values. Indeed, rushing out to meet Vlashkin at the end, Aunt Rose even instructs Lillie on the proper "couple wishes on my wedding day. A long and happy life. Many years of love" (22).

One problem arises, however, in considering "Goodbye and Good Luck" as a performance, that is, short story qua dramatic monologue. It is suggested in the very first sentence—"I was popular in certain circles, says Aunt Rose" (9)—which is the only variation from consistent first-person narration *by* Rosie Lieber ("lover") in the story. Instead of an *implied* audience—like the Count's emissary to the Duke of Ferrara in Browning's "My Last Duchess" or the chance patron of the China Grove, Mississippi, post office in "Why I Live at the P.O."—with whom the reader may identify at once with absolute neutrality and on whom the reader may then project the appropriate emotional responses to the narration and the narrator, we now have an identification of the immediate audience with the *author* of the story.

In other words, Paley's persona is not Rose in a tour de force but Lillie in a strategic distancing of reader from situation. The question then becomes, echoing the title of another Welty performance story, "Where Is the Voice Coming From?" That question becomes a crucial issue in analyzing several of Paley's stories, as well as a general focus of analysis for her short story technique. An approach to an answer comes from rephrasing the question: How do we hear the voice? through what or whom? The stories, taken as a whole in generally chronological order, will move toward a more and more clearly explicit answer: The voices we hear are heard voices, the medium of communication being the story hearer.

Much admired and anthologized, "Goodbye and Good Luck" has attracted far more affectionate tribute than analysis. Kathleen Coppula suggests why, in calling Rose's narration an "old-fashioned story, . . . a tale to be retold, and there is a sense of living happily ever after, slightly tongue in cheek."[11] Saul Bellow selected it for his *Great Jewish Short Stories* and suggests another explanation:

> Laughter and trembling are so curiously mingled [in these stories] that it is not easy to determine the relations of the two. At times the laughter seems simply to restore the equilibrium of sanity; at times the figures of the story, or parable, appear to invite or encourage trembling with the secret aim of overcoming it by means of laughter. Aristophanes and Lucan do not hesitate to involve the Olympian gods in their fun, and Rabelais's humor does not spare the heavens

either. But these are different kinds of comic genius. Jewish humor is mysterious and eludes our efforts—even, in my opinion, the efforts of Sigmund Freud—to analyze it.[12]

Leonora Hornblow and Bennett Cerf, including the story in their *Take Along Treasury* in a section called "Other Loves," drew attention to Paley's reliance on a "direct, gravelly prose to tell [a story] full of compassion and feeling. *Goodbye and Good Luck* may not be a love story in the usual sense but the reader will find it an authentic one."[13]

One idiosyncratic reading of the story merits particular attention: the sympathetic treatment by Ruth Wisse in the "American Dreamer" chapter of her *The Schlemiel as Modern Hero*. After summarizing Rose's tale, Wisse concludes,

> Fat, romantic Rosie is played off against the flat, middle-class values of her sister, obviously to her own advantage. The energy of the monologue is the extension of her emotional nature which is her one and only asset. She loves Volodya because of the emotions he is able to arouse in his audiences, and she is satisfied with herself because by feeling, she too has lived. The story is soaked in irony, there being some distance between the monologist's interpretation of her actions and the reader's independent judgment. Yet Lillie, the silent witness, is with her Aunt, not her mother. . . . Objectively, Rosie's life is such a failure that her mother and normally settled sister bemoan her pitiable fate. By her pathetic insistence on a life of virtue once her lover is free. . . , she confirms that her values are in no way different from those of her family. Only her priorities are different, and these, in her own eyes, make Rosie the most fortunate "lieber" of all—fat, aging bride though she is. Actually, her romantic attachment is rewarded: albeit on the rebound, she does get her man.[14]

One of Wisse's perceptions is supported in a way she may not have known. Revising the story from magazine to book, Paley made only two substantive changes. One was to add an allusion to the grave as "a bed not so lonesome, *only crowded with a million bones*" (19; my emphasis on addition), a recurrent image in Paley. The other occurs in the reference to Rose's experience, when she was given the "pleasure" ("privilege" in the *Accent* version) of standing on stage in crowd scenes. Originally, she calls this "a special pleasure, to stand behind his back and hear him [Vlashkin] breathe."[15] But in the revised version, that phrasing is deleted and we hear her *account* for the pleasure, because it allowed her "to see like he saw every single night the hundreds of pale faces waiting for his feelings to make them laugh or bend down their heads in sorrow (13)." The difference is striking. Rose has been moved from being preoccupied with her feelings for Vlashkin to gratefully being able to see things through his eyes. In other words, Rose's development parallels that of Paley, who became a storyteller only when she could hear stories told to her and, speaking with the other's voice, see through the other's eyes.

In other ways, Wisse seems slightly off base. Rose's "emotional nature" is not "her one and only asset," her insistence is hardly "pathetic," and her fatness doesn't merit such emphasis except as a focus of Rose's wit, good nature, unselfconsciousness, and acceptance of her physical/emotional/experienced self. She is proud and happy even while self-deprecating. Moreover, Wisse should know better than to call her a schlemiel (if I may guess at her motivation, she may have wanted to include a discussion of a story by Paley, a writer she admires enough to put in lofty company). Rosie Lieber fails to match Wisse's own definition of *schlemiel:* "vulnerable, ineffectual in his efforts at self-advancement and self-preservation, . . . berated for his foolish weakness . . . exalted for his hard inner strength . . . the model of endurance, his innocence a shield against corruption, his absolute defenselessness the only guaranteed defense against the brutalizing potential of might" (4–5). That description should be complemented, in any case, by reference to Sanford Pinsker's *The Schlemiel as Metaphor,*[16] but in the case of Paley's first female narrator, we need only observe Rose's effectiveness and strength in standing up not only to her mother and sister, to other men, and ultimately to Vlashkin but to her garment-district forelady as well. Instead of ineffectual bumbling, we find lovable efficiency. And it needs to be urged without fear of giving offense: A woman cannot be a schlemiel, because the schlemiel's genesis, tradition, and heritage do not allow it.

Aunt Rose has lived her life her way. Her niece Lillie, the silent audience in the story, must be saying with us, "More power to her." In Paley's comic irony, the woman becomes independent, Americanized, modernized, and radicalized by moving away from her middle-class family and its values into the world of the Yiddish theater. Yet she trails those bourgeois values with her, like clouds of glory, and her triumph—marriage, security, propriety, happiness, love, creature comforts—is registered in the voice of her family, on precisely the grounds its members have always imposed. But the choice of weapons has been her own—good-natured wit and self-determined behavior—and those weapons carry the (wedding) day against the passive, lifeless endurance of the others. It is for Lillie, after all, that Aunt Rose performs, and while we may feel sorry or at least uncomfortable for the mother who isn't there to defend herself against the triumphant sister's well-aimed barbs, we are glad that Lillie has a choice of models and wish her well. However much Rose's apologia reveals about herself, her instructions extend to the whole of her audience.

One of Grace Paley's first three stories, "A Woman, Young and Old" grows directly out of the set of experiences that first gave impetus to her prose narratives: women alone, with or without families, in wartime. The narrator is the first of her precocious, worldwise, teenage women, into whose characters their own idiosyncratic speech breathes life. Josie, a month shy of her fourteenth birthday, is innocent only in the sense that she tells her tale totally without guile. That tale is structured in a characteristic way, beginning with a present-tense depiction and moving through a past-tense reporting of momentous events—an initiation rite of sorts—to a new present-tense picture of the revised state of affairs.

Initially there is a glimpse of three generations of women without men. Josie and her about-to-be-age-twelve sister Joanna live with their mother, Marvine, who "was born not too very long ago" (25). Their father has returned to France. Josie's "imagination-minded" (25) Grandma, who has named her sons Johnson, Revere, and Drummond, says, "Everyone's sons are like that. First grouchy, then gone" (29). Unfortunately Grandpa is still around, beating up members of the family, but we never see him in action because the story takes place at Josie's house, where Grandma spends a lot of time, along with Marvine's seventeen-year-old sister, Liz. The happiest time occurs in the kitchen, Josie cooking while Marvine prepares the French sauces, Joanna sitting on Grandma's lap. As Josie says later, Grandma, "always philosophical with the advantage of years" (39), appreciates the moment: "Women have been the pleasure and consolation of my entire life" (28).

When Aunt Liz appears, with her current boyfriend, Corporal Brownstar, contentment gives way to excitement. Josie's combination of childlike freshness and knowing opportunism is too much for Browny (as the title suggests, she is all woman, regardless of age). He is flustered and flattered, just a boy eager for affection and adulation, really, and when Lizzie acts out in jealous anger, he turns gratefully (and perhaps a touch spitefully) to accept Josie's proposal of marriage.

Her mother's sullenness—she has been the one most vocal in lamenting the absence of a man of her own—in turn enchants the next man Liz brings along ("I'm beginning to feel like a procurer," Liz says [39]). The only marriage the story celebrates is Marvine's. And Josie, who describes her life finally as "living . . . on a turnpike of discouragement" (40), having heard nothing from Browny after he flunks his Wasserman test but a single postcard with "an aerial view of Joplin, Mo." (equaling and recapitulating her mother's correspondence from her Frenchman), is nevertheless content with hearing the happy sounds from her mother's bedroom and with the new respect she has earned from her own kid sister since her engagement to Browny.

Josie, barely in her teens, has learned what all women are supposed to know: Men are forever disappointing, irresponsible, unreliable, foolish, and violent, but they're nice to have around with their life-charging energy. There's a bit of bravado in the narration. When Josie says about Grandpa beating her mother, "If anyone ever touched me, I'd reduce them to fall-out" (25), one is reminded of Flannery O'Connor's Mary Fortune Pitts in "A View of the Woods," who, beaten regularly by her father, regularly tells her grandfather, "Nobody's ever put a hand on me and if anybody did, I'd kill him."[17]

Yet the tone of the narration smacks less of denial than of acceptance. Still tender and romantic, Josie has constructed a set of mature defenses that will allow her to cope with "wars, deception, broken homes, all the irremediableness of modern life" (25), whether or not she accepts the theory that "it's all part of the violence in the atmosphere" (25). Survival is not all—no more than ripeness is—but women endure in the knowledge of the weakness of men and in the self-knowledge of their own weakness for men. They endure, and they know how to enjoy.

A meeting with an ex-husband is a recurrent motif in Paley's stories, appearing first in "The Pale Pink Roast." Most nearly like the traditionally constructed kind of story Paley typically shuns, it has nevertheless been cited frequently as an example of her method. "The Pale Pink Roast," a third-person story with a surprise ending, effectively conveys its meaning in action and imagery. Anna, the protagonist, is moving into a new apartment. She has been trying to reach Peter, her ex, to ask him to take their little daughter Judy for the weekend so that she can concentrate on the transition. But they meet, perhaps not really by chance, in the park.

All the action is seen through Anna's eyes, though she rarely comments directly on what she sees and we get only limited glimpses of her inner consciousness. What is typical of Paley is the way incident and character are carried by dialogue. What is atypical for this first collection is the relative volume of physical activity and the outdoor setting for much of the action. The story begins and ends with Peter seen outside in motion. Anna's spotting him in the park is followed by a father-daughter reunion, also presented in vigorous physical action. Peter goes to the apartment with Anna to help her settle in: He is "crazy about heavy work" (45). Even indoors the action is vigorous and fast paced. Peter loads records into cabinets, puts up Venetian blinds and curtains, stacks books in bookcases, repairs a bureau, shelves toys, and sweeps up debris. In short order he takes Anna to bed—she is "faint and leaden" (50) while he does the unbuttoning and presumably most of the other required activity—and quickly dresses afterward.

Only then does he—and the reader along with him—learn that Anna has remarried. The action is suddenly arrested: "Petey sat absolutely still" (51). Shocked and angry, disillusioned because he has expressed the wish for repeat performances "every now and then" (50), he asks Anna if her motive was "revenge" or "meanness." In tears now, she says, "I did it for love" (51). When she repeats it, convincingly, his cold look is replaced by a smile, and "embarrassed but happy" (52), he leaves and she watches him cavort out the door into the street.

It is difficult to understand why a critic like Rose Kamel gives Peter as an example of the "uneasy, sometimes predatory men [who] inhabit Paley's stories."[18] Anna's Petey is so easy, so comfortable in his own active body, that she finds him irresistible. And far from being predatory, he would not have "preyed" on Anna, we understand, had she told him the truth first. Even so careful a commentator as Anne Z. Mickelson has missed the point by overlooking the *indirect* effect of Paley's language. This story, she says, "with its reference to cannibals who, once tasting man, see him thereafter as 'the great pig, the pale pink roast' . . . , leaves no doubt concerning the woman's feelings about her former husband."[19] She goes on to contrast the $8.50 a week he sends Anna for child support to what he spends on vitamins, not realizing that Peter says that amount facetiously, as one would say "pound of flesh." Anna's memory of the cannibal image is triggered by Peter's direct request for admiration ("Look at me, what do you see?"[47]) and her spoken response is "Peter, Peter, pumpkin eater" (48, which he hears as reference to his health-food diet but which we, with Anna, extend to his inability to keep a wife).

Ronald Schleifer is another critic who takes this atypical story as representative of the "goal of Paley's storytelling." He cites the dialogue at the end of the story as offering "a sense of their whole married life together: how Peter is not able to notice what is happening right before him, but seeks instead to find the meaning and explanation of his experience. There is no symbolic significance in this ordinary conversation after lovemaking—Paley offers us no psychological analysis—the conversation is simply there, calling for interpretation rather than providing explanation."[20] Again, I would respond that the psychological analysis that Paley offers, through Anna's perception, is present in the language. One need only hear it and see it, because its explanation makes "interpretation" unnecessary.

"The Pale Pink Roast" is a song-and-dance routine. It is a musical number seen and heard through the instrument of Anna's consciousness. She sees Peter kicking, straddling, standing on his hands, and finally cartwheeling. No wonder she says she knows him, "theme and choreography" (44). She watches him hugging their daughter, after Judy leaps over a bench and lunges into his arms, and then dropping her to her "springy hind legs but [holding] onto one smooth front paw" (43–44): a father-daughter pas de deux. Friends hailed by Peter "soft-shoed it over" (45) to him. For musical accompaniment Peter sings "in tune" the first line of Cole Porter's "What Is This Thing Called Love?" (44), whistles a "dozen bars of Beethoven's Fifth Symphony" (47) when he sees the apartment, and whistles again "while he worked" (49), and when he suggests they make love he does so by way of a Rodgers and Hammerstein song title, "Shall we dance?" (50).

The central image in the whole pattern occurs early in the park scene: Peter, turning into a silence between himself and Anna, sings "like a summer bird, 'We danced around the Maypole, the Maypole, the Maypole'" (44). The Maypole is a recurrent image for Paley, but at this first occurrence it is exposed in blatant irony. Peter, the penis, the Maypole, is dancing around himself, singing the praises of his physical self. In this context, by which I mean the story and its over-whelmingly dominant pattern of song-and-dance imagery, the image of the cannibal that flashes through Anna's mind is actually of man devouring himself.

In "about the third flush of youth" (43), Peter is perfectly happy to nourish himself in admiration of his physicality. Instantly refreshed by sex with Anna, rewarded for his physical efforts on her behalf (less hunter than gatherer), he need only have his self-esteem reinforced by her emotional reaffirmation of love to be able to carry on his self-celebration. His handstand and cartwheel, as Anna sees it, are ritual reenactments of his penis-centric dance around his totem of ego. The pig,

15

chauvinist, has little to do with Anna's perception. Peter is the pink reflection of the full-bodied sanguinity he imagines himself to be.

Early on, Philip Roth singled out "An Interest in Life" as Grace Paley "at her best . . . displaying an understanding of loneliness, lust, selfishness, and fatigue that is splendidly comic and unladylike." Jonathan Baumbach went further, fourteen years later, calling it "probably the best piece" in *The Little Disturbances of Man* and "one of the best American stories of the past twenty-five years." Its achievement, he says, is "to bring us, unburdened by melodrama, to an awareness of the character as if someone known to us intimately for a long time." In general, "Paley's comic stories deal in exaggerated understatement, disguise their considerable ambition in the modesty of wit"; in this story in particular, the "matter-of-fact, ironic voice of the protagonist, Ginny, distances the reader from the conventions of her pathos [and] makes light of easy sentiment."[21]

The instrument of achievement is that voice. Through it are projected not only the articulated environment and its social components but also a fully realized set of attitudes and values produced thereby and therein. Diane Cousineau listens to that voice and hears statements of feminist theses: "Sexual experience fails to provide Paley's women with that experience of unity which will belie their deep sense of fragmentation and loss. They know that man's gift will not fulfill their longings for wholeness, for it is rooted in irony and ambiguity."[22] Thelma Shinn, on the other hand, hears "an advertisement for the feminine mystique, and we have to remind ourselves that it is written by a woman." Shinn locates the irony in Virginia's situation, not in her telling voice: "Hers is the contentment of the circumscribed life; it can only be maintained as long as she is exposed neither to the mainstream of her society nor to the failure of her support systems. . . . That the mystique can be best maintained only in a dependent subculture reveals how hopelessly impractical it is for modern woman." Shinn describes the world of Paley's stories as a matrilineal or at least matrilocal American subculture: "Women may not own the houses . . . , but they do hold them, while the men do come and go; and childraising is obviously the woman's exclusive responsibility, as is the household governance."[23] Shinn's sociological description may be closer to Paley's creation than Cousineau's political labeling, but neither the latter's sense of "painful" irony nor the former's assessment of Virginia's "blithe acceptance of life" seems to do justice to the idiosyncratic quality of that narrator's voice. When in *Enormous Changes at the Last Minute* Paley retells this story from the vantage of another character, that quality becomes clearer while the generalizations recede.

Virginia's narration follows a logic of her own, so that the chronology loops and dissolves without the slightest sacrifice of coherence. She is telling us how she got to where she is and how she understands the meaning of it all. Along the way she is completely candid about what she sees and hears and those she encounters, unapologetic and unforgiving about her own feelings and behavior. She begins with the trauma of desertion and ends in a dreamlike reverie of homecoming. The middle is a story of travail and accommodation with, at its heart, the scene that gives the whole collection its name.

Her husband leaves her just before Christmas, going to the army, he says, and giving her a parting gift of a new broom with a fancy dustpan. Cousineau calls it "an unconsciously mean present, a present that simultaneously speaks his absence and affirms his presence" (60). But Virginia herself knows better: "No one can tell me it was meant kindly" (81). One may dismiss suggestions that associate the broom with witches or phalli, since her husband's accompanying message— "A new broom sweeps clean" (96)—tells her all she needs to know. He has been harping on the mess and the stink of their three-room apartment ever since her mid-March announcement of pregnancy. It is too much for him; they already have two boys, four and three, and a five-month-old baby girl. All this motivation—his growing alienation; his mounting annoyance, agitation, and frustration; his crescendo of complaints about her size and slovenliness throughout the pregnancy—is provided much later, during her courtship by John. She shares the information with the audience, not with John; she would never betray her husband to John in this way.

At the start, the scene of the desertion is interrupted by an encounter with Mrs. Raftery, who has instructions for every occasion for anyone who will listen. Enjoying a good cry as much as her wine, Mrs. Raftery tells Virginia about the death of a neighbor and exactly how to behave during the condolence call at home and the viewing in church. After Virginia's husband "skip[s] off into the future," Mrs. Raftery has two sets of wisdom to share: how to deal with the welfare system and to "look around for comfort" (84). In time, Virginia heeds both pieces of advice, Paley's satiric treatment of the welfare system giving way to the irony that comfort comes in the form of Mrs. Raftery's only son, John. Virginia sees her young children getting out of control and her own "face . . . curling up to die" (87) when John, sent upstairs during his regular Thursday visit to his mother, comes to Virginia's rescue. He had once wanted to marry Ginny, had been scared off by his mother's reaction, and had moved to New Jersey and acquired a wife and family of his own and a good name in the building trades.

On the third Thursday upstairs, John offers "to place his immortal soul in peril to comfort" her (90). She has three reasons for refusing: (a) she knows he is a good, devout man who "would in the end pay terrible penance and ruin his long life" and she doesn't want that "responsibility on" her; (b) the baby might wake, wander in, and see a "vision" to "affect a kid for life"; and (c) everyone in the building is too nosy (90). But John keeps coming, bearing gifts, so that the children rely on his visits as much as Ginny does. He deals with their problems so satisfactorily that she tells him he "should've been a social worker" (92)—one of Paley's most direct statements of her preference for social-work measures, as opposed to the bureaucracy of Social Services.

At this plateau of relative calm in the story, Virginia ruminates on what her life has taught her:

> Once I met my husband with his winking looks, he was my only interest. Wild as I had been with John and others, I turned all my wildness over to him and then there was no question in my mind.
>
> Still, face facts, if my husband didn't budge on in life, it was my fault. On me, as they say, be it. I greeted the morn with a song. I had a hello for everyone but the landlord. . . .
>
> But for his own comfort, he should have done better lifewise and moneywise. I was happy, but I am now in possession of knowledge that this is wrong. Happiness isn't so bad for a woman. She gets fatter, she gets older, she could lie down, nuzzling a regiment of men and little kids, she could just die of the pleasure. But men are different, they have to own money, or they have to be famous, or everybody on the block has to look up to them from the cellar stairs.
>
> A woman counts her children and acts snotty, like she invented life, but men *must* do well in the world. I know that men are not fooled by being happy. (93–94)

What must be made perfectly plain is that this is neither Paley playing Margaret Mead in observing a whole population nor Paley playing Betty Friedan in politicking for change. It is Virginia, speaking out of her own experience, absolutely in character, with never a wrong note.

From this vantage, now, she can let us in on those final months of her marriage. But she has much yet to learn about herself and life.

Two Thursdays ("Johndays," the children say [97]), John doesn't appear, and as Virginia sits crying in the kitchen, she suddenly decides to go on "Strike It Rich." The bitterness begins to recede as she contemplates her list of troubles, realizing, "All that is really necessary for survival of the fittest, it seems, is an interest in life, good, bad, or peculiar" (98). Now John arrives, confessing that he can't go on with things as they are. Ginny, "looking at it from his man point of view" (98) and thinking about her life with "strongest consideration" to the kids, decides that, "given the choice" she'd "choose not to live without him" (99).

John sees her list and dashes her hopes for a TV appearance: "In addition to all of this—the little disturbances of man—[those people] *suffer.* They live in the forefront of tornadoes, their lives are washed off by floods—catastrophes of God" (99). Virginia sadly accepts these words and contentedly acts on the earlier decision; they become lovers. John learns to accommodate his conscience, Mrs. Raftery hypocritically approves (her son's visits, at least to the house, are assured, and the slight to his New Jersey wife is relished), and Ginny, behaving as carefully as she knows how with him, envisions her husband's eventual return. The story ends in her fantasy renewal of their powerful sexual attraction: "On that polka-dotted linoleum, he got onto me right where we were, and the truth is, we were so happy, we forgot the precautions" (101).[24] The audience is not called on to extrapolate philosophy, morality, or code from Virginia's thinking, behavior, and experience. What we do, though, basically, is what she does, that is, learn to accept the selfhood of the other (which is, in fact, what has enabled Paley to tell her story) as a possible way to self-acceptance. And we applaud Paley's full realization of our neighbor Ginny.

Charles C. Charley is the most likable of Paley's male narrating personae, but the other male figures in the tale Charley recounts in "An Irrevocable Diameter" fare poorly. The women, for that matter, are hardly objects of admiration, though the narrator is gracious, forgiving, and accepting. That archetypal patriarchal institution of our society, the law, is the most ridiculous figure of them all. Despite the robes and the blinded female symbol of justice, the court operates as paternalistic enforcer in rituals of aggressive competition, and—as "An Irrevocable Diameter" succinctly shows—can be made to look foolish by such simple virtues as truth, absence of rancor, and passive resignation.

There is no clear evidence of a particular audience implied in Charley's narration, but his language sometimes echoes judicial phrasing ("I, Charles C. Charley" [105]; "if it may be sworn" [107]) and therefore suggests a setting down of testimony, an affidavit, to be used at some future time of reckoning. Charley's free-flowing wit, however, echoes a variety of sources, so that any inferences must be tentatively drawn. This is a man, after all, who, in describing his response to Cindy, says "little factories of admiration had started to hum" (108); who thinks to lie about his age "quick as nighttime in the tropics" (106); and who is reading Eileen Powers's book, *Medieval People*, an approach to social history by way of the lives of ordinary people, when Cindy calls with the news that will change his life.

The plot is a familiar one, that of a man trapped into marriage with an underage bride rather than face prison for statutory rape. But Charles not only pleads guilty; he consoles himself with the prospect of "a period of self-revelation under spartan circumstances" (116) with thoughts of fate, God, and Nehru. It is not that he considers marriage to Cindy a fate worse than jail but that he is willing to accept whatever life has in store for him. And so he accepts the marriage—not gratefully but gracefully—because it is the solution that least upsets the most people.

The macho bombast of Cindy's father is a caricature, as are the lesser roles of the mothers of bride and groom, and the whole trial scene is a cartoon of legal proceedings. That it is a political cartoon is made clear in the final settlement, which includes a good home in the upscale neighborhood and an upgrading of Charley's business into a first-class appliance franchise "obtained right out from under the nose of a man" who had labored thirty years to get it (123). This is the only story in the collection to take place in the suburbs (what Eddie Teitelbaum, a character we have yet to meet, calls "superbia" [151]), and as a product of that social setting Cindy is a willful, spoiled-brat indictment of its values and life-styles. Still, her husband speaks kindly of her. As a narrator and an actor bridging the stages of a generation gap, he is optimistic about her future, though he concludes that he will not share it.

Passive and accepting as Charley is—the story could be called "Zen and the Art of Air-Conditioning Maintenance"—there is no false modesty about him. His charm and openness, his ability to make a smiling best if not jest of everything, are admirable. But what he admires most about himself, "breathless with self-respect" (119), is his silence regarding the truth of Cindy's sexual experience before she met him. Charles C. Charley accepts his nature as just one irrevocable diameter of "the Great Circle of Life" who is also "just tangent" to it in his meditation upon it (121). In geometric terms this is an apparent paradox, but as actor and narrator he both passes through the center of existence (experiencing life egocentrically through his senses) and touches it only at a single point from the outside (distanced, viewing it intellectually, yet from an idiosyncratic angle or bias). The title, then, is a metaphorical reference to the paradox of all first-person narration.

Once again, in "The Loudest Voice," the play of verb tenses locates us in a space-time setting and informs us about the context of a first-person narration. "My voice is the loudest" (55) ends the first paragraph, and "My voice was certainly the loudest" (63) ends the story. At first the narrator, Shirley Abramowitz, introduces us to the scene that lives perpetually in her memory—"There is a certain place where dumb-waiters boom" (55)—that is, her tenement world with the old brick school around the corner. Then when we are there with her, she walks us through an episode she lived through there. But twice along the way she stops to remind us of the distancing of time—once by praying for the soul of her mother, very much alive in the historical narration, and again by thanking her father for the kindness of his estimation of and accurate prophecy for her.[25]

The plot itself is barely more than a skit. For the school's Christmas play, Shirley, who not only has the loudest voice but also reads with expression, gets the star role of narrator. Most of the major parts in the pantomime are also played by Jewish children. There is debate among parents concerning the propriety of all this, but there is great satisfaction in the narrator's performance. The mothers tend to question, on principle, the idea of casting Jewish children in the Christmas play, while the fathers are proud of their children's accomplishments, implying steps toward assimilation. Shirley's father jokes with the mother of the girl who plays Mary: "How's the virgin?" (62) but the secularization or socialization of religious ritual seems important to him.

The eternally surviving voice dominates the action and gives it its significance. The richness of the story is in its texture, not its structure, but it is worth observing that the play-within-a-story, in which Shirley as Jesus narrates the story of his life and crucifixion while the other kids act it out, is a cameo of the story's design, in which Shirley narrates an episode from her early life while the audience sees it played out on the page. The language of the play's first line underscores the mirrored structure: "I remember, I remember, the house where I was born" (61). Shirley's voice is the "remembering tongue" (62) of the play's Jesus and the projecting, projected instrument of the whole story.

Some confusion has occurred about the tone of "The Loudest Voice." Irving Malin and Irwin Stark refer to the theme of exile as taking a comic turn and conclude that Shirley "ironically . . . experiences a sense of pity for all the poor 'lonely' Christians." And Allen Guttmann, appropriately discussing the story in the context of the acculturation of American Jews, also notes that Shirley "feels sorry that the Christian children did not play important roles" and "goes to sleep—with a prayer for the 'lonesome Christians.' "[26] But it is a proud and happy Shirley who sleeps the sleep of just rewards, of rave reviews, at the story's end. She has "prayed for everybody" (63), *even* passersby and lonesome Christians, believing in the efficacy of *her* prayer by virtue of the volume of the voice that utters it. Self-satisfaction is the tone, condescension the attitude, as when she tosses "a kiss of tolerance" with both hands at the corner tree decorated with Christmas lights, since in this neighborhood, "poor thing, it was a stranger in Egypt" (60). Augie March says, "First to knock, first admitted," announcing both his rationale and his way of going at things. Five years after Bellow's rogue-hero's roar, in Shirley Abramowitz's voice, Grace Paley lets us hear that knocking and experience the feel of the world in which it reverberates. The memory speaks but briefly, but it breathes life into a faded world more effectively than the long-winded, repetitious droning of Bellow's insistent intellectualizing.

"The Contest," Paley's first completed short story, is a very nearly fully realized dramatic monologue, lacking only a specific audience and a context for the narration. Freddy Sims, who is telling the tale of his relationship with Dotty Wasserman and the "Jews in the News" contest they won together, is offering an *apologia pro vita sua*. But his rationalizations are betrayed by his tone, his language, and his self-satisfied, self-pitying, self-indulgent values. His narcissism, in other words, reflects back on him an image of self-destroying, alienating male ego. Seeking sympathy, he evokes contempt; however, Paley's performance is too funny to be mean.

Paley says the story chronicles her attempt to understand what makes guys like this tick.[27] What she has come up with is a study in self-deception. Freddy professes to "like girls" (67) and believes what he says. Yet for all his talk of "slim and tender or really stacked, dark brown at their centers, smeared by time" (67), he expresses hostility for his sister, his mother, and every other particular female he encounters. Even Dotty—or especially Dotty—whom he describes as a type made familiar through later generations of J(ewish) A(merican) P(rincess) jokes.

Given Dotty's relationship with her mother and the way Freddy construes her values and attitudes, "The Contest" may be read as an ironic mirroring of Muriel, her mother, and Seymour Glass in Salinger's "A Perfect Day for Bananafish."[28] But it is Freddy who is dehumanized by narcissistic, creature-comforted indolence and Dotty who enunciates an everlasting refusal to be compromised. More power to Dotty Wasserman. No wonder she turns up in a later story as an object of love. She is affectionate and practical, romantic and resilient, strategic and principled. Her campaign for Freddy's hand and soul is determined, even admirable, but when the final prize proves unclaimable, Dotty, having made the best of things all along, cuts her losses and moves on.

The contest that gives the story its name (though it surely refers, more broadly, to the battle of the sexes) is a gimmick serving several purposes. In its own right it provides a vehicle for comic playfulness. Structurally it provides an ongoing sequence of action with complication, suspense, climax, and resolution. Thematically it provides contrasting models: for Dotty's view of teamwork (togetherness), reasonable expectations and tangible reward and for Freddy's demonstration of superior wit and above-it-all cool. And its inherent satiric component provides windows of ironic opportunity, through which Freddy affronts the world and the world recognizes Freddy.

Freddy's final message to Dotty—"This is your *last* chance" (77)— is the summary irony of the story. It is Dotty who is Freddy's last chance, and by now we know that he can't take that chance, because he basically cannot accept Dotty's acceptance of (and hopes for redeeming) him. He has the Groucho Marx/Woody Allen syndrome of not wanting to join a club that would accept his membership. A womanizer who hates women ("the hideous examples of your mother and all the mothers before her" [77]), a heartless Jewish anti-Semite, Freddy fronts his essential self-loathing with contempt for others and their values. His carefully articulated value statement reveals an absence of values, and when he is left, in the story's last line, with "nothing at all" (78), we have removed that ironic tongue in cheek as he tastes the ashes of tongue-of-arrow poetic justice. Nothing more from

23

Dotty means nothing left for Freddy. Attempting to project his "guilt" (76) and "unconscionable behavior" (77) onto her, he confirms his own lonely, alienated fate.

In the months between its publication in *Accent* and the appearance of the book, Paley made a few slight changes in "The Contest." One is the addition of the phrase *of my old-fashioned window* (67) to the description of Freddy's house in the storm scene of his first encounter with Dotty. That Freddy's view of the world is outmoded may be obvious to present readers, but in the context of no-so-ancient social history this detail is telling. The major emendation, though, is the insertion of a new paragraph spelling out Freddy's preoccupation while Dotty tours Israel and three European capitals: "The lean-shanked girls had been brought to New York by tractor and they were going straight up too, through the purgatory of man's avarice to Whore's Heaven, the Palace of Possessions (76)." Perhaps the harshest indictment in the story and the bitterest inversion of an allegorical model of morality, the passage may have originated in Paley's feeling that it was necessary to underscore the valueless venality of Freddy's attitudes. There may have been too many laughs in the story or it may have seemed too comfortable an accounting for too many men, but for whatever reason Paley seems to have slapped on a ham-handed appendage to an otherwise deft piece of karate chopping.

The "Two Short Sad Stories from a Long and Happy Life," "The Used-Boy Raisers" and "A Subject of Childhood," mark the first appearance of Faith, a character who shows up in six stories in the second collection (narrating four of them in the first person) and ten in the third (narrating six). Perhaps equally important, those two stories make up the first of Paley's diptychs, pairings of stories that stand independently but take on more complete significance, to fuller effect, in conjunction with each other.

Dena Mandel refers to them as "two stories which bear [a] collective title" but goes on to treat them separately.[29] Kamel calls them "companion pieces" but treats them separately anyway (34). Coppula joins them in a single paragraph, suggesting that though they both "have a resolution or sense of closure, the endings are more like the end of a visit or the end of a day." She concludes, "If, as readers, we are left with a heaviness or a desire to sigh at the end of these two episodes, Paley offers release in the knowledge that for the character Faith, this is but a small portion of her 'long and happy life'"(64).

It should hardly be surprising that a writer whose idea of storytelling is to wait until she hears two things—incidents, characters, scenes, and so on—"bumping into each other" before she has a story to tell should use the diptych form. Three pairs in *Enormous Changes at the Last Minute* and perhaps one more in *Later the Same Day* can be considered in this way (and, arguably, a threesome in each as well), yet only this initial pair from *The Little Disturbances of Man*, joined together by more than a joint title, was so designed.[30]

Both these stories address Faith's relationships with men, with ex-husband and husband, called Livid and Pallid (the epithets extend the title image from "Pale Pink Roast"), in "The Used-Boy Raisers" and with a lover called Clifford in "A Subject of Childhood." But though the action of the stories has in their foreground the comings and goings of the men in Faith's life, the real focus is on the constant background of her relationship with her children. This point is reminiscent of Auden's commentary on Breughel's Icarus in "Musée Des Beaux Arts": However dramatic or traumatic the man's feat or fall is, life goes on with hardly a skipped beat "and the torturer's horse / Scratches its innocent behind on a tree."

Perhaps that is why the two parts are told in reverse chronology. In "The Used-Boy Raisers" the men exchange macho posturings, saving face with each other in the process of teaming up to put Faith down. These pale-faced Tweedledum and Tweedledee were both raised as Catholics, and when they argue about what they have taken with them from the church they left ("faith" for Pallid, who recommends parochial schools, and a "unifying memory out of childhood" for Livid, who threatens violence at the idea of the boys going near "that church" [131]), Faith is eventually confronted about her own version of Judaism.

Her statement, which interrupts her embroidery of a traditional American God-Bless-Our-Home pattern, is actually a refusal to participate in the men's dispute, which she dismisses as "your little dish of lava" (131). Her furious restatement of "opinions" they both know "perfectly well" moves away from the issues of their dispute. Faith's notion of the secular value in being Jewish; her anti-Zionist view that the Diaspora serves a useful, humanistic function; her statement that Jews "aren't meant for geographies but for history . . . not supposed to take up space but to continue in time" (132)—all these things may coincide with Paley's own views, but in context that is not the point.

25

What Faith does is to defuse and diffuse the dispute, redirect the discussion, and dismiss the men—all without their being aware of it. And their views of the children's development—distanced, intellectualized, and self-serving—are dismissed as well. These "clean and neat, rather attractive, shiny men" are sent off to "the grand affairs of the day ahead of them . . . in pride on paths which are not [Faith's] concern" (134), while she straightens up her home and "organize[s] the greedy day; dinosaurs in the morning, park in the afternoon, peanut butter in between, and at the end of it all, to reward us for a week of beans endured, a noble rib roast with little onions, dumplings, and pink applesauce" (134).

"A Subject of Childhood" flashes back to another Saturday morning two years earlier. Clifford, mentioned in passing by Livid in the other story, is the between-marriages resident male. He overplays his role, his roughhousing with the boys predictably[31] ending in injury, anger, and tears for all concerned. Faith gets the boys—clutching one another's thumbs in the image of "love that myth or legend has imposed on brothers" (138)—to take a nap and returns to deal with Clifford's wounded vanity. What he does, this "gentle person, a consortment of sweet dispositions" (140), is to blame her. The kids, in his rationalization, have ruined the relationship, and his criticism of Faith's parenting is a Parthian shot.

Faith wants to give him every opportunity to retract. Slow to accept the termination of their relationship, she takes time to assert, for the reader, "a compendium of motivations and griefs, life to date" (139). She begins with a brief statement of her Monday-to-Friday, on-the-job success, and there follows an abstract of her single parenting, worth citing substantially:

> On Saturday mornings in my own home . . . I face the sociological law called the Obtrusion of the Incontrovertibles. For I have raised these kids, with one hand typing behind my back to earn a living. I have raised them all alone without a father to identify themselves with in the bathroom. Laugh. I was forced by inclement management into a yellow-dog contract with Bohemia, such as it survives. I have stuck by it despite the encroachments of kind relatives who offer ski pants, piano lessons, tickets to the rodeo. Meanwhile I have serviced Richard and Tonto, taught them to keep clean and hold an open heart on the subjects of childhood. We have in fact risen mightily from toilets in the hall and scavenging in great cardboard boxes

at the Salvation Army for underwear and socks. It has been my per-
versity to do this alone. (139)

When Clifford persists in his view that she has done a "rotten job"
(138) with the kids, a "lousy" job, a "stinking" one (139), Faith, armed
with justified and righteous anger, launches an ashtray missile at his
head, slicing an earlobe. His departure, as we know from "The Used-
Boy Raisers," is terminal, but Faith is not left alone. She barely has
time to ask herself "the sapping question: What is man that woman
lies down to adore him?" (143). As Kamel suggests, that is more than
a rhetorical question (34). It carries the concreteness of visual imagery
and the thematic implications of Faith's (here equivalent to Paley's)
quest for understanding the other.

But her jesting life does not stay for an answer: "At the very question
mark Tonto came softly, sneaky in socks" (143). Refusing every argument and plea of his mother to be alone, even for a couple of minutes,
Tonto climbs into her lap, forming a living statue of a *Pietà*, assuring
her of his love and the permanence of his place right next to her.

The closing image, singled out by both Kamel (38) and Mandel (91)
for special attention, poignantly expresses the pleasure/pain in the life
sentence of their connection: "The sun in its course emerged from
among the water towers of downtown office buildings and suddenly
shone white and bright on me. Then through the short fat fingers of
my son, interred forever, like a black and white barred king in Alcatraz,
my heart lit up in stripes" (145).

One of only two stories in *The Little Disturbances of Man* without a
first-person narrator, "In Time Which Made a Monkey of Us All"
nevertheless leaves no doubt about its narrative voice or, for that matter, about the listener's role in the narrating context. The whole narrative—it is the longest in the collection—is framed by two paragraphs
in present tense. In these paragraphs the storyteller directs the attention of her audience to a pair of snapshots from life, candid stills but
full of suggestions of movement like the best "decisive moments" of
all action photography, less a matter of stop-action than of tableaux that
prompt and initiate and then conclude (before a fade to black) the
momentous action of the tale.

That first paragraph introduces if not all the explicit ironies of the
story then at least the ironic mode of its presentation, including the
polysemantic language, multiple frames of reference, and directly playful paradox. Look at this still shot, the narrative voice says to an im-

plied "you," and proceeds to identify the protagonist first by what he is *doing:* dredging, twitching, sniffing, snarling, and swallowing. But his observed actions do no justice to his heroic nature, as we are told what he *is:* "knee-deep . . . in man's inhumanity" (149), reconciled to his relationship with his father and his pet monkey, resigned to his place in the tenement world, and a knowledgeable citizen of that world. "For the present," the narrator teases her audience at the paragraph's end, "no names" (149).

The term *present* refers to the grammatical tense of this opening shot, as well as to the time before the beginning of the story's action. And *no names* refers to a presumed confidentiality of the storytelling context, as well as to the subservience of other characters to the already-seen star. But the irony is deeper than that, because of all the names already uttered: Eddie Teitelbaum, the hero (the unintentional Edward Teller of the Stink Bomb, perhaps "devil-tree" or deviltry, as suggested by the Yiddish echo of the German *teufel*);[32] Fudgsicle (the brand name pinpointing a time-space reality); Itzik Halbfunt, the pet monkey (whose first name is Yiddishized Hebrew for "laughter," the name of Abraham's son offered up to God to confirm the covenant with the chosen ones, and whose last name is a typical Yiddish pormanteau combining the German *halbpfund*, "half pound," with the American slang "half-pint," an affectionately insulting diminutive); and Utrillo (evoking the urban scene of the paragraph picture and initiating a series of references to Paris). Moreover, Itzik is called a "hair-shirted Jacob" (149) to Eddie's father, shifting generations in biblical chronology to make Isaac the son of Isaac, the one who steals the birthright of his brother Esau the hunter by disguising his hairlessness. Clearly, Eddie is no Esau, his principle being to limit hunting of all species to necessary food, and the "Jacob" is the naturally hairy "son"; nevertheless, for both Eddie and his father, Itzik is the hair shirt that signifies self-affliction, sacrifice of creature comforts, and humiliation before higher powers. Finally, there is the namelessness of the setting, the house known simply by its number, 1434, with no reference to street, never mind crossing avenue. If this factor alone does not suggest dehumanizing in general and the destruction of identities by numbering inmates of prisons or tattooing concentration camp detainees, then that allusion becomes clarified in subsequent references to the camps, the Holocaust, and psychological/historical issues of identities.

I have indulged so elaborately in details of one paragraph not so much to take issue with aspects of the interpretation of Adam J. Sorkin, whose essay is commendable as one of the few to undertake analysis of a particular Paley story against the backdrop of the whole corpus,[33] but to demonstrate against the repeated critical disclaimer that inhibits such analysis. Paley's individual works are at least as susceptible to and worthy of explication and discussion—of whatever critical stripe—as those of any other major writer.

Sorkin identifies the themes of this story as "talk, art, laughter, and hope as man's triumph over his silent fate in time" (148)—a bringing together of the central concerns in the book. Such a reading resonates with a generally prevailing attitude of the collection but does little justice to the wealth of specific concerns in this story. Among its explicit subjects are segregation versus integration, the dangers of technological advancement without ethical considerations, ecology, the Holocaust, adolescent sexuality, psychotherapy versus mental health, nuclear destruction, animal rights, and—in a multitude of forms—politics. And into its texture are woven many topoi, including scatological humor, classical hubris ("I am the vena cava and the aorta" [158]), footnoted references à la Borges or Nabokov to imagined texts, Orwellian Newspeak (nourish = suffocate), fashions in the art world, and a wonderfully slanted allusion to Marvell's "To His Coy Mistress" (a more direct allusion appears in "The Loudest Voice" [55]).

It is a tribute to the storytelling style of the narrator that given this freight of material, she maintains the story's highballing pace, moving exterior and interior actions forward while keeping in the air the twists and turns of phrase-juggling precocity. "Now look" (149) is the way she begins the second paragraph, but by its end she is into the simple narrative preterit that she pursues, through the multiple closures of all lines of action, only to move in the last three paragraphs through the imperfect or continuing tense (*has retained, has received, has been bottled, have been translated*) back to the present that suspends time. The final sentence, "She smiles and praises Eddie" (171), applies primarily to Mrs. Goredinsky but with greater impact to the storytelling voice, emblematic of her tone. In a sense, this is Paley's first tentative step toward metafiction.

The operant phrase of the title—*to make a monkey of*—is a metaphoric cliché meaning to make a fool of, to turn [someone] into something less than human. Since an important character is literally a monkey, the figurative quality of the phrase is rendered concrete, inverted, played with. So much is clear, but what is the meaning of *time* in this context? One meaning is "history," the history of man's inhumanity to man, epitomized by the Holocaust, which Eddie's experiment, in Sorkin's phrase, recapitulates in its "murderous efficiency" (151): The Teitelbaum monkey is named for Eddie's great-uncle "who had died of Jewishness in the epidemics of '40, '41'" (157); that particular time had turned that one Jew into his monkey look-alike. But *time* also carries the meanings here of "living" and the "ongoing action of the story." The remaining question, then, is about the meaning of *us*. More than a cast of characters in a story, whose mixed fates are summarily accounted for, the first-person plural includes the narrator and her audience. We need not assume identification with the neighborhood of 1432, 1434, and 1436. "We" have been fooled by our hopes for Eddie and what he represents, rendered less than human by what he does and what happens to him, turned into monkeys when pacifist intent falls prey to the thoughtless application of technology.

"The peaceful guy who listens to the warning of his senses will survive generations of defeat" (164), says Eddie, instructing his troops on the lesson of his inventions. First, there is a "cockroach segregator," which electrically encourages a return to its "gummy environment under the linoleum" (153) while killing "only that cockroach which emigrated out of its pitchy crack into the corn flakes of people" (151). The meek, according to Eddie's gospel for cockroaches, will "inherit the entire congressional district" (151).

The last invention is the "War Attenuator," a supposedly nontoxic stink bomb, an "instrument of war that will not kill" (163). Eddie's weapon would thin out, dilute, the destructive capacity of war, while those who shunned its effects would be the survivors. Eddie's pacifism is thus the principle of Tolkien's Hobbits before Gandalf, Bilbo, Frodo, and others enrich their understanding of the great world and what is required for human beings to survive as such.

If, for Paley the antiwar activist, pacifism is the subject of this story, then what it says about pacifism (survival through avoidance, ghettoization, or isolation) is a far cry from laughter, hope, or triumph. The best pacifist intentions in the world, motivating the technological experimentation of the protagonist, produce bitterness, despair, death, failure, alienation, and catatonic withdrawal. The laughter is not that of the narrator, the reader, or Eddie but of Carl Clop, whose thoughtless application of the antiwar technology results in the climactic recapitulation of the Nazi gas chambers and who goes on "to become an atomic physicist for the Navy" (171). To give the last laugh to the scientific-military establishment is hardly an effective strategy to support pacifism. What the story seems to say is that time, which is also evolution,[34] has fooled us all by accelerating technological advancement, while we, in acquiring humanistic control of aggression, remain painfully close to the troglodytes. The nineteenth-century myth of progress is one-sided, distorted, ultimately alienating and polarizing.

Paley herself does not count this story among her activities in the cause of peace. She sees it as a case study, an admiring account of that outstanding young leader she shows us first as a dominating presence on the topmost step of his tenement. At the end, institutionalized and choosing both consciously and unconsciously to remain incommunicado with the world, he is a terrible figure of not only a wasted mind but an embittered heart as well. The phenomenon of mind-blown youth is not new to the post-1960s effects of a drug culture, Paley shows us here. There have always been those who, their reason having been affronted by the unreason of the world (nature or society, systems or persons), choose an aberrant attitude, an apparent mindlessness. They "go mad" (or "go ape") as a determined destination, because in fact they perceive the world as mad (or subhuman). Paley calls them "kids who dropped out of sanity."[35]

The satiric mode of "In Time . . . ," however, does not allow it to be a straight psychological study. Paley mocks both psychodynamic interpretation of behavior (Shmul's "That's how you got so smart. Constant competition with an oddball sibling . . . Aha" gets Eddie's response of including him among the "bunch of jerks" [161]) and psychotherapy (in the practice of Dr. Tully, whose self-fulfilling prophecy of Eddie's relapse leads to admiration from his peers). Rorschach tests are ridiculed, occupational therapy is lampooned, the idea of "identity crisis" is travestied, and even the well-intentioned social-work approach to mental health is caricatured in the figure of Jim Sunn (a "Sunny Jim" but perhaps also a subconscious allusion to jimsonweed or locoweed),[36] whose good-natured encouragement of Eddie leads to his final relapse and withdrawal.

The story is the darkest of the whole collection, its images definitively depressing. Mrs. Goredinsky on her knees at the end, blessing Eddie for all the wrong reasons, in her fatness and ignorance has unwittingly supplied the power for Eddie's experiments. Taxed to support the war effort against war (the notion of having to destroy villages to free them resonates prophetically of Vietnam), she is grateful for the trickle of social services. Like the most effective satire, "In Time . . ." imprints the terrible state of things on the audience, hoping to prompt reform. But whatever hints of "talk, art, laughter, and hope" are picked up by Sorkin, the story makes no positive recommendation. If we know what we're up against and how absurd and powerful it is, perhaps we can find a way out or around or through or over. But this story never shows us how. The darkness and silence that come here predict some of the weathers to come in the later collections.

The last story in *The Little Disturbances of Man* is probably the first that suggested the word *surrealistic* be applied to Paley's work. And yet "The Floating Truth," once you get past its oddities of character, situation, and language, can be seen as one of the more traditional stories in the collection. The narrator is a young woman, six weeks out of school and beginning to think she is unemployable, but the situation of the narration is unclear. That is, the narrator tells her story of her first job—within the framework of her dealings with her "vocational counselor"—in simple past tense and without any specific audience to hear it or context to hear it in.

Although Paley has said that the story is about work (it has been reprinted in a collection subtitled "Fiction about Work by Contemporary American Writers"),[37] its two main themes are (a) sexist attitudes in the American workplace and (b) the meaninglessness of work in entrepreneurial capitalism, and its main appeal is in the comic-absurdist character of the employment agent.

The employment agent lives in and works out of a hearse; he raises philodendrons in the spring, crocuses in the fall, on the back window ledge. We never learn his name, because the narrator refers to him successively as Lionel, Charley, Marlon, Eddie, Bubbles, Roderick the middleman, Everett, Poor Dick, Surly Sam, and Morton (a cop's name for him is Squatface). All the names connect, by association, with a broad, comic frame of reference, but the jokes are sometimes limited by topicality or generation.

What the employment agent does in the story, however, is perform the classic economic function in our society, an act of commercial prestidigitation: He creates a demand out of the air and conjures up a unique supply for it (or, in personnel terms, he fabricates a résumé to satisfy factitious conditions of employment). The irony is that the narrator is qualified to do nothing, and nothing is what she is hired to do.

When the employment agent asks the narrator what she wants to do, she can only stammer some social-conscience generalizations—"something worthwhile . . . make a contribution . . . help out somehow . . . do good" (176)—which are greeted with gross ridicule. Later, after she has quit her so-called job, he says, "Now if you were really sincere, you could take your shoes off and stand on a street corner with a sign saying: 'He died for me'" (188).

The most telling satire in the story, because the bitterness of much of that dialogue is replaced by comic inventiveness, occurs in samples from the résumé. For experience in advertising, he describes an eight-month, seven-pronged campaign she waged to bring the name of THE GREEN HOUSE before the public. When she asks what THE GREEN HOUSE is, he giggles that he doesn't know (183).

Under the public relations rubric, he describes how, using the name Gladys Hand, she toured the country for five months on behalf of *The Philadelphia* (an "association of professionals working in the Law and allied fields"), bringing "Law and its possibilities to women everywhere" (183). Her results were impressive: more customers for legal services, higher fees for those services, and such crowded court calendars that seven states had to revise their statutes. The joke is that an already-litigious society, characterized by the proverbial shrewdness of Philadelphia lawyers, expands its counterproductive energy and earnings by sending a glad-handing agent (no relation to Learned Hand) to co-opt women.

And then he credits her with inaugurating a "high-pressure plan to return women to the kitchen" (183) on behalf of THE KITCHEN INSTITUTE. In sum, what he has done is to override her social values, however vaguely expressed, with a set of credentials that costume her as the embodiment of a manipulative, subjugating, sexist system. Moreover, it is clear from his exchanges with the prospective employer and their initial interview that it is her beautifully dressed body he is packaging for sale.

The title of the story comes from that meeting, lunch for three at the Vilamar Cafeteria, and the dialogue of Jonathan Stubblefield, whom the hearse dweller consistently refers to as Edsel (with all its appropriate associations).[38] When she acknowledges being "not innocent but ignorant," Stubblefield says, "Of course. You can't deny it. The truth finds its own level and floats" (180). Then, having gently touched "that part of the decolletage furthest from my chin," he hires her, "pending résumé" (181).

Stubblefield's free-floating, liquid-asset, free-market definition of truth is acted out in the subsequent telescoping of the narrator's months in his employ, as is his reduction of history/tragedy to brand-name appearances. All she does is read and file the news, keep her pencils sharpened, and answer the phone. He in turn is happy to have an employee, so happy in fact that he hires another because "we're in the middle of an expanding economy" (186). The narrator is perhaps jealous that Serena, the "camel-hair blonde, all textured in cashmere" (185), is a recent Sarah Lawrence graduate—a kind of prophetic inside joke, since the story came a half-dozen years before Paley began teaching there—but she focuses her anger and resentment on Stubblefield. She feels insulted and inadequate, especially since "there's nothing to do." But his response is belligerent: "If I want to, I can hire forty people to do nothing. NOTHING." Her childlike behavior is accompanied by tears, but he is "a man nevertheless with truth on his side" (186).

She returns to the hearse for new direction, and in the process a cameo shot of the whole story is seen. She has brought the employment agent a gift of some food, he rejects it, and it is given to a passing child. The child rips off the wrapping, dumps the food, and puts the folded aluminum paper in her pocket. Packaging is more important than substance.

The story ends on a scene in which the bile seems purged. The narrator has shaken the employment agent's hand, without anger, and walked away. Looking back before going down into the subway, she sees him "pee [not] like a boy who expects to span a continent, but like a man—in a puddle" (189). In this nine-to-five workaday world, where nothing is accomplished, where packaging is all important and substance—especially when it is the substantial sustenance offered by a woman—is devalued, where a man is entitled to have two women or forty, if he wants to and can, the waste and impotence find their own level in the gutter.

The middleman, service-oriented, nonproductive agent-magician at work is at home only in a vehicle for corpses, a death's-head symbol of a self-destructive capitalism. Thus when she looks at him carefully, she sees that on "the outside he was a mirror image of a face with a dead center" (176); he is merely a pale, blank reflection of lifeless superficiality. Even while subjugating his female client, he can operate only when she buys his fuel, and in anger he demands that she clean up the mess his mode of living makes.

In the context of Paley's work as a whole, "The Floating Truth" is interesting for those images, for the characteristically witty verbal effects, and for the swinging emotional affects. But perhaps most interesting of all is the way the story is "directed to the future" like its narrator. Although she finds it "hard . . . to part with experience" (188), she can walk away, move on, remember, make judgments, and live according to newly discovered, rediscovered, or reinforced values. Her decisions—her final decisiveness—are emblematic and prophetic of Paley's characters in the later work. Over and over, her women let the floating truths evanesce as they stand firmly on their own solid grounds.

Enormous Changes at the Last Minute

From the opening pages of her second collection, the reader encounters a Grace Paley significantly different from the cherished voice of the first. We recognize the voice, the phrasing is familiar, but we find a speaker more confident in her own speaking persona and thus also more comfortable with stretching her story forms to adopt or hear the voices of other personae.

"Wants" and "Debts" are the first two stories, though they were among the latest written. They had appeared together in the *Atlantic* (though in reverse order) under the heading "Two Stories by Grace Paley,"[39] and since they are numbered there and then kept together for the book, it seems appropriate to consider them as a diptych after the manner of "Two Short Sad Stories" (*LDM*). Like more than half the seventeen stories in the book, they are shorter than the shortest in *The Little Disturbances of Man;* like the majority, they are first-person narrations. But unlike anything in the first collection, here the speaker is a persona we can identify as the Grace Paley storyteller/story hearer. Paley says she did not conceive them as companion pieces; it was a matter of developing a form in which to tell "the stories of those stories" and using it as appropriate.[40] Nevertheless, they stand together in text and because of that format, along with the matching form, they serve critics' purposes by being treated together.

"Wants" and "Debts" are so short that each was printed on a single magazine page (facing the other, a graphic if not authorial diptych), each filling barely three pages of type in the book. Irving Howe included "Wants" in his selection of "short shorts," a form he describes as "fiercely condensed, almost like a lyric poem; it explodes in a burst of revelation or illumination; it confines itself to a single overpowering incident, it bears symbolic weight." Grouping "Wants" with Sholom Aleichem's "A Yom Kippur," Howe says that "the short short appears to rest on nothing more than a fragile anecdote which the writer has managed to drape with a quantity of suggestion. A single incident, a mere anecdote—these form the spine of the short short."[41]

Despite the brevity of these pieces, the reader must take exception to Howe's notion of singleness. For Paley, elements must bump into each other before there is a story at all. And then, in a pairing of stories, pairs bump into other pairs. In "Debts," in a space of ten paragraphs, stories of lives bump into stories of lives to prompt a life of storytelling.

The "I" of the story identifies herself as a writer who had "already used every single thing I knew about the Yiddish theater to write one story" (9). In other words, she is the author of "Goodbye and Good Luck." Then, "There is a long time in me between knowing and telling," she says (9), accounting in a way for the fifteen years between two collections of stories. This frank new element of self-reflexivity may justify identifying the narrator completely with the author, but it is safer to identify a new character: a Grace Paley persona.

In any case, the narrator rejects the offer from a stranger to transmute that lady's family archives into literature. But her friend Lucia, whom she tells about it, says that it is "a pity to lose all this inheritance just because of one's own mortality" (10). Yes, the narrator concludes upon reflection, perhaps "I did owe something to my own family and the families of my friends. That is, to tell their stories as simply as possible, in order, you might say, to save a few lives" (10).

She proceeds to tell about Lucia's family: "Because it was her idea, the first story is Lucia's" (10). It is a story about Lucia's mother, Anna; her grandmother, Maria; and two husbands named Michael. It is a story, as Howe might say, of fierce condensation and draped with manifold suggestions. But the "burst of revelation" is that narrator's glimpse of the obligations of writers. It is not, however, the first story in the collection, because for the purposes of the book, Paley found it better to begin with a clearer focus on theme than on form, because she thought "Wants" was an easier way into the collection for the reader and because "Wants" and "Debts" sounded better to her, felt better rhythmically, than the other way around.[42]

Alone among the commentators, Baumbach groups "Debts" with "Wants." He says, "It is an impossible obligation—impossible like the 'wants' of the story of that title—which the narrator tries hopelessly (and successfully) to fulfill" (304). And then he turns to a brief discussion of "Wants," in which the narrator "bumps into" her ex-husband while returning to the library two Edith Wharton books eighteen years overdue (perhaps another ironic reference to Paley's collection, long "overdue," coming eighteen years after her first story was published).

Coppula describes the "collision" as "between the narrator's view of herself as fluid, capable of change, and her ex-husband's view that characterizes her in the past" (66). Their differences he sums up as "I wanted a sailboat . . . you didn't want anything" (5). When he leaves, she feels accused and defends herself by itemizing what she does want. As Coppula says, the list—which includes wanting to be a person who ends wars, effects changes in the school system, addresses the Board of Estimate, and returns library books—"turns the clash of the two characters in the story into a reflection of culture" (67).

There are political overtones: The narrator's values as pinpointed by her wants include social philosophy, whereas her husband's reflect crass capitalism. But the essence of character revealed by her wants combines her emotional nature with her writerly temperament: "I wanted to have been married forever to one person, either my ex-husband or my present one. Either has enough character for a whole life, which as it turns out is really not such a long time. You couldn't exhaust either man's qualities or get under the rock of his reasons in one short life" (5).

Baumbach likens their encounter to "a creation of the narrator's imagination, a day dream or obsessive fantasy." He calls the story's "occasion . . . metaphoric, its details hyperbolic" but feels it "touch[ing] us through its humanity and perception—Paley's vision like nothing else—as strongly as if it were taking place in that literary convention we call the 'real world'" (304). The movement back in time (or place and therefore time, as in "The Long-Distance Runner") can trigger fantasized encounters for the Paley narrator-persona. It is difficult and probably unnecessary to make that distinction for "Wants," but Baumbach's notion is supported by the passage at the end in which the narrator accounts for the whole cycle of reminiscence and action: the blossoming of sycamores "dreamily planted . . . before the kids were born" (6).

What is clear is that time itself is a subject of the story. Baumbach, again: "her best intentions, her 'wants' defeated by fleeting time and the ordinary, quirky circumstances of a life" (304). Blanche Gelfant is more ambitious for Paley's time theme. She cites the narrator's line "I don't understand how time passes" (3) at the very beginning of her essay "Chronicles and Chroniclers," crediting Paley with "putting her finger on the enigma of life as well as of fiction and history, the narrative forms that show how life passes in time."[43]

The question "Whose life is it?" is thus superimposed on "Whose voice is it?" The ex-husband attributes the dissolution of the marriage to the narrator's failure to invite the Bertrams to dinner. Her telescoping response—"if you remember: first, my father was sick that Friday, then the children were born, then I had those Tuesday-night meetings, then the war began" (4)—extends self-reflexivity beyond Paley's stories to Paley's life as mother, neighborhood organizer, and peace activist. In "Debts" the references are to earlier stories (not only "Goodbye and Good Luck" but in the final paragraph echoing "An Interest in Life") and in "Wants" to other activities. It is all of a piece, this first pair of stories in *Enormous Changes at the Last Minute* says to us in the voice of a writer/narrator/persona/character.

Addressing an unspecified audience-at-large in "Distance" but doing so in an implicitly one-on-one setting, Dolly Raftery's voice—strident, New York Irish, idiosyncratically mixing idioms—speaks of a situation we know well from its very successful earlier treatment in "An Interest in Life." Her son John, married and with a family in New Jersey, spends two evenings a week in Mrs. Raftery's house with her neighbor Ginny, being a father to Ginny's kids and attending to her needs so that "he hasn't enough time to visit" (26) Ginny and his mother both.

It is as if Grace Paley had decided to heed George Eliot's epiphany as announced in the twenty-ninth chapter of *Middlemarch*. In what has been regarded as the most significant single paragraph in the history of English-language narration, culminating the tradition of eighteenth- and nineteenth-century fiction and looking forward to the twentieth, Eliot stopped in midsentence to say, mutatis mutandis, "Hey, wait a minute, folks, why should we look at this marriage just from Dorothea's side—or at anything from just one point of view?" The result for Paley's "Distance" is what Mickelson calls "another view of the improvised domestic scene and another distribution of sympathies" (226).

Yet is it hard to see the narration accomplishing Mrs. Raftery's strategic objective when her tactics are self-defeating. As Baumbach says, her point of view is "self-justifying [but] self-denying," and "victories Mrs. Raftery claims for herself are undermined by events, defeated by her own story" (304). I should have said "hard to hear," rather than "hard to see," because the story achieves its ironic effects through the recognizable voice of its contrary teller.

Of the material we know from "An Interest in Life," Mrs. Raftery gives a different slant to several aspects: her opposition to Ginny when John wants to marry her; her histrionic gesture with a kitchen knife to bring John back in line; her motivation for trying to protect John—her other son, "clever" Michael, had died—and for not sending him to college; Ginny's marriage to "Blackie" and why he left her; John's nature as naive and "not bright" (rather than simply pious and well meaning [18]); Ginny's nature and character as mother, wife, and homemaker; her own part in John and Ginny's getting together; and her relationship with Ginny. But the key word here is *slant*. Mrs. Raftery, who has more than a little taste for sweet wine, comes at her experience of life in this *apologia pro vita sua* from an extremely sharp angle, defined by the cutting edge with which she skewers everyone else. And so well do we understand the distortions built into her as viewing instrument—the proverbial unreliable narrator—that we consistently measure and discount her judgments.

Our interest is in the judge and her process of judging, not the accuracy of her judgments; her obiter dicta are more illuminating than her substantive decisions. Mrs. Raftery ends her monologue with a series of questions, rather existential than rhetorical; aware of the contraries of her life, she wants to understand the meaning of life. "You would certainly be glad to meet me" (15) is her opening line, and her whole narration with its compulsive put-downs convinces us otherwise.

The contradictions go on. Proclaiming herself "the lady who appreciated youth," she insists that hers, unlike others', "did not go by . . . like a flitting dream" (15) and then proceeds to present it precisely as a flitting, recurrent dream of her eighteenth year, when she "knuckled under again and again" (26) to Anthony Aldo, "mashing the grass of Central Park" (19). And the youth she appreciates includes neither Ginny's nor John's, neither Ginny's children's nor her New Jersey grandchildren's. One wonders about her vaunted success as "a famous widow babysitter" (25), though her self-styled ability as "grand storybook reader . . . like an actress, Joan Crawford or Maureen O'Sullivan, my voice . . . deeper than it was" (25) may be taken as self-criticism, Grace Paley acknowledging the deepening of her own capacity to speak in the voices of others.

John's father, Jack, does not appear in "An Interest in Life" (except for John's comment that he was "a weak earner" [*LDM*, 93]), so that Dolly's marriage is a total revelation in "Distance." Her "advice to mothers and wives: Do not imitate the dimwit's girl friends" (17) is less acceptable wisdom, given her description of the dubious success of her own practice. She says, "my old man, fond of me as he constantly was, often [fell for] terrible weirdos in a dumb way" (17). And when, after referring repeatedly to his lack of brains, she quotes him during significant scenes, he seems to us the more sensible and even sensitive of the pair.

In the series of eight existential questions Mrs. Raftery poses in the story's final paragraph, two refer specifically to Jack, one to John and Ginny, and one to Anthony. The rest have to do with herself and her wonderment about life, love, and sex, under the general heading "What's it all about?" The "distance" of the title measures the journey from here to there, meaning life's passage and destination. Its application is threefold: first to sex, "the noisiness and the speediness, when it's no distance at all" (26); second to mating, in which John's "lifelong trip to Ginny" (26) has been circuitously achieved despite Mrs. Raftery's own short-circuiting of the direct connection; and third to her own experience, "going off to live and die" (27), in which the meaning of love remains unfulfilled, unresolved, and undefined. Mrs. Raftery's certainties and assertiveness are thoroughly betrayed because running through her questioning is the strain of unknowing. She could not know the minds of John, Jack, or Anthony. And her perception of love's absence is beyond the knowing of the priest who once seemed more moved by her dilemmas than she was herself—and at the same time more certain in that unknowing. That is precisely the kind of confessor she has become in her own telling of her story.

"Faith in the Afternoon," though one of Paley's longer published pieces, is perhaps the least fulfilled as story. It seems to be a salvaged remnant of what was to have been a novel about Faith and, since it was published separately in *Noble Savage* in 1960, survived to be included in *Enormous Changes at the Last Minute* in 1974.[44]

Its raison d'être is announced early on: "Certain facts may become useful" (33). In other words, it is a story that is almost entirely explication. It accounts for things, it gives background material, it summarizes history and suggests broad patterns of motivation. It serves, therefore, to illuminate the other stories about Faith, since its novelistic function is academic. In its immediate function, however, it is an attempt to account for Faith's present state of mind, a period of "willful unhappiness" (34) after her husband Ricardo has left. Angry that her parents and siblings seem ashamed of "her ridiculous position right in the middle of prosperous times" (34), Faith buries her head under her pillow with her regular nightmares—and these, too, she attempts to account for with "certain facts."

Thus we are filled in, with some sardonic distancing from the consistent third-person restricted point of view, on Faith's family: her grandparents who settled in Yorkville among Germans and Irish, her parents who escaped to Coney Island, her prospering brother and sister, her first husband and his girlfriends. The afternoon of the title, however, refers to a visit to her parents, who have moved against their children's wishes and advice into the Children of Judea, Home for the Golden Ages. Occupying nearly three-quarters of the story, this flashback reenacts the only time Faith has visited after Ricardo's departure and explains why she has yet to return. "I can't come until I'm a little happy" (48), she has told her father, who then urges her, "Don't be selfish, Faithy, bring the boys, come" (48).

Marianne DeKoven has drawn appropriate attention to the virtues of "Faith in the Afternoon," especially to Paley's characteristic interplay of language and feelings, whether complementary, contrastive, or ironic. She also does justice to the comic figure, the sorrowful clown in her oiled wheelchair, Mrs. Hegel-Shtein, president of the Grandmothers' Wool Sock Association.[45] Structurally, the flashback scene recapitulates the useful chronicling of facts, as Faith's mother and Mrs. Hegel-Shtein tell sorrowful summaries of lives from the Darwins' old neighborhood. Perhaps more meaningful, though tossed off incidentally, is the change in Faith's father from having a lifelong concern with social and geopolitical matters to writing poetry. Faith has managed a big smile for him, though not the enormous one he deserves, to "meet the commitments of her face" (46). But when he takes her fingers and touches them to her cheeks, he feels her tears and turns away, saying, "'Aaah . . .' an explosion of nausea, absolute digestive disgust" (49).

That moment, in which Gersh Darwin preempts his daughter's own revulsion from aggrieved old age, is freighted with meaning. Neither, in their respective transitions, can properly hear the other's voice and story. And so the story ends in a suspended instant inside a flashback. But the reader's recognition, like the factual information he or she has acquired, may be stored for retrieval when subsequent stories like "Dreamer in a Dead Language" require recall.

It is tempting to urge that "Gloomy Tune" and "Living" form a diptych. They appear in sequence in the book, and they appeared together, in reverse order, in *Genesis West* in 1965. In fact, though "A Gloomy Tune," as it was then called, was originally published in *Genesis*

West three years earlier, it was reprinted alongside "Living"—a highly unusual occurrence for a little magazine, suggesting special consideration for a writer's intention. Moreover, taken together, the two stories complement each other stylistically, demonstrating an impressive range and forceful contrast of voice, pace, and diction.

Criticism, however, even like more exact sciences, must yield to the principle of parsimony. The simple truth is that Gordon Lish reissued "Gloomy Tune" because he liked it. Although Grace Paley has a fondness for *Genesis West* because it published her and Bob Nichols in the same issue before they had ever met, she never intended the stories as companion pieces, even though they remain juxtaposed in the book.[46]

With the release of the movie *Who Framed Roger Rabbit,* the ironic allusion to Looney Tunes in the story's title will be less remote to many readers. There is a kind of antic, frantic, cartoon lunacy about the world presented in "Gloomy Tune." Paley once described the story to Lish as a "documentary," which extends and compounds the cinematic frame of reference. But there are a detachment, a neutrality, and a quick-cutting succession of images that characterize both old-fashioned documentaries and cartoons.

The narrative voice in "Gloomy Tune" is distanced and nearly neutral. But however impersonal, it is by no means value free. The narrator pretends to reflect common knowledge in the community, introducing a family she says "nearly everybody knows" (53), with children named Bobo, Bibi, Doody, Dodo, Neddy, Yoyo, Butch, Put Put, and Beep (any relation to Seymour, Buddy, Boo Boo, Walter, Waker, Franny, and Zooey is coincidental). While the story emphasizes the kids' language, the narrator also records the distinctive voices of their mother, the sister from the parochial school, Chuchi Gomez, and Chuchi's "gramma." Common knowledge is extended to what all these people think, and the narrator also intrudes occasionally in her own voice.

For example, when she reports that the two oldest girls, "mean babysitters," sometimes "jerk people off," she adds, "They really like to" (53). After recording examples of the children's progressively vulgar cursing, she ends, "but I don't like to say" (54). The sister's attitudes and behavior are in turn judged, commended, excused, and explained by her own nature and experience as a teacher, a good person, a nonmother, and a nun. The children themselves are defended several times: about their language, because "I don't think they really understood what they were saying" (55); about their belligerent behavior in the playground, because "they never stole" and "wouldn't murder anyone I think" (55); and about both, because "they had a right to curse back or push back" (55).

The climactic incident in the story, if it can be called that, brings the narrator's voice into clearer focus. Chuchi slips in a puddle of olive oil, because the lady whose bottle broke picked up the glass and left the oil. The storyteller says, "I wouldn't know what to do about oil either" (55). The narrator's "neutrality" is here presented as a matter of not placing blame, and her attitude becomes an echo of what the story itself says. That is also the last time she intrudes as "I" in the story.

Chuchi blames Yoyo for his fall. They argue, curse each other, and fight. Picking up a board with two nails in it, Yoyo bloodies Chuchi's shoulder. As in a cartoon, the violence turns slapstick, graphic but not conveying pain, and the narrator's comment is comic caption: "That isn't such a bloody place, but with the oil and blood and all, if you got a little vinegar, you could of pickled Chuchi" (56). And that, she summarizes, is how Yoyo got his reputation for using a knife and his fame in the whole social-work and settlement-house community. "He is bold and hopeless" (56), we are told, and from this statement we might generalize about a population for whose condition nobody is to blame and for whom good intentions are misdirected: "In school he gets prayed for every day" (56).

"Living" is about dying. It gives us Faith at her lowest point. She is depressed, hemorrhaging, more depressed because of the hemorrhaging, and hemorrhaging all the more because of her depression. But the story is also about living in the face of death, living out a life in the contemplation of death while providing for others' lives afterward. Perhaps most important is the story's ironic theme: the discovery that some meaning in life comes from shared experiences, even when the experiences are metaphorical living deaths or literal dyings.

William Peden describes Faith's voice here as "harsh and strident,"[47] but I hear bitterness, despair, and mostly tiredness. When her friend Ellen calls to tell her she's dying, Faith can't even summon up the strength to register the news properly, never mind acting on it. Her "clear sentence"—"Please! I'm dying too, Ellen" (60)—is uttered from the pits of self-involvement in the perfect pitch of New York isolation/alienation. Her physical sense of her own lifeblood hurrying to leave her prompts an attempt at sardonic consolation that only comes out as sarcastic whine. "What's so great?" she asks, escalating her discontent from issues of cockroaches, men, and poverty to imminent disaster in "heat blast firewaves" (60).

Ellen, frightened and worried about who'll take care of the kids, is dead within five weeks of their conversation, and by that time Faith has recovered. Two weeks before Christmas she had been thinking, "You have to be cockeyed to love, and blind in order to look out the window at your own ice-cold street" (59). But after an uninterrupted rest while her kids were at her sister's, Faith "was in such first-class shape by New Year's, [she] nearly got knocked up again. [Her] little boys came home. They were tall and handsome" (61). Two weeks later, at Ellen's funeral, Faith asks Ellen's son Billy if she should adopt him, but Ellen has provided a future for him with his uncle in Springfield. Faith has made the offer in good faith, not knowing how to provide the money, room, and time for another child, and so is relieved.

Her psyche as well as her physical health restored, Faith can now miss and remember Ellen, with the proper poignancy of mingled nostalgia and irony, as someone with whom she shared "a million things in these scary, private years" (61). The most vivid surviving image is of the time when the boys were babies; the tired young mothers would scream at them, and as "a joke we stapled their snow suits to our skirts and in a rage of slavery every Saturday for weeks we marched across the bridges that connect Manhattan to the world" (61).

In the *Genesis West* version, the last sentences read, "We shared apartments, jobs, stuck-up studs. With Ellen, two weeks before last Christmas, I was dying."[48] In the book, the final sentence has become, "And then, two weeks before last Christmas, we were dying" (61). More than anything else in the story, it seems to me, that revision underscores Faith's recovery from self-absorption to a degree of shared experience that defines "living."

Not the shortest but arguably the slightest story in *Enormous Changes at the Last Minute*, "Come On, Ye Sons of Art" takes place on a Sunday morning in the bed of Faith's friend Kitty. Single mother of three and pregnant again, Kitty is with her lover, Jerry Cook, an unsuccessful businessman, and the narration is consistently restricted to her third-person center of consciousness. We get brief glimpses into her thoughts and feelings ("life on Sunday was worth two weeks of waiting" [72]), but mostly what we get is what can be heard, dialogue—or rather monologue, since Jerry is delivering a harangue on the subjects of business, family, and self. Jerry's routine includes other voices, and at the end it gives way to a radio show and the sounds from the kitchen of Jerry making breakfast. But most of what we hear is Jerry's voice, its brassy bitterness and bluster muted only by the ambience of comfortable warmth in Kitty's bed. What is significant, then, is the format: the story hearer at the story's center, listening to a storyteller; it is the content of that teller's story that I have called slight.

In Jerry's hierarchy of businessmen, two Jews are better than twenty-five Syrians, one Greek exerts more pressure than fifty Jews, and the Japanese are beyond comparison. But the real focus of his tale is his sister Anna Marie, who, like their two brothers and their wives, is crooked and smart but is smarter and more crooked. Her acumen is demonstrated by her bribery of unscrupulous auctioneers to acquire a warehouse that foresightedly (a) receives the supplies and equipment she has her brothers steal from the big builders they work for and (b) gives visual evidence of collateral for bank loans she uses for her real estate ventures. "High risers" are her triumph, in Harlem and the Village, and she shrewdly ensures their success in advance by choosing appropriate names: Harriet Tubman Towers, Egypt, and the Franz Kline.

Listening with Kitty, we hear the irony in Jerry's references to businesspeople as "artists" and "the masters." These are hardly the painters who, to Auden, were never wrong about suffering; to Jerry, Cézanne and van Gogh are place-names in the Village. But we do, after all, hear Jerry with Kitty's ears. When he shakes his head sadly about not being "in on it" and asserts "I'm crooked too," we understand her response, "Sure you are" (68), as being encouraging and accepting at the same time as it denies his claim.

Why does Kitty, who is "loving" and has "tolerance" (70), accept a man who disparages "shvartzes, spics and spades" (70), "mockies" and "Yids" (71)? Perhaps it's because she understands that it is all merely manner of speech for him, like his New Yorker's equation of "everywhere in America" with "New Jersey and Long Island" (65). Perhaps it's because she knows that the real Jerry is the good-hearted man who would put their unborn child through Harvard if he could, who enjoys his role as "Sunday-breakfast chef" (72) for her other three kids, and whose joke, "I hate a dumb kid. I always think it's me" (72), has a sad truth in it. Or perhaps it is just because at this hour, warmed by the affectionate presence and attentiveness of her man; glowing with her pregnancy, which is theirs; and overflowing with nurturance and indulgent satisfaction, she can accept almost anything.

In the final paragraph, as Kitty snuggles under "Faith's grandmother's patchwork quilt" (72), it may be that when we hear the radio commentator say, about the Purcell piece just played (which gives the story its title), that "it was on account of the queen's birthday . . . that such a lot of joy had been transacted in England the busy country" (73), we are hearing Paley's voice. She has taken Jerry's performance with its metaphor of business as art, which has after all brought joy to Kitty, and turned it on its head—joy bringing art to the country of business—where it properly belongs.

"Faith in a Tree" is actually two stories. The first story is a brilliant evocation of the young-single-mother-in-the-park scene, in which ongoing concerns with child raising and PTA-related politics are constantly being undercut or conflicted by ongoing sexual urges. The second story has the park scene interrupted by a little political demonstration, Faith's son Richard's response to it, and Faith's epiphanic decision to change her life—in her children's behalf—to become active in the larger struggles of the world.

I mean literally that it is two stories. In its first version in *New American Review* in 1967, called "Faith: In a Tree," it ends with Faith's acceptance, expressed with an appropriate mixture of irony, longing, and chagrin, that the new eligible man in the park is going to be coupling with her friend Anna, not her. There is no miniparade, no activist gesture by Richard, no dramatic movement by Faith—not even back up into the sycamore. The story begins with erotic imagery ("Just when I most needed [a] companion who could translate my friendly language into his tongue of undying carnal love" [77]) and ends with erotic imagery ("as I watched his blood descend from his brains [I thought] that I would like to be the one who was holding his balls very gently . . . when all the thumping got there" [97]). The final sentence—"I felt his keenness, though the cutting edge was standing over that nice white airy spongy loaf, my pal Anna"[49]—does not appear in the later version, but here it maintains the sharp focus on the sexual issues at hand and the personal presences in the playground.

From Faith's strategic position, she can see out and over her immediate surroundings and, looking down at them, comment (in a first-person narration that can resemble omniscience because of her physical vantage) on her friends and neighbors and the passing scene. "What a place in democratic time!" (77) she thinks, locating us precisely in both with her observations. That location includes the context of Paley's stories about Faith and her world: We see Kitty during her fourth preg-

47

nancy (same time frame as "Come On . . ."), hear news of Faith's ex-husband Ricardo, and catch glimpses of Ginny and Mrs. Raftery. Moreover, the new eligible man is Phillip Mazzano, who by the time of "Dreamer in a Dead Language" has become Faith's lover, not Anna's, and has lost one *l* from his name.

The story's technique is interesting, as it moves seamlessly between the objective realism of Faith's vantage point (from which we get her—and Paley's—intimately caring attention to all the children) and a kind of surrealistic interior associational monologue. (It is the latter, no doubt, that disturbs the sensibilities of the father in "A Conversation with My Father.") Unlike Paley's customary avoidance of conventional punctuation, "Faith: In a Tree" uses quotation marks to record dialogue as separate from the interior monologue. But it may be somewhat disconcerting to discover that her friend Kitty, her neighbor Mrs. Junius Finn, and especially her son Richard are capable of responding to Faith's unquoted thoughts as if they hear them.[50]

The apparently simple device of the tree itself is richly evocative. Rituals of tree climbing are widespread in many cultures and seem in fact to be universal in shamanic societies, where their function is to *connect* individuals essentially with the world (world-tree = *axis mundi*) by *separating* them physically (rite of initiation, death/rebirth, prophetic trance, etc.).[51] Paley would not consciously have chosen a self-consciously symbolic motif, but it could well have been something, as she appropriately says, "that was in the air."[52]

One other element in the story demands attention. When Faith reports to a mutual acquaintance, Alex Steele, about her ex-husband Ricardo, she reads to Alex from a letter that gives Ricardo's exotic address as "Guerra Verde c/o Dotty Wasserman. Am living here with her. She's on a Children's Mission. Wonderful girl. Reminds me of you ten years ago" (82). Alex then remembers Dotty as "a funny plain girl" (83). We, of course, remember her from "The Contest" (*LDM*), in which she failed in her mission to get Freddy to marry her. Are we to take this self-reflexivity as an inside joke; as a suggestion of the "reality" of created characters à la Borges, Nabokov, García Marquez, or Bioy Casares; or as a linking of pieces in the jigsaw of Paley's created world of Faith? Dotty's similar reappearance in "Love" in *Later the Same Day* complicates the issue, but there is a possible clue in the second story of "Faith in a Tree."

With only minor emendations, the version in *Enormous Changes at the Last Minute* takes over the whole presentation of the playground world and uses it as a literal and figurative point of departure for Faith. This is the story that Mandel cites for "the progression from personal to social awareness" (92). When Faith, who has come down to earth to meet, perhaps to mate, Phillip, sees that it would be Anna "in that affectionate position" (97), she decides to reascend her tree. At this point, "luckily," a short parade appears, "four or five grownups, a few years behind [her] in the mammy-and-daddy business, pushing little go-carts with babies in them, a couple of three-year-olds hanging on" (97).

The demonstration has three posters, Burma-shave style, showing first "a prime-living, prime-earning, well-dressed man" with a little girl and a printed question: "Would you burn a child?" (97); second, the same man putting a burning cigarette on the child's arm, with the printed answer: "when necessary" (98); and third, without words, a picture of "a napalmed Vietnamese baby, seared, scarred, with twisted hands" (98). Kitty, Anna, Mrs. Junius Finn, Phillip, and Faith all react in different ways, until Douglas, the friendly neighborhood cop, orders the "meeting" to "disperse" (99). And then it is third-grader Richard, disgusted with Faith's feeble protest, who acts appropriately. Taking another child's chalk box, he reprints the message of the parade in fifteen-foot-high letters "so the entire Saturday walking world could see" (99).

The story ends as social protest ideally always would—in commitment, dedication, and change, all founded on loving appreciation and perception: "And I think that is exactly when events turned me around, changing my hairdo, my job uptown, my style of living and telling. Then I met women and men in different lines of work, whose minds were made up, and directed out of that sexy playground by my children's heartfelt brains, I thought more and more and every day about the world (99–100)." Clearly this story is dramatically different from the first version. But beyond the thematic urgency and the structural addition, what sheds light from this later one onto the whole corpus of Paley's stories is the phrase *style of living and telling*. Both for her and for Faith, the two gerunds are inseparable, a verbal equation for the storyteller's life, in which all the pieces are of a coherent whole.

Can it be that the living/telling essence of Faith is a clue to the meaning of Dotty Wasserman here? It is possible that Paley at this point was moving in the direction of Salinger's work, where over time everything comes to be seen as the creation of Buddy Glass. She has said that she became aware of the tendency and that she thought it was unfortunate (I understood her to mean unfortunate for her *and* for Salinger), so that in *Later the Same Day* she took pains to alter the perception, even jar the reader out of it. But in this story in *Enormous Changes at the Last Minute*, there is, aside from Dotty Wasserman, also Marilyn Gewirtz, cited in a footnote (!) as the source of a third-grade incident and as "the only real person in this story" (84). Assuming Gewirtz to be a "living teacher and child admirer," one still wonders whether in the construction "told me this," the personal pronoun refers to Grace Paley or Faith Asbury.[53]

"Two Stories from Five Boroughs" appeared in 1968 on facing pages in *Esquire* (though the second required a dozen column inches at the back of the magazine for completion). Although that cover title disappears in the book, "Samuel" and "The Burdened Man" remain in tandem, joined irrevocably by common subject matter and treatment even more than by juxtaposition, achieving their effect in concert with each other. They are not, strictly speaking, a diptych. The original idea was for a series of stories in this form or format, perhaps one for each borough, but Paley decided that the stories of these two stories were all that would properly be served by the form; accordingly, the "Boroughs" heading was dropped from the book.[54]

Both stories relate incidents that could be taken from back-section items in newspapers. "The Burdened Man," in fact, includes a graph from "The Midnight edition of the morning paper" (114). Both stories are told in a flat, distanced, uninvolved, third-person narration. The point of view is very nearly omniscient, since the narrator is able to report on cognitive processes (long- and short-term memory, daydream, fantasy, conscious bias and its rationale, awareness of anxiety and defenses against it, associational sequences, strategizing, and prioritizing) of whatever character she wishes, though the voice's flatness of affect precludes any expression of judgment, feeling, or empathy.

The two stories are identical in structure, beginning with present-tense sketches of their subjects, moving briskly into past-tense narration of the incidents, and closing with projections far into the future to summarize the incidents' effects. And though the first has to do with the accidental death of a child on the subway and the second with a shooting that changes the course of several lives, there is never a stooping to the kind of melodrama ironically suggested by the *Esquire* title's allusion to the "eight million stories in the naked city."

Samuel is one of four boys playing dangerously "on the platform between the locked doors of the subway cars" (103). The immediate cause of his death is that he has "let go of his hold on the chain" (105) just when an angry passenger has pulled the emergency cord. But the meticulous detail of the narration makes clear that the accident is determined (or overdetermined) by many factors, including the backgrounds and learned attitudes not only of the boys but of several passengers as well. Even the simplest incident cannot support a simple cause-and-effect, here-to-there plot line, because every event in life is part of the weave of an infinite number of strands.

In "The Burdened Man" the flattening is accentuated by the absence of names for characters. The man, his wife, his son, the neighbor, her husband the cop—all remain anonymous until the newspaper item names three of them. The man's burden is economic. The demands on his life, though ordinary, exhaust whatever supply of enjoyment he might have had. A squabble with the woman next door leads to a friendship between them, and they spend many Sunday afternoon hours talking "when both their families are on duty or at the movies" (111).

After a summer-vacation separation, he senses a coolness in her toward him, and so he decides it is "time to consider different ways to begin to make love to her" (111). But before he can act out any of his fantasized stratagems, he is surprised at her dinette table by her husband, drunk, waving a gun, spewing vulgar venom (the *ECLM* version is far more offensive—and realistic—than *Esquire*'s), trying to reclaim the bravery that once earned him a medal for killing a crazy farm boy in Central Park. The wife's appearance and reaction bring the cop's performance to a climax, and he shoots "the man, the woman, the wall, the picture window, the coffee pot [and] the floor, right through his shoe, smashing his toes for life" (114).

Now, the point of these stories does not lie in the results of the incidents. The contrast is ironic. "Samuel" is about a senseless death and is therefore potentially tragic. The participants and observers have immediate reactions. Samuel's mother is hysterical. She soon has another boy, but "immediately she saw that this baby wasn't Samuel. She and her husband together have had other children, but never again will a boy exactly like Samuel be known" (106). The potential for pathos is barely touched and then set aside, perhaps because, as Coppula says, Paley refuses "to let the reader dismiss the story as finished, set in the past" (68), or perhaps because, as in Gelfant's view, the mother's realization of Samuel's uniqueness gives way to Paley's realization: "Then he lives on in the story and in our consciousness, a unique being" (1975, 143).

The burdened man survives his incident. After three days in the hospital (nearly all of his stay covered by insurance), he sells his house and moves to another (similar) neighborhood. He has changed. No longer troubled, "he was hardly unhappy again" (115). The cop's career has been shot along with his kitchen and foot, but of the others we hear nothing. But "survival and renewal," pace Baumbach (305), are hardly the subject of "The Burdened Man." Though bravery and anger are central to both stories, their result of tragedy in the one and triumph in the other are not the issues either.

The point of these conjoined stories, it seems to me, is Paley's double-edged observation: that we tend, on the one hand, like newspapers, to trivialize the most horrible of everyday events and that we try, on the other, to exalt common human experience to a level of tragedy or heroism by inventing conventional plot lines superficially to explain them—which is another form of trivialization. What *her* stories can do is quite something else.

They can produce a sense of ongoing, open-ended, multifaceted (and overdetermined) human experience. By withholding explicit judgment on the judgments implicit in central focus, conventional structure, and generic choice, they can extend the characters' freedoms to the reader. And finally, by drawing us back to the recognition of the familiar narrative voice, they can remind us that we are hearing stories, which is why at the end of this pair, Paley plays with the newspaper's wise-guy tone and then ends with a sentence that rings true for the particular story but plays in perfect pitch for the particular storyteller at work: "In fact, for several years, he could really feel each morning that a mixture of warm refreshments was being pumped out of the chambers of his heart to all his cold extremities" (115).

For all that it is a direct and evocative treatment of certain major themes in Paley's work—forging links between generations, seeing the world from a social-work perspective—"Enormous Changes at the Last Minute" is a freestanding story. That is, although the characters may inhabit familiar Paley terrain, they neither appear in other stories nor cross paths of those who do. The protagonist is Alexandra, whose father happens to be a physician like Grace Paley's (and Faith's older brother), and Alexandra's visits to her father in the hospital somewhat resemble formats of "Faith in the Afternoon," "A Conversation with

My Father," and "Dreamer in a Dead Language." Like Dr. Goodside, Alexandra's father can quote Pushkin in his native Russian, taught himself English by reading Dickens, and worked his way through medical school to shoot "like a surface-to-air missile right into the middle class" (122). But superficial similarities aside, they are quite different men/characters. And Alexandra, whose irony is rather gentle and self-targeted, is significantly different from Faith or her creator, whose tough, quick-tongued comedy wreaks verbal vengeance on the world they confront. Moreover, Alexandra, in Renee Winegarten's words, exalts her "own sense of social responsibility, by engaging in social work."[55] Alexandra is a full-time social worker, whose social-work values inform not only her attitudes toward life but her entire life-style as well.

Throughout most of the story, the narration follows Alexandra in traditional, consistent, third-person-restricted storytelling. The scenes in which she meets her young lover, Dennis; begins their affair; becomes pregnant; and insists that he leave so that she can deal with the pregnancy on her own are intercut with visits to her father. This structure mirrors Alexandra's situation in life, poised between generations: her old father at one extreme, with his hospital roommate and her ex-husband "Granofsky, the Communist" on that side, while ranged on the other are Dennis, her pregnant and addicted teenage clients, and ultimately her baby-to-be. It is not that Alexandra engineers reconciliation across generational gulfs; rather, she mediates a passage, in herself, tending and loving and nourishing and nursing.

Alexandra meets Dennis on her way to the hospital. Paley has said that she couldn't get on with the story until she realized that he had to be a cabdriver so that they could meet. More important, he lives in a commune and writes songs for "The Lepers," who used to be "The Split Atom" (they changed their name because "they became too popular and their thing is anonymity. That's what they're known for" [125]), are thinking of becoming "Winter Moss," and do become "Edible Amanita" and eventually "Fair Fields of Corn."

As Alexandra attends to Dennis's lyrics, listening to his reality as an experience quite distinct from their enjoyable lovemaking, she hears a generalized sentimentality also quite distinct from her own—a sentimentality in which she supplies beef stew to supplement methadone and knows "there are all kinds" (126). Glossing his own lyric, Dennis explains that despite the "terrible troubles [that] hang over them, such as the absolute end of the known world quickly by detonation or slowly through the easygoing destruction of natural resources, [the kids] are still, even now, optimistic, humorous, and brave. In fact, they intend enormous changes at the last minute" (126).

Alexandra tries "to look at things in this powerful last-half-of-the-century way." Although she "had always had a progressive if sometimes reformist disposition . . . she could see straight ahead over the thick hot rod of love to solitary age and lonesome death" (126). Thus Alexandra hears—rather than stating or embodying—Paley's antiwar and ecological concerns, but she personalizes her care for the kids into her role as caseworker and recognizes how personal passions subsume philosophical positions. That "hot rod" is an image less phallic than generational from her reality-tested perspective.

Dealing with her father is even more problematical for Alexandra. The two are concerned with each other's mortality, but when their immortality is implied by her pregnancy, he can't handle it. From the attacked heart of the middle class he orders her to marry, so that Alexandra has to hope he does not survive the pregnancy and ruin "his interesting life at the very end of it when ruin is absolutely retroactive" (133).

At the end of seven sections, the story's consistent point of view ends with Alexandra's refusal to move into Dennis's commune or to allow him to move into her apartment. We stay with her to this point: inside her behavior as she bites "her lip to the edge of blood to show pain politely" (134) and inside her mind as she thinks about "the continuity of her work, how to be proud and not lose a productive minute" and "about the members of her case load one by one" (134). And we hear the final exchange of their dialogue, she: "I know exactly what I'm going to to" and he: "In that case, this is it, I'm splitting" (134).

But there is an eighth section of the story. Where we had listened, intimately, to the sounds of Alexandra's voice and thoughts, hearing with her ears Dennis's lyrics and lines and her father's wisdom and limits, now we hear the familiar voice of Paley as storyteller. It is the aural equivalent of a camera pulling back or a film cutting from subjective close-up to wide-angle panoramic overview, this shift to an omniscient voice that telescopes time and events to summarize what happened and comment wryly on the results.

Alexandra opens her apartment to three pregnant teenagers, thus ensuring "their health and her own" and taking notes to establish "a precedent in social work which would not be followed or even mentioned in state journals for about five years" (134). Her "father's life was not ruined," because he cracks his skull in a fall and loses "twenty, thirty years in a flood. . . . His eyes were rounder, he was often awe-struck, but he was smart as ever, and able to begin with fewer scruples to notice and appreciate" (134).

The baby is named Dennis Granofsky. In "his tiny honor" his father records a simple lyric that says "Who is the father? . . . I am the father" (135)—an acknowledgment that gets him kicked out of his commune. But on the baby's third birthday, Dennis produces a new folk-rock al-bum called "For Our Son." Its featured song, a dialogue between fa-ther and son, "was sung coast to coast and became famous from the dark Maine woods to Texas's shining gulf. It was responsible for a sta-tistical increase in visitors to old-age homes by the apprehensive mid-dle-aged and the astonished young" (136).

The story, in its last sardonic words, vetoes Alexandra's resistance to the general. Her personal, personalized social concerns, placed within the larger context—but with a tart tongue to cut through any cloying sweetness—of Paley's overseeing view, indirectly effect a universalized inching toward closer ties across generations. There may be some irony in the agency of this movement, but that its vehicle is poetry of any sort is surely part of the point. A Shelleyan strain in Paley wishes her storytelling words scattered among mankind as from an unextinguished hearth. Even folk-rock lyrics and short stories have their incantational force.

Though spread out over a decade of composition, the next three stories appearing in sequence in the book, "Politics," "Northeast Play-ground," and "The Little Girl," can usefully be grouped together as a triptych. Not only do they have a playground itself as a focal point of activity ranging from the healthiest to the most heinous, from public politics to private passion, but they may be taken together as a para-digm of three different registers of the Paley voice's narration.

The first is an impersonal third-person account (bordering on omni-scient, as appropriate to satire), except for a single phrase, "our neigh-borhood" (139), in the first sentence and then a consistent tone suggesting that the narrator is one who simply knows everything that happens in that neighborhood. The second is a first-person narration in which the "I" is implicitly the Paley writer-persona herself, as cer-tain self-reflexive passages unobtrusively suggest. And the third is a first-person performance, in which Paley's presence is felt in her role of story hearer.

This is not to say that they were conceived as a triptych, only that they might be considered together. Their sequential arrangement makes sense. Had they been designed as companion pieces, they would surely have more in common than a unity of setting (many of her stories, after all, have that) and a complementarity of point of view.

"Politics" is a story that goes swiftly around in a broad satirical circle like the best of Jules Feiffer's cartoons. Some mothers from the Lower West Side go in a group to the Board of Estimate to plead for a fence around their park because the children need protection from bums, tramps, perverts, junkies, whores, and Commies. They are successful, having been inspired to present their petition in song by a midwestern media man who "loved our old moldy pot New York" and who "was also clean-cut and attractive" (139).

Five of them take turns singing their request "before the high municipal podiums" (140), while all the women join in on a recitative chorus. The board members, including the mayor, are impressed and murmur their approval "in a kind of startled arpeggio round" (141), and the comptroller calls Parks, Traffic, and Child Welfare to expedite the project.

The next day, the fence is up by noon. That night, a Tactical Patrol Force cop snips a large hole in it to get the baseball equipment from the locker room inside. Surprised by a *Lower West Side Sun* reporter, he impresses her with his rhetoric, his copy of Camus's *The Rebel*, and his good looks and "inject[s] her with two sons, one Irish and one Italian, who sang to her in dialect all her life" (142).

The music goes round and round in this story, and it comes out when the valves of sex, seduction, rhetoric, and embarrassment are pressed. One note of political storytelling may be added. When "Politics" first appeared in *Win* (1968), the phone calls of the comptroller, that "famous financial nag" (141), were reported this way: "He threatened each laughingly with a grand jury investigation. All were agreeable in response and by noon the next day, the fence was up."[56] In the book, this passage has become, "All were agreeable when they heard his strict voice and temperate language. By noon the next day, the fence was up" (141). To the readership of a magazine subtitled "Peace and Freedom through Nonviolent Action," the pressure based on assumption of corruption was a pointed and appreciated joke. To the general readership, the open-ended irony of the adjectives *strict* and *temperate* is more palatable and thus more effective. The storyteller's song is attuned to her listeners—that is the politics of aesthetics (or vice versa), which is the story's subject, object, and model.

"Northeast Playground" seems to have more to say about politics

56

than "Politics." It is the story that Gelfant uses to exemplify Paley's ability as "wonderfully economic and elliptical. . . . In a four-page story . . . she spans a generation of mothers, their manners, politics and sociological self-definitions into 'special-interest group[s]'" (1975, 142). "When I went to the playground in the afternoon," it begins, "I met eleven unwed mothers on relief. Only four of them were whores, the rest of them were unwed on principle or because some creep had ditched them" (145). Connected thematically with "Enormous Changes," the story proceeds as if the narrator were like the reporter in "Politics" who asks questions "because she was trained in the disciplines of curiosity followed by intelligent inquiry" (141). The line of questioning might also suggest a field-worker in cultural anthropology, except that her tone persists in betraying the narrator.

Tonally, the use of "some creep" for absentee father and "very funny and lovable" (146) for all the babies sets up certain polarities. As the narrator catalogs the group, other attitudes enter. A certain nostalgia for the times with her own babies in the park is undercut by her romanticizing of the present group. What begins as a nonjudgmental observation gives way to conscious admiration: "What a wonderful calm unity in this group!" (146). She contrasts this state with the past, when the mothers quarreled by criticizing one another's children, using psychoanalytical jargon.[57]

Only two of the women and two children are given names. The others tend to be paired up: twin sisters dressed alike; a pair of "handsome dykey women," who are "whores and junkies and watched each other's babies when working or flying" (146); and two who are depressed, embarrassed to be on relief, "young and pretty, the way almost all young girls tend to be these days, and would probably never be ditched again" (147). Again the narrator's sentimentality is undercut by irony, because when she tries to reassure these last two, one of them says, "My mother says don't feel bad, Allison's a love-child," and the narrator understands: "The mother was accepting and advanced, but poor" (147).

The most beautiful child is dark brown Claude, whose white "mother" Leni got him from "some dude" who couldn't pay her what he owed and paid her off with "the first little bastard he had" (146). Leni seems satisfied to be an Aid to Dependent Children mother with time for "a trick a week" at most. The most articulate of the group is Janice, "a political woman, conscious of power structure and power itself" (146).

Her cataloging done, the narrator reports that she asked "one or two simple questions and made a statement" (147) on the afternoon of her visit. When she asks the women if it wouldn't be better if they mixed in with other mothers and babies, "really a friendly bunch," they reply, "No." When she asks what "this ghettoization will do to" their children, they just smile "proudly" (147). The statement follows: "In a way, it was like this when my children were little babies. The ladies who once wore *I Like Ike* buttons sat on the south side of the sandbox, and the rest of us who were revisionist Communist and revisionist Trotskyite and revisionist Zionist registered Democrats sat on the north side" (147–48).

When most of them respond "NO kidding!" to this statement, Paley omits all description. We can probably hear the mixture of tones, making assumptions based on the catalog. But Janice is their political spokeswoman, and she has the last word in the story because absolutely nothing more needs to be added. Themes and attitudes, subject and object, the feelings behind the story told and the story heard—all are reduced to the kernel of irreducible truth in Janice's message: "Beat it" (148).

It is difficult to reconcile "The Little Girl" with the prevailing view of Paley's hopefulness.[58] It is a story, after all, about a blonde fourteen-year-old runaway from the Midwest who is raped, brutalized, and killed. Moreover, the repeated experiencing of this child's death, as it might seem to her parents and as it apparently is felt by Charlie the storyteller, is a living curse worse than death.

Charlie cannot get the event out of his head. He is obsessive about details, about getting every word spoken just right, about sparing no item—just as he has been spared none in the report of "Hector the beat cop" (156). Nor, as an older black, does he spare social commentary from his perspective: "Park is full of little soft yellow-haired baby chicks. They ain't but babies. They far from home, and you better believe it, they love them big black cats walking around before lunchtime, jutting their apparatus. They think they gonna leap off that to heaven. Maybe so" (151–52).

The questions that keep coming to Charlie are existential ones: Why this girl? Why this time? Why wasn't it the way it usually was? Why did Angie show up just when Carter finished? Why my place? Why me? He asks all these questions, knowing they cannot be answered, and so he focuses his efforts on answering the questions of exactly what happened, piecing together a plausible—however unpalatable—scenario. (The defense mechanisms are called displacement and sublimation.)

Carter had asked to use Charlie's place before Charlie knew with whom he'd use it, and Charlie had agreed, even though his white junkie "lodger" might be around. The girl had agreed to have sex with Carter, but because of their relative size he had had to force her. He admitted having slapped her "once or twice" (154) and left her "bleeding out between her legs" (155). But investigation showed that she had been assaulted with a blunt instrument or fist, bitten and torn as if by an animal, and died on contact with the ground at the bottom of the airshaft. "She just tossed out that toilet window wide awake alive," Charlie says (156), and the accurate rendering of the dialect allows the verb to be active or passive.

Charlie's present speculation ("That what I think right now" [158]) is that Carter used the girl and left her wounded, that Angie found her and used her worse, and that the girl then somehow found "some power" to "raise herself up that windowsill and . . . just topple herself out" (158). When Charlie concludes, "That is what happened" (158), he seems to be trying to persuade himself. He has convinced some (including William Peden), while others may share with me the possibility that either Carter or Angie "picked her up like she was nothing, a bag of busted bones, and dumped her out the fifth-floor window" (157). For Charlie, perhaps, there is some consolation in spreading out the misery of guilt among the company.

When the story first appeared in *Paris Review* (1974), just months before publication of the book, it began with this paragraph: "My old friend Charley that I've known for 20, 25 years stopped me in the street. He said, I've got something to tell you. Now, sit down. Right here. That was the steps of the Cafe Zipp in the middle of Macdougal Street. He put his hand on my knee. Then he said, now you listen, this is what happened."[59] That this passage is omitted entirely from the book's version requires critical speculation, because the whole nature of the performance is changed thereby. Instead of placing the audience inside the story (like the hearer who says "says Aunt Rose" in "Goodbye and Good Luck" [*LDM*, 9]) and identifying his or her relationship with the storyteller, thus defining the reader's place concretely as well, we are now asked to infer the storytelling urgency and accept a generalized story hearer.

Several explanations are available. The context of the book with its surrounding stories and its nature as *collection* makes the encounter of a writer-persona with Charlie superfluous. On reflection, the specific allusions to Macdougal Street and Cafe Zipp diminish the story's broad effect. The insistence on details of the writer's connection with Charlie smacks of special pleading and distracts or distances the reader, perhaps even supplying an unwanted cushion for the horror. Or—and this would be my choice—there is new confidence in method so that the presence of the story hearer is clearly sensed in Charlie's telling of his tale; a new collection of Paley's stories has made the Paley persona a prominent player among the performers.

No Paley story has received more attention from critics than "A Conversation with My Father." Baumbach called it his "favorite of the second collection" (305) and Peden "just about the best story about writing a story that I've ever read" (723). Theodore Solotaroff, who published the story originally in *New American Review* (1971), coupled it with a Leonard Michaels contribution as stories in which "the issues of writing fiction become a paradigm of the complexity of experience and vice versa, while what is imagined and what is not become inextricably mingled."[60]

In the story, the narrator visits her ailing, eighty-six-year-old father in the hospital. The book says, before its table of contents, "Everyone in this book is imagined into life except the father. No matter what story he has to live in, he's my father, I. Goodside, M.D., artist, and storyteller" (facing contents page). We cannot, then, as Kamel has mistakenly done (45–6), confuse matters by calling the narrator Faith, who is not Dr. Goodside's daughter but Gersh or Sid Darwin's. We may call her Grace, as long as we understand that we are talking about a Grace imagined into life as the Paley storytelling persona.

The narrator's father asks her to write "a simple story . . . the kind de Maupassant wrote, or Chekhov, the kind you used to write" (161). She tries to comply, writing down "a story that had been happening for a couple of years right across the street" (162). In a single inset paragraph, she reads to him of a mother who became a junkie to maintain a close friendship with her teenage-junkie son. When the boy gives it all up, leaving "the city and his mother in disgust," she is left grieving, hopeless, and alone. "We all visit her" (162) is the closing tag.

The father objects, complaining incidentally (Paley's self-reflexive mode) about her "Faith in a Tree"—"people sitting in trees talking senselessly, voices from who knows where" (162). He asks for details, she answers specific questions about the characters, and she tries again. Now she produces a full-length (seven-paragraph inset) Paleyesque version, complete with telling details, a snatch of verse, an adolescent love story bringing together the juvenile editors/publishers of mimeographed journals called *Oh! Golden Horse* (for the junkie audience) and *Man Does Live by Bread Alone* (for the apricots-and-nuts trade), and several wry, ironic, satiric comments imbedded in the indirection of an offhand tone and play of diction.

In the dialogue that follows, the story-within-a-story is brought up to the surface of the main story, the conversation. Her father makes three points: to compliment her sense of humor, to disparage her storytelling style, and to inquire about the mother in the story. He rejects the possibility of change in that woman's life, takes some nitroglycerin, and plugs himself back into the oxygen tank.

Now the storyteller, though she "had promised the family to always let him have the last word when arguing," asserts "in this case . . . a different responsibility. That woman lives across the street. She's my knowledge and my invention." Thus she composes a hopeful epilogue, not an ending but a continuing of the woman's life as employee "in a storefront community clinic in the East Village," praised by the head doctor. The narrator's father is still listening, dismisses this addition as another joke, and predicts that the woman will backslide. And Dr. Goodside does get the last word, asking his daughter, "When will you look [tragedy] in the face?" (167).[61]

Clearly, when a story includes not only a telling and retelling of a story but also discussions thereof, its nature as metafiction makes it a cynosure of commentators' attention. Harry Blake, for example, has his version of postmodern fun with the story, identifying its "conflict . . . between writing as the writing up of the old reality principle as exemplified by the father distrustful and critical of the expansion of the story into the storyless story anyway and writing out the new into something important as exemplified by the writer."[62]

For most commentators the story turns on the issue of responsibility, that of the storytelling character and that of writers in general.[63] DeKoven carefully distinguishes between Paley the writer *of* the story and Paley the narrator-persona writer *in* the story. The ultimate responsibility she believes Paley to have accepted as storyteller is both moral and political: Her "structures . . . are rooted not only in an assertion of openendedness and possibility, and in a nonlinear vision of life's events, but also, ultimately, in a profound commitment to freedom as a primary value" (219).

Two full-length treatments of the story, by Nicholas Peter Humy in *Delta* and by D. S. Neff in *Literature and Medicine*, testify to its provocative capacity.[64] Though both treatments have reference to Paley's use of the Scheherazade motif and both engage the story in a spirit of intellectual challenge, a reader with only these two commentaries would wonder if they were engaging the same text. Humy, invoking the names of Roland Barthes, Victor Shklovsky, William Gass, and Harold Bloom and employing some of the vocabulary and tactics of deconstruction, nevertheless reaches an interpretive, quasi-feminist conclusion. When the narrator speaks of "a different responsibility" toward her father, Humy says, "She will demonstrate to him that it is not in the end that meaning is found by changing the ending of the woman's story" (94). But where Humy talks of a narrator of a story in which the narrator tells versions of a story to *her* father, Neff talks about "Grace Paley, the daughter of a physician, [who] seeks to establish a new dialectical balance between medical and literary efforts to cope with mortality" (119).

Humy sees the piece as "the story of a conversation [tracing] for us the struggle that we all encounter when we acquire language, the tool of the father, and use it with, for, or against him. . . . The narrator, by telling the stories within the father's story, has demonstrated what the responsibility of the storyteller is not. She has not formed the lives of her inventions to *his* given end and meaning, to *his* law. And, in the telling of her father's story, she has commuted his sentence, and, like the narrator of 'Debts,' fulfilled her true responsibility: 'That is, to tell their stories as simply as possible in order, you might say, to save a few lives'" (94–5).

In Neff's reading, the father as physician is trying to get his daughter to accept his own mortality, trying "to heal [her] psychic wounds resulting from his impending demise." That is why he calls for "traditional tragic plot structures with 'closed' endings." The daughter, by contrast, is using "'extraordinary means,' open-ended stories which magically negate death." Thus her "metafiction . . . simultaneously reinforces and undermines the aesthetic integrity of fictional remedies for death's sting, forcing art to wrestle with its artifice as it investigates ethical complexities of healing." Neff sees the story concluding "in ironic stasis. . . . The expressive wars of Paley's characters make us realize that love exists beyond the confines of tragedy and comedy, and that the most mature art, like the most ethical physician, must revel in a capacity for self-transcendence in an endless quest to encompass life's inexplicable mixture of endings and renewals" (119–24).

When a story can evoke rhetorical flights on such divergent trajectories, its open-ended capacities are proved, which may or may not be a tribute to its aesthetic excellence. It is interesting that Humy and Neff both, though to different ends, discuss the metaphorical language of the story. Humy, whose careful analysis of Paley's use of tenses and punctuation is instructive, nevertheless can say that the father "and his condition are not described with language, but created in it. The metaphors which the narrator uses do not help to make her father 'recognizable' to the reader, rather, they call attention to the language and testify that the act of writing will intrude upon the tale" (88). Neff, for his part, says, "The writer's desire to deny or postpone the process of dying manifests itself through her formulation of metaphors . . . that temporarily reduce the terrors of death by disguising them in language which insulates and distances them from reality" (119–20). They are talking about the *same* metaphors, the ones labeled as such by the narrator.

What needs to be clarified is that the father's language—hardly "the plainest words possible" that Neff claims, preventing "him from hiding amidst the refuge of figurative language" (120)—is made up of a different set of metaphors. The phrase *potassium shortage* may have a "scientific" ring to it, but it is no less figurative than *bloody motor* and *brainy light* (161). In fact, what Paley does as the story goes on in its structure of conversation, dialogue, and dialectic is to produce a synthesis of the two metaphorical sets, as when she says, "Guilt is the stony heart of nine tenths of all clinically diagnosed cancers" (164) and when the imagery of life-preserving medical apparatus serves as analogy for the life-rendering apparatus of the storyteller's open-ended art. The story's achievement lies in this synthesis, transforming, just as it says it does, life-and-death incidents into stories of mortality and immortality.

Sandwiched between Paley's two most frequently discussed stories, "The Immigrant Story" suffers from inattention. Short enough to be printed on one page of *Fiction* magazine in 1972, it is nevertheless significant enough for the author to draw attention to it often, in discussions and interviews. The story has two distinct parts. The first is a conversation, an argument really, between Faith (the first-person narrator, though unnamed here) and Jack, her longtime friend and present lover. It is as nearly abstract to the point of allegorizing as Paley ever gets. The second, what Paley calls "the story of that story," is Jack's story of his parents. Paley says she had that story in mind for more than twenty years but didn't know how to tell it until the dialogue of the first part showed her the way.[65] The two sections are unified by two visual images Jack has of his parents, two snapshots from his memory book that still cause him to rage against his parents and to account for the grayness of his view of the world.

That's what the argument is about: Faith's "rotten rosy temperament" (173), as Jack calls it, remembering as far back as her sixth-grade show-and-tell of patriotism, versus his unrelieved grayness. "Rosiness is not a worse windowpane than gloomy gray" (174) to see the world clearly, Faith says, having grown "up in the summer sunlight of upward mobility [that] leached out a lot of that dark ancestral grief" (171). But for all the story's references to long-range historical factors, political philosophy, and religion, it is the personal emotional history at the heart of Jack's memories that matters.

His opening gambit, "Isn't it a terrible thing to grow up in the shadow of another person's sorrow?" (171) leads, after a brief abstract exchange, to the first of Jack's fixed images: "One day I woke up and my father was asleep in the crib" (172). Even now, this image evokes rage at both the "bitch" who avoided sex and tried "to make him feel guilty" and her husband—"Where were his balls?"—who smilingly accepts his wife's commands.

Faith has another explanation. Jack, who was five at the time, and his sister "had scarlet fever and needed the decent beds and more room to sweat, come to a fever crisis, and either get well or die" (173). Paley has spoken of Jack's being "awful" toward his parents, but in this passage she has Faith utter her most virulent attack on psychiatry: "Anyone whose head hasn't been fermenting with the compost of ten years of gluttonous analysis . . . could tell you" (173).[66]

Again this exchange gives way to spiraling generalization until Jack insists that Faith just listen. The rest of the story is his summary of his parents' immigration to New York from Poland. Jack's father came first, but by the time he could send for his wife the famine had eaten up "the bodies of the [three] little boys" (175) left behind. Jack pictures his parents' life in New York, never going anywhere, the two holding each other's hand. The closing picture focuses on them at the table, the father holding "both her hands in his as though they needed warmth," reading the newspaper to her "in that old bulb light." And beyond the table and their heads lies "the darkness of the kitchen, the bedroom, the dining room, the shadowy darkness where as a child I ate my supper, did my homework and went to bed" (175). The "terrible thing" of Jack's experience, that icon upon which the rage of his uncomprehending "awfulness" is fixed, has now been presented for Faith and us all to see.[67]

Like "A Conversation with My Father," "The Long-Distance Runner" has drawn the attention of many commentators. But unlike the earlier piece of metafiction, this topical fantasy, the last story in the book, has received no full-scale treatment, nor have the reasons for the attention been fully understood. Whether in brief commentary such as Julia Wolf Mazow's remark that the story is "about the need to re-establish a connection with the past . . . Faith literally runs to her past and back to the present" or in the misguided attempt of John Crawford to identify "archetypal patterns," critics have either focused too narrowly on one piece of a complex structure or obscured, in a cloud of extrapolation, the way the story works. What is even more dismaying is that Crawford, Kamel, and Mandel, to name a few, in making errors of fact are led inevitably to distortions of meaning (though, to be fair, Mandel is generally accurate in her description).[68]

Faith takes up running in middle age and one day leaves her family, takes the subway to Brighton Beach, and runs back to the old neighborhood, now completely black, "where her childhood happened" (198). She takes sanctuary in her old apartment, where Mrs. Luddy, her son Donald, and "three little baby girls nearly the same age" (188) give her an intensive three-week course in family processes—love, learning, continuity, communication, tradition, and storytelling—more shared among different populations than divergent. When Mrs. Luddy says it is time to go, Faith runs all the way home, where she is greeted as though she had just jogged once around the block.

The allusive quality of the story is announced in its title. Various meanings attached to running in Sillitoe's "Loneliness of the Long Distance Runner" and Updike's *Rabbit, Run*[69] are suggested by Paley in the sense that Faith is escaping from perceived, experienced, conflicted reality. But for Paley's protagonist there is also a quest for another reality, another truth, implicit in the running. Perhaps more to the point of the story, Faith's running can be compared to the swimming in Cheever's "The Swimmer," so that its function on a metaphorical, allegorical, or symbolic level can be recognized. The submerged allusion to Cheever's story is embedded in the opening passages, when Faith starts her training in Connecticut, "in the wide-zoned suburban hills" (179).

Most of the allusions in "The Long-Distance Runner," however, contribute to the significant element of self-reflexivity. The presence of Faith, Richard, Tonto, Jack, and Mrs. Raftery provide the immediate placing of this story in the larger context of Faith's family and neighborhood. References to Faith's parents in the Children of Judea, to ex-husband Ricardo in Chile, and to sister Hope, brother Charlie, and Grandpa and Grandma when they all lived together in Brooklyn enrich the detailed evocation of that "realistic" context. But back in the old neighborhood, Faith makes connections of another kind. She remembers "Mrs. Goreditsky, [a] very very fat lady" who lived in the "first floor front, 1B" apartment (184) and "Crazy Eddy's house . . . famous 1510" (190), which the reader must associate with the Mrs. Goredinsky and Eddie of 1434 made famous in "Time Which Made a Monkey of Us All" (*LDM*)—a story unconnected with Faith, until now. In this story, Faith keeps making a point of how she is resisting that effect of time, even while her trip back in time reinforces its power and that process.

The changes in spellings and numbers are somewhat disorienting, but they alert the reader to pay attention to what is going on. When Faith volunteers the information that her mother is dead, only to wonder why she says that when the Darwins are ensconced nearby at the Home for the Golden Ages, we understand the confusion between Faith and Paley, a kind of crisis of consciousness in slipping back and forth between created writer-persona and creating writer-persona. On her return run home, Faith stops "at the northeast playground where I met a dozen young mothers intelligently handling their little ones" (196). Again, the reference to "Northeast Playground" and the deliberate echo of its first sentence place Faith in conjunction with a story in which she had no explicit part.

It would appear that in "The Long-Distance Runner" Paley is drawing together many of the elements of her storytelling in what is both a summing up and a looking forward. Familiar topics, attitudes, methods, and experiences—hers *and* Faith's—become elements in this story or are at least alluded to within it. And the structural device employed to accomplish all this is the running. It is characteristic of Paley's evolving art that she can treat the running itself as part of literal description, social observation, cultural history, and the like, on the one hand, and as a figural vehicle for movement backward (while looking forward) in time and place, on the other.

The commentators so far have treated Faith's run as an event taking place in the "real time" of her life with Richard, Tonto, Jack, and the rest. But the text does not support this reading. The fact that she takes the subway to Brighton Beach to start her run and then three weeks later runs all the way home—not to mention the swirling about her of all those disparate, representative voices and faces or her family's be-havior concerning her absence—should sufficiently put the reader on guard. What is especially important to observe, however, is how the whole experience back in the old neighborhood and in the old flat with Mrs. Luddy's family—including getting there and back again—has only the coherence of a dream. Whether we call it dream, fantasy, sur-realism, allegorical mind-trip, or mythic voyage of discovery, the main body of the story is separated from real time and place, precisely the way the voyage of Coleridge's Ancient Mariner is separated from—but impinges on—the Wedding Guest's reality.

Like the Mariner, Faith tells her story again and again. At its heart, with Mrs. Luddy telling how *her* mother had stories to tell and raised her on them, with her and Faith trading stories between them, and with her son Donald taking them all in, this too is a story about stories, storytelling, and story hearers. But unlike the Mariner, Faith elicits from her audience the uncomprehending response, "What?" (198).

Neither the story nor the book can end with that interrogative. The final paragraph answers more than the explicit question: "Because it isn't usually so simple. Have you known it to happen much nowadays? A woman inside the steamy energy of middle age runs and runs. She finds the houses and streets where her childhood happened. She lives in them. She learns as though she was still a child what in the world is coming next" (198). This passage relates the story to Paley's work as a whole in a way no critical commentary can. The voice is no longer Faith's; it is Paley addressing her reader. And the reader, cherishing that steamy energy, wonderingly anticipates what is to come.

Later the Same Day and Later

In its very first story, *Later the Same Day* announces a new emphasis on self-reflexivity in Paley's work. While it is not, strictly speaking, meta-fictional in structure or content, "Love" does refer to the creative process of a poet and to the interrelationship of life (love) and art.

The first-person narrator is unnamed, and so is her husband. Ordinarily, this arrangement would suggest Paley in her role as her own narrator-persona, as in "Wants," "Debts," and "A Conversation with My Father" (*ECLM*). The fact that the narrator is a poet, like Paley, adds to the suggestion. The situation is complicated, however, when the narrator mentions her friend Louise. Is this Faith's friend Louise, and should we therefore infer that the narrator is Faith? Or does the reference suggest that Faith and Grace Paley, with a friend in common, exist on the same level of "reality"? Or do we cop out on coincidental names?

What makes this issue crucial is that the whole story turns on another character who bridges levels of reality—and explicitly so in the text—Dotty Wasserman. Instead of two things bumping into each other to form a Paley story, "Love," which barely fills a single *New Yorker* page,[70] has at least four matters crossing and colliding.

The story begins simply enough with the narrator's poem about love-evoking memory, a poem that seems less Proustian than it does a Paley version of Hammerstein's "Hello Young Lovers" from *The King and I*. The narrator's husband's response is to rehearse his own annals of love memories from adolescent summer lakes through his years as a poet and ending the sequence with Dotty Wasserman. Now, Dotty Wasserman is a character in Paley's first story, "The Contest" (*LDM*), who despite (or perhaps because of) disparaging treatment at the hands of that story's narrator emerges as a relatively attractive figure. She is subsequently mentioned, as we have seen, in "Faith in a Tree" (*ECLM*). Not only does the narrator's husband profess to have loved that created (by his wife?) character, but he has imagined an existence for her that extends beyond the time frame of "The Contest" and crosses his and his wife's lives at several stages in their own history.

The narrator marvels about the way love "glides to solid invented figures from the true remembered wraiths" (5–6). She goes shopping (thereby getting an opportunity for some socioeconomic observation) and begins "to mumble a new poem" (6). At this point the final bumping element intrudes when she sees Margaret, an old associate with whom she fought two years previously. Their politics diverged, and her best friend (her "lifelong park, P.T.A., and antiwar-movement sister"[7]) Louise was lost to Margaret's position. Now the narrator and Margaret exchange instinctive smiles, and "so foolish is the true lover when responded to" that the narrator takes Margaret's hand, presses it to her cheek, and kisses it (7).

Later, the narrator's husband interprets the kiss as meant for Louise, and their evening together touches on diplomacy, disarmament, economics, poetry, family, and sex. The punch line of this cameo of a story, this digest of the several intersections among Grace Paley's life and the lives of her created world, is given to the husband the next morning. "You're some lover," he says, ". . . you remind me a lot of Dotty Wasserman" (7).

With "Distance" (*ECLM*), Paley had reworked material from an earlier success, "An Interest in Life" (*LDM*). With "Dreamer in a Dead Language," she rethought material from "Faith in the Afternoon" (ECLM), a story about Faith's visit to her parents at the Children of Judea, Home for the Golden Ages, Coney Island Branch, because she was not entirely satisfied that she had used it successfully. For the reader who comes to "Dreamer" with a clear memory of "Afternoon," the onomastics may be confusing. Gersh and Gittel Darwin have become Sid and Celia, and Mrs. Hegel-Shtein, who had been Celia, has lost her Christian name. In the story Faith's mother tells about Anita Franklin, the villain is named Arthur Mazzano. Now he has become Philip Mazzano (though at our first meeting in "Faith in a Tree" and still in the *American Review* version[71] of "Dreamer" he is Phillip), but we know it's the same person because Faith warns Philip not to let on to her folks that he is "the guy who dumped" Anita Franklin (15).

I do not mean to suggest that we are talking about two versions of the same story. Most of the characters are the same, several topoi or motifs recur, and the basic situation overlaps, but each story has its own identity and integrity. I am arguing, however, that "Dreamer" is the more fully realized story, with a more thoroughgoing integration of its elements into a centered, cohesive whole. Perhaps in part that is a function of the more consistent third-person-restricted point of view, but it may also be true that without the excursions into omniscience—the setting down of "certain facts [that] may become useful" (*ECLM*, 33)—in the earlier story, the later one would not work so well as it does.[72]

Faith at the time of the story is much put-upon, misunderstood, unrecognized, and unacknowledged. The people around her simply ignore or override the identity that she is discovering in herself and struggling to assert. Three generations of significant others move and interact around her, but they almost seem to collude in treating her as an object.

Philip, her lover, professing to admire the poetry her father is producing out at the Home, seems bent on competing with her ex-husband Ricardo for entrepreneurship over publication and promotion rights. He demonstrates his wit by table-hopping around the Green Coq to repeat whatever clever line he comes up with, by parodying "Twelve Days of Christmas" in putting down Ricardo ("Who's that jerk know? Four old maids in advertising, three Seventh Avenue models, two fairies in TV, one literary dyke" [14]), and by conceiving the title for a proposed book of Sid's poetry—and of this story.[73] That Faith does not encourage Philip to pursue the project costs her not only his anger and sarcasm but "the longed-for night in which sleep, sex, and affection would take their happy turns" (15).

Faith's visit to the Home with Richard and Tonto is a series of inopportune incidents that pile up on top of one another like the choreography of a Marx Brothers movie—only the effect is anguish, not laughter. The behavior of Faith's father with the kids, the attitude of both her parents toward her (though when her mother presses Faith's hand to her cheek, we recognize that Faith has come naturally by this characteristic gesture), the oppressive presence of Mrs. Hegel-Shtein, the depressing glimpses of the incapacitated old—all push Faith toward an angry bitterness.

When they are alone together, Mr. Darwin succeeds in escalating his daughter's alienation. First he confesses that Ricardo has been visiting, and he actually defends Ricardo to Faith, the wife he deserted, the mother of children he fails to visit or support. Then Mr. Darwin tells Faith that the way he feels about himself and about life has made him want to leave the Home, that he would divorce her mother if he could—but cannot, because they were never married.

Faith responds to this revelation in the cold irony of "the real and ordinary world" (31). When her father tells her the reason he and her mother never married was their "idealism," Faith tells him she has three lovers and says, "Which of my three lovers do you think I ought to settle for, a high-class idealist like me" (31). His reaction is reversion to middle-class cliché: Do you do it for money? Where did we go wrong? We did our best; never tell your mother. Faith runs back to get the boys from her mother, when Philip, with the timing of a great comedian, shows up to discuss Mr. Darwin's poetry with him. "This is probably a comedy, this crummy afternoon," Faith thinks (34), and leaves with two words, "Goodbye" and "No."

In the sand of Brighton Beach, Faith regains her sense of self and place. She shares childhood memories with her sons and an image of the Russian grandfather she never saw. When Richard tells her she has to get the Darwins out of that place, she says, "Why is everything my responsibility, every goddamn thing?" (36), and when he says, "It just is," she wants to scream, "Help!"

In a characteristic authorial intrusion, undercutting sentimentality or pathos just before the conclusion, Paley says, "Had [Faith] been born ten, fifteen years later, she might have done so, screamed and screamed." Then, distancing us from the sadness of her character with idiosyncratic phrasing, she adds, "Instead, tears made their usual protective lenses for the safe observation of misery" (36). When Faith lies flat on the beach and tells the boys to bury her, sensitive Richard takes her seriously and tells her he was joking. "I was only joking too," she says, and saying it she does joke: "Only up to here . . . so I can give you a good whack every now and then when you're too fresh" (36).

Richard, "his heart eased in one long sigh," joins Tonto for the closing image: "Giving her lots of room for wiggling and whacking, the two boys began to cover most of her with sand" (36). Under that October sun, with all those other relationships not discarded but eclipsed, Faith plays her one fully realized role. As single mother she is nearly covered by what her sons pile on her, yet she is free to be her wiggling, whacking self.

For three paragraphs toward the middle of "In the Garden," the tense of the narration shifts to the present before returning to the past for the rest of the story. It is practically the only indication, in an otherwise disorienting tale, of the controlling (if hardly comforting) presence of the storyteller.

Set in a Caribbean island, the story focuses on a man whose daughters had been kidnapped eight months earlier. The man is very successful, with money and property and a beautiful wife, and his bravado sustains the illusion that his daughters will return, that no tragic loss can happen to him. But that is merely the *object* of the story; its subjects are those who observe the object, learning, judging, interpreting, and placing in perspective.

The structure is familiar; it is the three-level or double-envelope setup that charts a process of discovery. At the outside is an elderly lady who is a neighbor. She is "wasted and stiff" (39), suffering from a degenerative disease, and she is the only character whose thoughts we are permitted to know. She understands the pathos and the irony in the beautiful young mother's sentences that begin "When they come home" (39), and she cannot bear the rich father's shouting voice.

Into the neighborhood comes a stranger on vacation, who, during the few days of his stay, talks to several of the friendly neighbors about the kidnapping. At the innermost level we hear those neighbors: a woman who bursts into tears remembering the children; a man who attributes the father's insults and hatred to his having been "driven mad" (41); and another man who presents the prevailing view of the whole scenario, the botched kidnapping, the delayed ransom, the probable results for the children of the crossed miscalculations of kidnappers and father. Those successive paragraphs in present tense take us from elderly woman to stranger to neighbors, thereby signaling the process that the structure supports.

There is a political dimension to the story. The father is anti-Communist, the stranger a Communist ("tenderhearted but relentless" [41]), but one of the story's points is the way human drama and character transcend politics, rendering political explanations of behavior and events pointless.

The stranger's farewell visit to the elderly woman closes the story, bringing us back to the woman's perspective. She says to him, "You see, sir, what the world is like" (43). As he leaves, she watches him, moving only her eyes, practicing what her life will soon be like when that is the only movement left her. She admits to herself, sadly, "that the eyes' movement even if minutely savored was not such an adventurous journey" (44). And then the final sentence—"But she had become interested in her own courage" (44)—blends her thinking with the observing vantage of the omniscient storyteller.

It is difficult for the reader not to accept the elliptical, understated, implicit view of "what the world is like" in this subtly ironic Eden. "In the Garden" is less "about hearing stories," as Coppula says (68), then, than it is about discovering possible meanings of a story.

In a short piece in *The Villager* in May 1978, Judy Slawson reported that Grace Paley "is now working on a story about a trip to China," a statement that seems to contradict an earlier observation: "She was very impressed with what she saw on her trip to China but doubts its relevance for American problems."[74] The story to which Slawson refers could have been "Somewhere Else" or "The Expensive Moment." Though neither is *about* a trip to China, both have reference, direct and indirect, to that experience—and both, in fact, clarify its relevance.

"Somewhere Else" begins with an incident on a tour to China. Faith, along with her friends Ann Reyer and Ruth Larsen, are among a group of twenty-two touring Americans who are all "to a tourist in love with the Chinese revolution, Mao Tse-tung, and the Chinese people" (48). They all "take pictures in order to remember the Chinese people better, to be able to tell our friends about them after supper and give slide shows in churches and schools later on. Truthfully, we do it with politics in mind, if not in total command" (47). But the Chinese, feeling betrayed by Antonioni's film on China, with its "denigrating attraction to archaic charm" (47), insist that permission be requested of and granted by any subjects before they may be photographed.

Their "political guidance counselor" (47) lectures the group members when this rule has been violated, and before the accusation is specified Faith guiltily thinks about the "terrible temptations for photograph-taking" (48). The picture in question, when identified, Faith imagines as a wonderful contrast of a peasant pulling his cart of country produce, a boy sleeping on top, down a narrow street of "buildings lined with first-class plumbing for the English empire's waste" (49). The accused is Fred, a "poor-people's lawyer" (53), who is defended by Joe Larsen (Ruth's husband, we assume, but don't know for sure until "The Expensive Moment"), who admits to having led Fred astray. The explanations are irrelevant to the Chinese, who use the incident to reemphasize the rule: "You must ask the people first, do they wish to be photographed" (54).

Three months later, most of the group reassembles for a Chinese reunion "full of food, slides, insights, and commentary" (54). Joe arrives forty minutes late and insists on telling a story. He has been working in the South Bronx, leading a group of Youth Corps kids in the making of a movie. But when he does some shooting on his own, panning a long background shot that may include a group of Puerto Ricans

on the stoop, one of the members of the group runs after him and
snatches his musette bag, camera and film and all, off his shoulder.
The film is ripped out and exposed as Joe tries to reason with the
group. But when the group members return the camera to him, Joe
insists on giving it to them against their wishes. This action precisely
mirrors the incident in China, where the counselor rejects Fred's gesture to surrender his camera.

Paley has said that she could not tell the story about the incident in
China until the similar incident in the Bronx bumped into it.[75] But she
puts the two together in what seems a casual, circumstantial way, carefully avoiding any explicit moralizing. The elliptical narration of
events, much of it a matter of Faith's repeating what others say, leads
readers to draw their own conclusions. The "somewhere else" of the
title is any place where someone else's behavior is determined in ways
different from the familiar. Good intentions cannot excuse actions offensive to others, nor can ignorance of different, strange, exotic, or
foreign attitudes and values do so.

The phrase *somewhere else* recurs in a central passage in "The Expensive Moment," set off by dashes for emphasis and perhaps to draw
attention to the connection between stories. It is part of an explanation
Faith gives Ruth, but it occurs in a scene later than the one in which
Faith impulsively kisses Ruth's hand—mirroring the characteristic,
crucial gesture in "Love" and thus forming another link among stories.

The passage in question, which I have called central, explains why
Faith has ended her affair with Nick, "the famous sinologist." She has
realized that the man wasn't the attraction but what he represented
was: "It was travel she longed for—somewhere else—the sexiness of
the unknown parts of far imaginable places" (190). Those last seven
words make up the original title of the story, as it appeared in *Mother
Jones* in 1983, and so they give a fair indication of what is a primary
focus of it—Faith's romanticism, which colors her politics and her personal relationships. The allure of the remote and different, as long as
they can be imagined into hopeful, beautiful, and concretely "real"
form, is a key to her aesthetic.

The story is presented in the third person, straying only incidentally
from Faith's center of consciousness (to Jack's), and it constructs a
loose weave of several themes or pieces of material. Friendship is one,
the bond between Faith and Ruth growing stronger as they share yet
another phase of their common problems in parenting. In the story's
final scene is an image of Ruth standing in the doorway: "Faith's

friend, the listener and the answerer, listening" (195). The image links Ruth with the various mother figures in Paley's stories and more specifically with the sequence of listeners and story hearers in the succession of six stories that ends *Later the Same Day*. Perhaps most important, the image suggests the possibility that it is Ruth rather than Faith—at least in this story—whom we should identify as an authorial persona.

The parent-child relationship is another theme, especially Faith vis-à-vis Richard and Ruth's with her absent daughter Rachel (a motif carried over from "Ruthy and Edie" and shared with Selena in "Friends"). A third theme deals with Faith's "monogamy" with Jack and her affair with Nick. She says, "if one is living a whole life in passionate affection with another, this differentness on occasional afternoons is often enough" (184). But it is not enough for very long. As she tells Ruth, "it never got thick enough. I mean woofed and warped" (190). And as the story's first sentence says, "Faith did not tell Jack" (179).[76] Yet toward the end, even as she acknowledges her Chinese visitor's observation that "in time you love the children more and the man less," Faith wants "to run home and find Jack and kiss his pink ears and his 243 last hairs, to call out, Old friend, don't worry, you are loved" (194).

Other themes surface throughout, such as the relationship of politics and art, Faith's conflicted memories of her father, and her memory of participating in a draft-resisters' action. But it is the theme of China that pulls separate strands together. Nick's rationalistic position on China has prevented him from being granted permission to visit. While Ruth and Faith have been there, he in his expertise has tried "to free us all of distance and mystery" (180). This clear-cut conflict with Faith's romanticism is dramatized in the scene where they both imagine Keats working in the fields of Shanxi, trying to compose poetry acceptable to the Great Leap Forward and the Cultural Revolution. Nick's parody of the opening lines of "La Belle Dame sans Merci" (183) has added force if taken in the context of Faith's remark to Philip in "Dreamer" (15) that it is one of her two favorite poems.

Faith's questions about China's foreign policy first evoke Nick's contempt and then exacerbate her differences with her ever more radical son Richard. (What infuriates him is that she continues to mother him when he talks politics.) A meeting with Chinese artists, a "cultural event," produces some ironic quips about culture, about aesthetic and social politics, and about the sexist component at every level of life East and West. Finally, a Chinese woman named Xie Feng (who remembers meeting Ruth) visits Faith. She takes pictures (asking permission first, a deliberate echo of "Somewhere Else"), they walk around the neighborhood, Faith introduces her to Eddie the butcher (vide "The Story Hearer"), and they return to the apartment, where Xie Feng—with Ruth now listening—draws the three of them together beyond geography, beyond politics, beyond culture, in the eternal, universal woman's questioning of how to raise children in the real world.

By changing the title to a phrase from a different passage, Paley has redirected our attention to her focus. The "expensive moment" is "a moment in history" (187) when mothers' children are called upon to act in conscience or passion or peer pressure. And that act, in a political world of danger and violence, has repercussions for mothers, not only in the tangible matter of future contact with those children but in the interminable and unanswerable questions of whether they are responsible—the psychological issue of guilt, the ethical issue of making right decisions in dilemmas. The cost of those moments accumulates for life, and the mothers never stop paying.

Twice published before *Later the Same Day,* "Lavinia" in the process lost its lead and gained a subtitle. The original beginning—"Mrs. Grimble said: That day I told Robert"—was dropped between the *Delta* version (1982) and the *Harbinger* ("A Journal of Social Ecology") one (1983).[77] And the subtitle, "An Old Story," was acquired between *Harbinger* and the book (1985). That first change is crucial to form, the second to the theme.

The *Delta* version announces the presence of a story hearer. Revised, the story instead begins as a performance, a dramatic monologue, in which Mrs. Grimble is telling her own story to Robert in an attempt to explain her opposition to his marrying her daughter Lavinia. In either case, more than 80 percent of the story consists of Mrs. Grimble's case presented to Robert.

The remaining fraction is splintered in three. First comes Mrs. Grimble's report of Robert's response, second a transitional sentence, and third her report of her recent perception of Lavinia's life with Robert. In the later versions, the shifts occasion a surprised realization of context, of an *implicit* story hearer. Mrs. Grimble has always been talking to someone other than Robert, but only in *Delta* was the reader aware of that fact from the outset. The formal surprise in the other versions arrests the reader's attention and virtually compels a regard for statement and not mere performance.

The poor, black speaker of this story—the three versions demonstrate Paley's scrupulous efforts to get the sound of the voice just right—presents a strong feminist statement. Her dreams of being a teacher and independent have been co-opted by Grimble's male dream of submissive wife and dutiful mother, though he courts her with lip service to her agenda. She has learned from her own parents to want better, from her own observations that all women are either "on their back providing for men or on their knees cleaning up after them" (65). In time, after bearing Grimble many children, of whom five survive, she becomes the victim of his self-destructive act of pure macho bravado.

Now, alone among her progeny, Lavinia has what it takes "to be a lady preacher, a nurse, something great and have a name" (67). Mrs. Grimble wants this one to break out of the cycle, but of course she doesn't. I say "of course" because that is the point of the "old story." Robert gets his way because Lavinia is happy in her active mothering. Laughing, appealing, smart, hopeful Lavinia is, as her mother sees her, "busy and broad." The story ends with Mrs. Grimble's anguished, heartbroken curse: "Damn you, Lavinia, ain't nothing gonna come of you neither" (68). She has staunchly endured her own lot, even knowing what is wrong with the way things are, but it is the prospect of the cycle being unbroken that breaks her spirit.

With "Friends," Paley returns to a situation tentatively explored in "Living": the death of an old friend. This story is not a reworking of the other but an enrichment of its themes achieved by a fleshing out of its context. Originally published in the *New Yorker* (1979), it was selected by Stanley Elkin for inclusion in *Best American Short Stories 1980*.

Attachments within and across generations are presented here, as Faith, Ann, and Susan travel five hours each way on a train to visit Selena, whose struggle with cancer ends—perhaps hastened by her own overdose of painkillers—later the same day. Again, the women's bonds have been forged over the years by their politics, their activism, and their similar experiences with and attitudes toward men. Most of all, it is as a sisterhood of mothers of a particular generation that they cohere. Selena spends her last hours thinking about her daughter Abby who died, and the pictures she most treasures show Abby as a child with the children of the others.

The three surviving friends do little to console one another. In fact, on their return train ride, they seem to demonstrate different phases of grief (denial, anger, commemoration) so insistently that they clash. Ann especially resents Faith's "good luck" with her children, whereas Ann's son Mickey is doomed to reenact Selena's Abby's drug-abusing fate. But Faith remembers how "a bond was sealed" the first day she and Ann "looked at each other" in the park, when their "babies had just stepped howling out of the sandbox on their new walking legs" (89).

Faith's younger son, Anthony, a.k.a. Tonto, now eighteen, provides some reality-testing corrective for Faith's sentimentalizing, but her own generous view of Selena and Abby, of Ann and Susan, prevails. More than a story about friendship and survival in memory, "Friends" insists on the ethical imperative of art. Paley's conclusion is this: "But I was right to invent for my friends and our children a report on these private deaths and the condition of our lifelong attachments" (89).

Faith's "report" is invention, mirroring Paley's own struggle to discover the form for this topic of friendship surviving death, as she says in her interview with Ruth Perry.[78] For both Faith and Paley, the material of the story *must* find artistic shape for the storytelling to accomplish its goals in the service of love and friendship, memory and commemoration, beauty and acceptance, value and meaning.

In form unlike anything else in the Paley corpus (except for its length), "At That Time, or The History of a Joke" is an experiment in comic allegory. It sounds like a cross between Doris Lessing and Woody Allen, one in which playfulness with language (idiom, image, phrasing, allusion) at the surface level gives way to the largest thematic, topical, satiric, and ethical concerns.

The alternate title could well be reversed. The story tells a joke on history, though it is also a joke on mythology, on medical and reproductive technology, on the media, on the criminal and civil justice systems, on social evolution, on religion and the role of the Jews, and indeed on ethics itself, all encompassed in about seven hundred words. Alone among Paley's stories, this performance could pass as mere tour de force, since for the most part the voice we hear could be that of anyone "doing" a dazzling "bit"—except for faint reminders of the Paley storytelling persona.

At the end, however, Paley's voice sounds clearly through. With the world rejoicing at the medical miracle of a black virgin girl born to a white virgin mother, certain Jews say, "So? . . . Praise to the most Highess! But the fact is, we need another virgin birth like our blessed dead want cupping by ancient holistic practitioners" (95). The tone, the rhythm, the English/Yiddish punning are unmistakable, and the final sentence includes a phrase, "workers in the muddy basement of history" (96), that evokes reflexive associations with "In Time Which Made a Monkey of Us All" and "The Used-Boy Raisers" (*LDM*).[79]

It has sometimes seemed to readers and reviewers that the figure of the father has cast a tall shadow over the figure of the mother in Paley's work. That impression, I think, comes from two factors: the prominence of stories concerning visits of the protagonists to fathers ("A Conversation with My Father," "Faith in the Afternoon," "Enormous Changes at the Last Minute," and "Dreamer in a Dead Language") and the assumed biographical prominence of Dr. Goodside in Paley's life. Yet images of the mother—not Manya Goodside herself alone or characters derived from her but a whole host of mother *figures*—are far more prominent in the texture of Paley's work.

Three stories in *Later the Same Day* augment that prevalence, hearkening back as they do to earlier appearances. "Anxiety," "In This Country, but in Another Language, My Aunt Refuses to Marry the Men Everyone Wants Her To," and "Mother" occupy, in sequence, the center of the book, and while they were not conceived as a triptych their complementary nature and cumulative effect suggest they be treated as such.

In 1975, *Esquire* was planning an all-American issue to celebrate the Bicentennial. The editors had come up with a "Mom and Apple Pie" concept and asked Paley to contribute "Mom." The result was a short essay called "Other Mothers," reprinted two and a half years later in a *Feminist Studies* issue subtitled "Toward a Feminist Theory of Motherhood," but—since the title was the essence of the idea for the magazine—called "Mom" instead of "Other Mothers" in *Esquire*.[80]

The first of five quick takes in the essay begins, "The mother is at the open window." Paley explains that it is not her mother but an "imprint," a "technical name of the first seeing" retained in her "head where remembering is organized for significance (not usefulness)" (85). No wonder the reader hears the echo of "every window is a mother's mouth" from "The Loudest Voice" (*LDM*, 55).

The essay makes a general comment on how contemporary psychology and literature have made villains of mothers, but it proceeds with specifics from Paley's own life. Besides the difficulty of dealing with her own mother's terminal illness and death, the essay is genuinely about "other mothers": her grandmother, her aunts, her older sister Jean (the "sister-mother"), mothers in the neighborhood caught in the act of being mothers, and finally herself as "mother to a couple of grown-up people" (86). What is especially interesting for the present purpose is how this material is transmuted into the stories.

"Mother" appeared originally in *Ms.* under the name "My Mother" with a subhead of "The times she stood in the doorway"[81] and, containing commentary of sorts on gender matters, was appropriately located in the magazine's "back page" department. Why, then, is it a story—and "Other Mothers" not—since the speaker (hardly "narrator"), the undisguised "I," is Paley? Part of the answer lies in its placement, anchoring this sequence of three pieces in the book. Part lies in its artistic arrangement of elements—the sequence of images of the mother in doorways (instead of windows, here), correlating with a sequence of statements on the theme of time passing, and the incremental refrain "Then she died" underscoring the irony of the mother's concerns weighing on the daughter's health and politics and the father's triumph and tiredness. And a small part lies in its glimpse of the narrator looking and listening: These are but snatches of sight and sound, but the reader senses the storytelling and story hearing behind them.

Even shorter, in fact the second shortest of all the stories in the three collections (and pared down by four precious words from the version originally published in *Threepenny Review* in 1983), "In This Country . . ." boasts Paley's longest title. Two of its main ingredients are taken from "Other Mothers." One is the aunt's advice about demonstrations and parades: Don't be the one to carry the flag. The other is the topic that provides the title: The aunt is described in the essay as "one who was mocked for not having married, whose beauty, as far as the family was concerned, was useless, because no husband ever used it" (86).

In the story, both these elements have been transformed by their storytelling context. That advice is more than conventional wisdom; it grows out of the grandmother's personal experience. The other topic derives from the grandmother, too, as she expresses the family's attitude that Aunt Sonia has "no life," since she is unmarried. The narrator assumes an ingenuous attitude in this piece, questioning why what people have or have left can't make up for what they don't have or have lost. In other words, Jack's darkness from living under "the shadow of another person's sorrow" (from "The Immigrant Story" [*ECLM*, 171]) is brightly attacked by the child's challenges to her aunt and grandmother.

If the implicit sense of art transforming the material of life seems remote, Aunt Sara renders it explicit when she refers the narrator to Dostoyevski for an understanding of her own feelings.[82] And finally all these elements are artfully transformed by the whole presentation of the warmth, the interaction, the ritual kvetching, and the laughter of the family-life setting.

In "Anxiety," which begins the sequence, the nuclear family becomes the human family. The narrator herself is now mother and grandmother leaning archetypally out her apartment window to cry advice to strangers, a couple of young fathers with their lovely children. She has seen one of them angrily respond to his daughter's irreverence toward him.

The story is psychologically profound on two levels, both in the narrator's wisdom in dealing with the father and in the perceptive (self-) analysis of the narrator's feelings as well. But at the same time it deliberately rejects a psychoanalytical approach. The narrator first praises the father as an example of progressive parenting. Then she engagingly leads him to identify with her in certain antiauthoritarian, antiwar attitudes, reminding him he has punished his child for being like him instead of cherishing her as a precious remnant worth saving from the destructive politics of history.

Finally, as they gallop happily off, each "fierce fast horse carrying a beloved beautiful rider" (103), the narrator leans further out the window to warn them all to be careful of the traffic. As she wonders "how to make sure that they gallop safely home through the airy scary dreams of scientists and the bulky dreams of automakers" (103), the anxieties of mothers stretch to embrace the mundane and the global. Careful to avoid the implications of the word *anxiety* as a psychoanalytical term for condition, affect, or behavior, Paley edited out the young father's remark, "We could get depressed," from the original version in *New England Review/Bread Loaf Quarterly* (1983).[83] The story presents, rather, the psychological rationale of mothers everywhere, giving a mothers-for-peace piece of advice through the window of regard for all children's safety and preservation. And as Thelma Shinn suggests, the story reminds us that "it is not only women who have come a long way and still have a long way to go" (xvii–xviii).

When the story called "Edie and Ruthy" appeared in 1980 in *Heresies* ("A Feminist Publication on Art and Politics"), it consisted of two almost equal parts. The first presents a scene from the life of two little girls; the second shows them many years later, celebrating Ruth's fiftieth birthday along with two other friends, Ann and Louise. The first part is now seen as a story Ruth frequently tells, but it occupies a very small part of the interactions among these women concerning their various involvements in political, professional, and family lives.

In *Later the Same Day,* the first part of "Ruthy and Edie" is virtually unchanged from the version in *Heresies* (except that the "stoop steps" are located in the Bronx). The second part, however, has undergone a wholesale transformation (far beyond the new information that the birthday is celebrated in Manhattan). It is now twice as long, Louise has been replaced by Faith, the other elements—including the significance of Ruth's story—are expanded, the political activities are clarified, and Ruth's daughter, son-in-law, and granddaughter appear.

The change in title suggests how much more clearly it has become Ruth's story. But there are many more significant aspects to the revisions and additions. Having by far the most extensive set of changes among Paley's published work, "Ruthy and Edie" reveals that her method is not simply one of constant "poetic" refinement of *le mot juste* or minimalist exercise of the less-is-more principle. What we find, instead, is the development of a self-reflexive dimension that is at the same time an enrichment of the story hearer/storyteller structure.

In the little-girl section, an omniscient narrator moves back and forth between the thoughts of Edie and Ruthy, revealing their attitudes and experience and accounting for their behavior. In the main section, as in the first, most of the narration is a direct recording of conversation, but brief descriptions are also interspersed, occasionally with internal views as well. We get glimpses of Edie's thoughts, Faith's, and even Ruth's granddaughter Letty's, and—somewhat more fully—Ruth's, especially in the closing paragraph.

The absence of a narrating "I" and the apparent omniscience of looking into several minds raise questions for the reader. Why are we not situated, familiarly, securely, with Faith? Whether as first-person narrator or third-person center of consciousness, she is our usual location whenever she appears in a Paley story. Does the absence of Ann's thoughts imply that it is she reading the others' minds? Does the relative weight assigned to Ruth's awareness—including the revelation that the story of her and Edie as children is her story—place her at the center?

To provide an answer is to suggest the story's significance in Paley's work and to touch on its constellation of themes. Over the years, Paley has acknowledged,[84] Faith Darwin had become closer and closer to

Grace Paley, even as the facts of their lives became more demonstrably divergent. And this closeness was a problem for Paley, who was comfortable with Faith's evolving point of view but uncomfortable with an association, even identification, with Faith that was misleading. The solution was to expand the center of consciousness from Faith to Faith's circle of friends. Accordingly, Ruth and Ann, who appear here, appear elsewhere; Louise, who was edited out of this story, appears elsewhere; and we also meet or remeet Kitty, Susan, Margaret, Selena, and finally Cassie.

In "Ruthy and Edie" the expanding role of these other women is directly related to the responses evoked by Ruth's story. Faith, saying that Ruthy tells that story only when she's "down in the dumps" (122), wants to confront the issue of the storyteller's psyche—a possible function of a story hearer as well as a glimpse of Paley's social-work perspective. Ann tells a little story of her own about Ruth, about her courage in the face of mounted police during a demonstration, in contrast to the little girl Ruthy's fear of a harmless dog. Edie insists that Ruth's interpretation of the little girls is wrong, that Ruthy did just what Edie would have done, only quicker.

Moving back for a wider-angle view, we see that the women's behavior makes indirect comment on the story. Edie, for example, told to look at herself by Ruth, does so and sees a schoolteacher who tells pupils that "history is a wonderful subject . . . all stories . . . where we come from, who we are" (119). With Ruth as historian, then, the story of the little girls tells us who Edie is. Faith, who is concerned about Ruth's depression, is more concerned about having the women address environmental issues of the city. But when she realizes how Edie takes this subject personally, weeping at the thought of "dumped" children, Faith is ready with a new topic of current local interest. Ann, however, is concerned with global political issues, on which she is ready ("I've been a witness of events!" [121]) to give firsthand reports cum slide show from Chile, Rhodesia, the Soviet Union, and Portugal (but not China, because Ruth was there with her and would "contradict every word" [122]). At this point the reader may be moved to ask several questions: Faith was there, too, wasn't she? Is it the same trip? Or is this reference another clue to the decentralization of Faith's point of view?

As for Ruth herself, the story, the group, and the politics are all secondary to her concerns about her family: her currently missing daughter Rachel and her granddaughter Letty (Sara's child), whose newest linguistic discovery—"Remember dat?"—makes her happy and proud to be able thus to "name so many pictures in her head" (125).

In some ways, then, "Ruthy and Edie" is also a piece of metafiction. Not only does it present a story within a story and then explore aspects of its presentation, significance, interpretation, and function, but it also causes us to rethink the facile identification of Faith as Paley's storytelling/story-hearing persona. All four of these gathered women represent aspects of Paley's activities, concerns, attitudes, and values. And what comes into sharpest focus as the story ends are two of Paley's primary themes as seen through *Ruth*'s eyes. One is the tightness of women's bonds—not only horizontal, as with the pair of the title or the team-of-four at the birthday, but especially vertical, as with the three generations of her family (reaching back through a fourth, in the story-within-a-story, as well). The other has to do with literature itself, the ability of language to weave an emotional safety net ("the hammock of world-inventing words" [126]) but its ultimate inability to keep human beings from life's harsh realities, from hitting "the hard floor of man-made time" (126).

"A Man Told Me the Story of His Life" is the shortest of all the collected pieces. Economically, in its title and first two italicized words, *"Vicente said"* (129), it accounts for the role and function of the Paley storyteller and the place of the reader or audience as identified with Paley as story hearer. It is a simple tale of a man who wanted to be a doctor, was told by his school (interpreting tests) to be an engineer instead, and was made a cook by the army. Now, with three children and a good job, he has saved his wife's life by diagnosing her condition (when the doctor did not) and telling the doctor she needs immediate surgery (which the doctor, in wonderment and surprise, confirms by a test).

What is "simple" about the tale is its telling. Vicente speaks so directly of these events, so sparely reporting what happened and what was said, that we hear the full range of emotions behind it—the disappointment, the frustration, the pride, the satisfaction. And finally the irony is felt precisely because it is unspoken, the underlying tone emerging from its very absence from Vicente's tone of voice.

The caring attention to cause and effect that would have made Vicente a good doctor presumably showed up on tests as an aptitude for engineering. The same quality of mind has allowed him to diagnose his wife's condition and save her life. The sensed irony circles the audience back to the narrator's place and view. In that way we can recognize the commentary on the systems that have written this man's story, that have told his life to him, without hearing his voice or understanding him even when heard.

If Grace Paley had not called a story "The Story Hearer," some critic would have had to invent the title, so aptly does it label the thrust of Paley's method. Henry James left ample testimony to the meticulous care he took in the development of his narrative techniques; Conrad wrote letters and prefaces to testify that he knew exactly what he was doing; but for Paley the evidence is included directly in the very substance of the stories.

"The Story Hearer" is primarily a dialogue between Faith, narrating in the first person (the name *Faith* does not appear in the text, though her grocer addresses her as "Mrs. A." [141]), and Jack, a dialogue in which she reports several other dialogues to him. Additionally there is the internal dialogue—or dialectic—in which Faith's aesthetic is evolving, and at the outside, containing the rest of the story, there is the implied dialogue between Faith as monologuist and her audience. It is at this circumference that Faith says, "Don't you wish you could rise powerfully above your time and name? I'm sure we all try, but here we are, always slipping and falling down into them, speaking their narrow language, though the subject, which is how to save the world—and quickly—is immense" (140). As John Barth says, addressing the reader in the "Seven Additional Author's Notes" to the Bantam edition of *Lost in the Funhouse*, the "deuteragonist . . . , antecedent of the second-person pronoun, is you."[85]

"The Story Hearer," then, has multiple referents. It is Jack hearing the story of Faith's day, it is the reader hearing more of it than Jack and hearing the story of its telling as well, and it is Faith hearing in the encounters of her day no fewer than seven stories. Most important, it is Paley, presenting in the voice of her narrator the story she hears her tell.

The story begins with this paragraph: "I am trying to curb my cultivated individualism, which seemed for years so sweet. It was my own song in my own world and, of course, it may not be useful in the hard time to come. So, when Jack said at dinner, What did you do today with your year off? I decided to make an immediate public accounting of the day, not to water my brains with time spent in order to grow smart private thoughts" (133). As topic paragraph it announces the story as a public accounting (representing a shift in Faith's artistic agenda, a shift that brings her yet closer to Paley's own storytelling stance), as a dialogue with Jack, and as a "song" cultivated[86] to function in the world and sung here in performance before a live audience of readers.

The report of the day is delayed by Jack's story, which Faith has heard "maybe thirty times" (134) but which moves her anyway. Then, as she begins, she contrasts the global politics and violence that produce death's success and the spring signs of life's renewal as abetted by neighborhood politics. The power and pleasure of language as a living thing is another topic introduced before other characters appear. Politics and aesthetics merge in Faith's exchanges not only with friends (Jim, the avant-garde theater artist, and Treadwell Thomas, fussy gourmet and Language Division specialist from the Defense Department) but also with the butcher and the grocer. Religion and sexism extend the list of topical concerns.

During these exchanges, Paley is careful to keep us aware of the dimensions of Faith's performance. We are reminded that Faith is telling her day to Jack ("Jack, to whom, if you remember, I was telling this daylong story" [136]) and that she is encapsulating that telling in a narration to us, as when she extrapolates from an interview that Jack once did with Treadwell Thomas in a magazine called the *Social Ordure* (in "The Expensive Moment" we learn that Ruth's husband, Joe, edited the *Social Ordure*, "a periodical which published everything Jack wrote" [188]). Such dual perspectives appear frequently. Talking with Orlando the grocer, Faith remarks on large issues of socioeconomics, but reporting that discussion to Jack, Faith focuses on individual lives and motivations.

When Jack goes off to bed, Faith mentions—to us—two matters she had not mentioned to him: "I hadn't said one word about the New Young Fathers or my meeting with Zagrowsky the Pharmacist" (142). The latter is a reference to another story ("Zagrowsky Tells," which like this one appeared first in *Mother Jones*, where it was called simply "Telling" [1985], thereby connecting it intimately with "The Story Hearer" [1982], since Zagrowsky "tells" his story in a performance for which Faith the story hearer is the immediate audience). The former is probably a reference to "Anxiety," so that, if we pursue the self-reflexive strain, we may identify the unnamed first-person narrator of that story as Faith again.

Sleep does not interrupt the dialogue. Faith remembers a song her friend Ruthy had made up, a sweet lyric about "the marriage bed"

(142) that ends in a cynical undercutting (or short-sheeting) of the sweetness. Jack and Faith both dream, and in and out of sleep they share their dreams and converse and reshape—as dreams do—the events and issues of the day. At the end of the story, Faith, sitting up to read "with interlinear intelligence" (144) the Old Testament story of Abraham and Sarah, applies it to her ongoing discussions with Jack about "perpetual bossdom and war" on the one hand and babies on the other.

Hearing biblical stories, we get both sides. Jack, contentious even in sleep, forces Faith to acknowledge the first. But she, remembering how "all our own old babies" just like "little baby Isaac . . . practiced their five little senses" and lay "around smiling and making up diphthongs and listening," urges the second. And that is what she insists, in the last line, that he accept. "Now all you have to do is be with me," she says (144).

This is not Matthew Arnold at the end of "Dover Beach" urging his love that they be true to one another because that is all they have to combat the ravages of time and war and loss of faith. It is rather the less despairing but no less urgent plea that Jack acknowledge Faith's movement and accompany her songs of public accounting. They need not, after all, tell stories that are personally isolated or that end in the sacrifice of babies. If, properly, hearing is believing, then that "open destiny of life" could be achieved by honest telling.

In his speech on the occasion of presenting the Edith Wharton Award to Grace Paley, William Kennedy singled out this story as an example of "her strength . . . in creating unusual harmony, in blending what is not ordinarily blended in daily lives, except by great writers or great minds." Of Faith's shopping trip, he says, "we dance through an entire world of guerilla theater, the lettuce boycott, the silk stocking boycott of Japan after the devastation of Manchuria, Antonin Artaud and the theater of revolution, Pearl Harbor, consumerism, and chicken legs, watercress and pork butts." The praise includes more than "harmony" because Paley takes "politics, . . . considered a heavy burden for American fiction writers, [and] humanizes it, personalizes it, and she carries the burden as well as any writer, male or female, ever has."[87]

Despite the first four words of its title, "This Is a Story about My Friend George, the Toy Inventor" raises the question of whether it is a story at all. And the possessive "My" raises another question, since the only first-person pronouns after the title are plural.

Alone among Paley's very short pieces, this one is essentially neither a story heard by a listening narrator nor a performance by an adopted storytelling persona. It is, rather, a dialogue in which George responds both to what "we" say to him about this invention and to what has happened with it as "we" report it.

To answer the second question first, the reader recognizes the presence of Paley as first-person narrator in the story's first, second, and fourth paragraphs. In turn, these passages provide envelopes that progressively unfold to reveal the dialogue at the center. The first paragraph presents George as an emotional child of immigrants, one who is often emotional about his own children, and states that the story is *not* about those children. The writer here is announcing *her* exclusive selection of story material. The second paragraph places the immediate circumstances in the larger context of George's whole life, again a deliberate labeling of the narrator's focus that instructs the reader about limiting responses to the story. And the fourth describes objectively the invention itself, a machine that has replaced the metal pinballs with jets of blue water.

Within the envelopes the voices are heard in dialogue. In paragraphs three, five, and seven, "we" speak as critics. We praise in critical phrases like "the poem of a pinball machine, the essence made delicately concrete, and so forth" (147). Then we separate our critical selves from the world at large by certifying the invention's beauty and calling it "so far ahead of its time that we were not surprised to learn it had been rejected" (148). And finally, we bring "political theory to bear on the matter" and suggest that "inside the opportunistic life of coopting capitalism" money could be "extracted" even from "beauty!" (148).

George responds in paragraphs six and eight and gets the last word in paragraph nine. Having rented and installed a couple of ordinary pinball machines in his boys' attic room, he has played and watched and finally understood. His "small innovation" could hardly have improved "that old invention of cumulative complication." It is "so remarkable, so fine, so shrewdly threaded . . . already beautiful in necessity and sufficiency of wire, connection, possibility" that to presume the *invention* of beauty is to commit artistic hubris in the first degree. The rejection, he concludes, was "fair. It's as though I had expected to invent the violin" (148).

To say that this story is an exercise in metafiction, however, is not to answer the initial question. The point is that it can fulfill its meta-fictional function only if it is first a story about a man's epiphany regarding true and false responses to his own work. Whatever else it accomplishes, in its envelopes of critical commentary and authorial voice, is peripheral to and dependent on its primary achievement in its story form. And to say that it has the integrity of a poem is not really to differentiate it from much of Paley's work (though the same issue of *Transatlantic* in which it first appeared in 1977 carried a poem by Nora Paley, Grace's daughter).

One of the most brilliant, fully accomplished performance stories in the whole short story canon is "Zagrowsky Tells." And despite its length (only two of Paley's stories are longer), it achieves its greatest success when read—told—to a live audience. Doing so is appropriate, since it is a story about telling (its original title in *Mother Jones* was "Telling"; Zagrowsky first appears under the name Zagrevsky in the 1982 *Mother Jones* version of "The Story Hearer"), yet to hear it is possibly to miss the extraordinary achievement of its structure, its nuanced shadings within its bold colors, its eye-catching subtleties within the robust sound of its voice.[88]

Iz Zagrowsky's idiosyncratic, idiomatic speech distinguishes him from all the rest of Paley's performers and characters. The combinations of humor and insensitivity, of bitterness and affection, of self-assertion and self-deprecation, of bias and sentimentality, flesh out a person you would not fail to recognize in the street or the park.

What is Zagrowsky telling? He is telling a life—that is, he has a story to tell. And he is telling a self—that is, like the best performances he is revealing himself more intimately and complexly than he intends. Whom is he telling? He tells for thee—that is, he is speaking to an unspecified general audience, on whom he projects assumptions and attitudes that may or may not be appropriate but are designed to tell us even more about him.

The pivotal device on which the structure turns is that most of Zagrowsky's telling is about a dialogue in which he tells his story—a first telling—to Faith. Faith serves several functions in the story. She had been a customer of his pharmacy, and in an emergency—Richie running a fever of 105—he made a lifesaving house call with the medicine. But Faith had also organized a picketing of the store because of Zagrowsky's racist attitudes; even now she chastises him for sexism as well. Her ambivalence is enacted during their meeting in the park— kissing and scolding—but it is her insistent curiosity about Emanuel, the black child with him, that prompts Zagrowsky's first cathartic account.

It is important to recognize that Faith is an object, not subject, of this story. She does not play her usual role of storytelling story hearer; nothing we hear is filtered through her consciousness. Yet *in the background* we glimpse her reporting to her women friends what she has heard from Zagrowsky, and they then intercede on his behalf when a young father in the park approaches him inquisitively. And in what the pharmacist says to her, remembers about her, and tells about her we get a more "objective" view of Faith here than anywhere else.

Paley's portrait of an old man matches anything I know this side of Muriel Spark's Atlantic or J. F. Powers' clergy. Zagrowsky's mind, memories, and associations work in mysteriously appropriate, stumbling-leaping ways. His irony is worldwide and time taught. His emotions can choke him with remembered and renewed anguish, resentment, or rage but can just as readily smother him with surges of nostalgia, pleasure, love, or protective concern.

At the heart of Zagrowsky's telling, however, is a world as ironic, idiosyncratic, and ambivalence provoking as its teller. It is a world in which his beloved daughter Cissy is a chronic schizophrenic with manic and hypomanic episodes symptomatic of bipolar (manic-depressive) disorder. She may bang her head against a wall in autistic withdrawal, or she may—on the model of Faith and her friends (Susan and Ruthy are mentioned)—picket her father's store; she may punch her mother in the face, or she may sing half of Handel's *Messiah*. While institutionalized, Cissy conceives a child by a gardener ("a black man with a green thumb," says Iz [169]).

Cissy names the child Emanuel, and Zagrowsky is pressured by his wife and all the mental health personnel tending Cissy to take him home. He is persuaded that doing so is the only hope for Cissy to lead anything like a normal life outside an institution. The result is that a man who had been outspokenly disgusted at the sight of interracial couples is now the custodial grandfather of an interracial child, a bright, sensitive boy who is his "little best friend" (169).

Prodded by Faith, making connections between her and Cissy, piecing together memories of Faith with images of peaks and valleys in his life, Zagrowsky is able to tell his story. And having directed it at her, he is now free to step back and enlarge its significance by reframing it in an at-large narration. Whether or not the theme of personal, loving involvement as effective antidote to the ignorance and fear behind bigotry is consciously intended by the narrator, it is clear at least that Zagrowsky is arguing that his experience is more enlightening about racism than any institutional prejudice or the organized abstraction of a demonstration can be.

Describing his wife, Nettie, Iz Zagrowsky says, "She says, Ai ai. She doesn't say oi anymore. She got herself assimilated into ai" (159). About his alleged sexual harassment, he pleads guilty to a lesser charge: "Maybe I patted, but I never pinched. Besides, I know for a fact a couple of them loved it" (165). When Nettie uses "we" to include themselves among the whites who kept blacks down for three hundred years, he says, "My two sisters and my father were being fried up for Hitler's supper in 1944 and you say we?" (159).

How is it possible to like such a man? It's not because he gives Faith (and Paley) yet another chance to explore the meaning of the Abraham-Isaac story. No, it is because his actions speak louder than his words, his socially evolving behaviors louder than his culturally devolved attitudes, his experienced love louder than his learned hate. It is because while his discourse speaks self-serving phrases and sarcastic one-liners, his story speaks volumes. The narration is compelling. The telling is— the word is irresistible and inevitable—telling.

The last story in *Later the Same Day*, alone of the thirty-four stories in two collections, was not published separately before inclusion in the book. This can be no judgment on its quality, for it is one of the more artful conjoinings of familiar Paley motifs bumping into each other. Perhaps it was finished too near the publication of the book to be placed separately (though Paley remembers "Zagrowsky Tells" as being the last completed).[89]

David Remnick says that "the voice [at the start of "Listening"] sounds much like her own."[90] It is, of course, Faith's voice as she tells a couple of little memory stories to Jack. They are conversations she overheard at the Art Foods Deli (where she and Ruth embrace in "The Expensive Moment" [187]), where her favorite sandwich is named for Selena and Max Ratelof (vide "Friends"). In the first conversation a young soldier tells his uncle he wants to settle down as a construction worker and marry "a good-looking American girl, someone nice" (201), leaving his Japanese wife and baby girl happily behind. In the second conversation two men discuss suicide: One doesn't want another child, because then he would have to defer his decision about suicide at least twenty more years; the other asserts his right to suicide rather than live with the indignities of ill health, but he is deterred by responsibilities to the men who work in his store and the "real work" (202) he wants to finish.

The middle part of the story begins at the breakfast table, where Faith, after rehearsing these heard memories, tells Jack, "One of those men was you" (202). When he complains that she tells him stories only about men, even though he is more interested in women, she answers that he has enough woman stories of his own, listing five categories of his memory stories and reflexively suggesting a similar list in "Love." They then pick up a dialogue from "The Story Hearer" about her wish to have another child now that she can't. Treating the matter seriously, in a "stately dance" (204) or ritual exchange, they move toward love-making: "So we lay down beside one another to make a child, with the modesty of later-in-life, which has so much history and erotic knowledge but doesn't always use it" (206).

The second scene of this section takes place back at the table, where Faith's son Richard, now eighteen and "known far and wide for his nosy ear" (206), challenges her remarks from the earlier conversation. His use of the word *intelligentsia* triggers memories in Faith of her mother and uncle. Then as Jack and Richard find common ground, share memories and attitudes about their fathers, and sit together smoking, Faith goes off to work, leaving them "breathing deeply, dangerously, in and out" (208), in an ironic mirroring of the breakfast scene in "The Used-Boy Raisers" (*LDM*).

Issues of politics, generations, sex, gender, memory, and story are threaded together by the tellings and listenings involving all the characters. And in the final section of the story, all of that material is set off as background for Faith's climactic listening to her friend Cassie. The scene takes place when, "as often happens in stories, it was several years later" (209). Jack is in Arizona for a year, to clear his lungs and hoping for "one last love affair, the kind that's full of terrific longing, ineluctable attraction, and so forth," that is, another "woman memory story" for him. Richard and Tonto are "in different boroughs trying to find the right tune for their lives." Faith, though living alone, is busier than ever "because of this planet, which is dropping away from us in poisonous disgust" (209).

Driving home from a meeting, stopped at a red light, Faith sees a man "in the absolute prime of life" crossing the street and is "stirred" because of "accumulating loneliness." Wondering why "man" has "slipped out of my sentimental and carnal grasp" (209), she turns to share her appreciation of him with Cassie, whose response is accumulated anger that Faith has told so many women-and-men stories but never *her* "woman-loving life." Cassie has just been omitted and she was there—"in the restaurant and the train, right there." Cassie claims friendship with Faith at least as close as Faith's with Ruthy, Louise, and Ann, and she asks, "Why have you left me out of everybody's life?" (210).

Faith stops the car. They sit in silence. Finally Faith acknowledges the truth of Cassie's charge, confesses she doesn't understand it, and empathizes with the feeling—"like a great absence of yourself." Then she asks, "Oh, but why did you wait so long? How can you forgive me?" The story—and the book with it—ends with Faith again as listener. The last voice we hear is Cassie's. Laughing, turning Faith's face with her hand to look into her eyes, she promises, "I won't forgive you. . . . From now on, I'll watch you like a hawk. I do not forgive you" (211). Self-reflexively referring to several of the earlier stories and their themes, here in the last story of the third collection Paley makes a gesture that pulls them all together while looking forward to a continuing process of developing her narrative art.

Hardly was *Later the Same Day* on the street than a new Paley story was heard from. "Midrash on Happiness"[91] is in a newly conceived form. As its title indicates, the form is borrowed from or suggested by an ancient tradition in which the Hebrews used their time in exile for the practical/theoretical purpose of composing exegetical commentary on sacred texts. In this story we find Faith and Ruthy "walking for some reason in a neighborhood where [Faith] didn't know the children, the pizza places or the vegetable markets." Interpreting the sacred word *happiness* in their own book of life, they set forth their values in a series of attempts to define and refine meanings. It is a dialogue of ideas, vocalized thoughts, and though the sounds of their voices are familiar we don't need reference to earlier stories to take in their full effect. There is no explicit self-reflexivity, but a general sense of their "history" carries over implicitly.

Faith asserts the values of personal connectedness as essential to happiness: children, a companion to live with, and "three or four best women friends" for intimate confidence and discussion of global, political issues. The midrash is rendered concrete by memories, images, allusions, and associations and expanded through them to include the necessities for happiness of responsible work and bread on the table. It is also moved along (and held together) by a kind of poetic structure in which the formula "by . . . she meant" is repeated many times.

Faith suddenly remembers that she has left out "Love [by which she meant] being *in* love," which produces "imaginings" and in turn "spiritual energy." Ruth takes exception, now, because love "seems like pride . . . when you look at the children and think we don't have time to do much (by time Ruth meant both her personal time and the planet's time)." She sees and hears "boom boom bellicosity" and knows "we have to change it all—the world—without killing it absolutely—. . . that'll be the trick the kids'll have to figure out. Until that begins, I don't understand happiness—what you mean by it."

Faith is shamed by Ruth's vision, which gives rise to her own: "Vast public suffering rose in reeling waves from the round earth's nation-states—hung in the satellite-watched air and settled in no time at all into TV sets and newsrooms."[92] She wonders how "happiness could . . . be worthwhile, with so much conversation and so little revolutionary change," and she ends by saying, "Sometimes walking with a friend I forget the world."

The dual third-person narration here is an extension of one development from *Later the Same Day*. We are inside Faith's head but Ruth's as well. Faith's interpretations, sentiments, values, and so on are essentially Paley's own, but so are Ruth's. And each, listening to the other, hears her story in a telling mode. And as we hear Paley telling it, particularly if we either imagine or experience a live reading of it, the performance of this midrash comes across as a kind of recitation on the most serious of subjects by a comic artist.

"Midrash" appeared in *TriQuarterly* in 1986 and was immediately picked up by William Abrahams for inclusion in *Prize Stories 1987: O. Henry Awards*. A favorite of audiences at Paley's readings, it has since been reprinted twice, once in the commemorative *Climbing Fences* (1987) and more recently in the *Peace Calender 1989*, published by the War Resisters League and subtitled "365 Reasons Not to Have Another War," with text by Paley and paintings by Vera B. Williams.

The calendar includes some nineteen poems (two of them reprinted from *Leaning Forward* and one, "It Is the Responsibility," that was presented at the American Poetry Review Conference on Poetry and the Writer's Responsibility to Society in 1984); three short personal essays that have some of the flavor of stories but have not yet found story form; two "Conversations" and another piece, "Cop Tales," reprinted from an earlier periodical (Dave Dellinger's *Seven Days*); a new piece in the "Conversations" series; and two other new pieces called "Answers I" and "Answers II." Two of the "Conversations" might be treated here: the first, since its main speakers are Faith and Richard, and especially "The Lion and the Ox" (not reprinted in the calendar), since it is the only piece in which a first-person Paley persona carries on a dialogue with Faith.[93] But like the essays (and like the earlier "Other Mothers"), they seem rather to be treatments of stories yet to come, sketches or studies for canvases not yet conceived—unlike the "Midrash," a conversation that has found its story form. The "Answers," however, are arguably a new form for very short stories.

"Answers I" uses 86 percent of its fewer than 150 words to ask its questions. And yet it covers an interval of twenty years, has the familiar unnamed first-person observer and hearer (in part, in her familiar window), contains the requisite bumping into each other of disparate elements, and touches on themes of violence, the destruction of youth in a destructive society, automobile mania as symbol and agency of a destructive materialism, and "true propertarian wrath."

"Answers II," fractionally longer, goes back "about eighty years." Asked in the summer of 1988 if any new short stories were in the works, Paley said that she had been thinking a lot about her uncle who had been deported in the early 1920s after being "arrested in the Palmer Red raids." "Answers II" is the first artistic product of that thinking. It contains four voices: the unnamed first-person narrator, setting down a story she heard once from her father, including a brief exchange with her uncle, and finally her aunt, the oldest sister, who says, "You're so crazy about your father; but if you had known Grisha, with your crazy ideas you would have loved him much more."

Apparent in the story are the revolutionary politics, the evocation of memory—and history—through the sound of voices, and the weighty strength of family ties and associations in determining values, mythology, beliefs, and language. Most prominent of all is the subject of storytelling itself. The story of that story has been part of Paley's awareness during perhaps six decades, awaiting a form in which it could be set down for literary as well as extraliterary purposes.

In the remarkable life, not to say career, of this remarkable writer, the ethical imperatives—to listen, to hear, to remember, to commemorate, and to tell—ensure continuation of the process that fashions her stories. Grace Paley began writing stories when she could hear the authentic voices of others. She continues to discover that lives revealed in those voices must be listened to, if the comprehensive, comprehending values of her own life are to be articulated.

Arranging most of the stories in three collections is largely a matter of chronological convenience and publishing expedience. It is also convenient and expedient for a critic to organize analysis with three discrete subdivisions. That is not to say that the separate volumes have no integrity of their own or that writer and editors have not attended carefully to meaningful, aesthetically satisfying, orderly arrangements of the stories within the collections. As we have seen, the groupings, the sequences, and especially the choice of beginnings and endings all serve authorial purposes and testify to conscious artistic design. But it is more important to see all the stories as part of an ongoing process, the continuing evolution of the lively art of a living writer.

Notes to Part 1

1. See Judith Arcana, "Grace Paley: Life and Stories," diss., Loyola University of Chicago, 1989. She "views Paley as a strongly autobiographical writer—politically as well as personally—and traces connections between the collected stories and the events and people of her life" (from Arcana's letter to me, 2 October 1988). Arcana's title for a book version of this work is "Cultural Dreamer: Grace Paley's Life Stories."

2. Natalie Robins, in "The Defiling of Writers," *Nation* (10 October 1987): 367–72, gives a preview of her forthcoming book-length study of the FBI's files on writers. Virtually every major American writer of this century is on the list, except for Robert Penn Warren and Wallace Stevens, but the FBI has not apparently caught up with the likes of Pynchon, DeLillo, or Albee.

3. Paley dislikes this word, preferring *storytelling* instead, because she finds the distinction between fiction and nonfiction false, misleading, and misguided (see Part 2). The title for this volume is dictated by the series in which it appears.

4. All citations are to the Penguin editions of *The Little Disturbances of Man* (1985) and *Later the Same Day* (1986) and the Farrar Straus & Giroux edition of *Enormous Changes at the Last Minute* (1974) and will be made parenthetically, by page number, in text. When necessary the title of the collection will be abbreviated parenthetically (*LDM, ECLM, LSD*).

5. The book's subtitle was printed as "Stories of Men and Women at Love," a transposing of Paley's "Women and Men" that was not corrected until very recent reprintings of the Penguin edition. No deliberate sabotage, that unconscious, automatic phrasing may serve as a reminder of how language reflects attitudes. See Jacqueline Taylor, *Grace Paley: Illuminating the Dark Lives* (announced for spring 1990 publication by the University of Texas Press), which promises to illuminate, from a feminist perspective, the ways that Paley's language, particularly language in performance, addresses these issues.

6. See Whitney Balliett, "Bob's Your Uncle," *New Yorker,* 23 February 1987, 126; my "Fiction Night at the Comedy Club," *New England Review/ Bread Loaf Quarterly* 11 (Spring 1989): 305–19.

7. "The Voice Project," in *Writers as Teachers/Teachers as Writers,* ed. Jonathan Baumbach, 91, 95–96 (New York: Holt, Rinehart & Winston, 1970). My experience at Brown in 1958, teaching the same course and listening to Hawkes talk about literature and about teaching fiction, was a valuable one; I am happy here to acknowledge that long-term indebtedness.

8. These principles are extended into dramatic renderings of stories, which themselves yield critical insights, by Jacqueline Taylor. See her "Documenting Performance Knowledge: Two Narrative Techniques in Grace Paley's Fiction," *Southern Speech Communication Journal* 53 (Fall 1987): 65–79. Further reference to this and other secondary sources will be made parenthetically in the text.

9. Flannery O'Connor, *The Habit of Being*, ed. Sally Fitzgerald, (New York: Farrar Straus & Giroux, 1979), 283.

10. Neil D. Isaacs, *Eudora Welty* (Austin, Tex.: Steck-Vaughn, 1969), 3–5. Since Frank Lentricchia has recently called Welty "the Cumaean Sybil of the New Regionalism" (in a lecture titled "Don DeLillo—Paranoia, Politics, and Other Pleasures," College Park, Md., 17 November 1988), the association of Paley and Welty could be embarrassing for a reading that rejects the notion of Grace Paley as a regional writer. A neighborhood in Paley always yields worldwide connections and contexts, but then for Welty, the Delta region or the Natchez Trace inevitably extends its mythology toward global application.

11. Kathleen Coppula, "Not for Literary Reasons: The Fiction of Grace Paley," *Mid-American Review* 7 (1986): 63.

12. Saul Bellow, ed., *Great Jewish Short Stores* (New York: Dell, 1963), 12.

13. Leonora Hornblow and Bennett Cerf, eds., *Bennett Cerf's Take Along Treasury* (Garden City, N.Y.: Doubleday, 1963), 265.

14. Ruth Wisse, *The Schlemiel as Modern Hero* (Chicago: University of Chicago, 1971), 84–85.

15. *Accent* 16 (1956): 160.

16. Sanford Pinsker, *The Schlemiel as Metaphor* (Carbondale, Ill.: Southern Illinois University Press, 1971).

17. Unlike Mary Fortune, Josie, according to Paley, has *not* been beaten (interview, 28 July 1988).

18. Rose Kamel, "To Aggravate the Conscience: Grace Paley's Loud Voice," *Journal of Ethnic Studies* 11 (Fall 1983): 34.

19. Anne Z. Mickelson, *Reaching Out: Sensitivity and Order in Recent American Fiction by Women* (Metuchen, N.J.: Scarecrow, 1979), 226.

20. Ronald Schleifer, "Grace Paley: Chaste Compactness," in *Contemporary American Women Writers: Narrative Strategies*, ed. Catherine Rainwater and William J. Scheick, 33–34 (Lexington: University Press of Kentucky, 1985).

21. Philip Roth, back cover of Meridian edition of *LDM* (New York: 1960); Jonathan Baumbach, "Life-Size," *Partisan Review* 42 (1975): 303–4.

22. Diane Cousineau, "The Desires of Women, The Presence of Men," *Delta*, no. 14 (1982): 60.

23. Thelma Shinn, *Radiant Daughters* (New York: Greenwood, 1986), 164. The treatment of this story serves the larger purposes of this illuminating book.

24. Schleifer, whose main concern is with the endings of stories, misreads this one as "John and Ginny on the kitchen floor making love" (37).

25. Why Kamel refers to "the child narrator" (32) is a mystery, unless she means the play rather than the story.

26. Irving Malin and Irwin Stark, eds., *Breakthrough: A Treasury of Contem-*

porary American-Jewish Literature (New York: McGraw-Hill, 1964), 5; Allen Guttmann, *The Jewish Writer in America: Assimilation and the Crisis of Identity* (New York: Oxford, 1971), 87.

27. See Part 2.

28. Paley acknowledged this possibility (interview, 28 July 1988) but took no responsibility—or credit—for designing it that way.

29. Dena Mandel, "Keeping Up with Faith: Grace Paley's Sturdy American Jewess," *Studies in American Jewish Literature* 3 (1983): 89.

30. "Wants" and "Debts," "Gloomy Tune" and "Living," "Samuel" and "The Burdened Man" (*ECLM*); "Somewhere Else" and "The Expensive Moment" (*LSD*); "Politics," "Northeast Playground," and "The Little Girl" (*ECLM*); and "Anxiety," "In Another Country. . . ," and "Mother" (*LSD*). In addition, "The Story Hearer," "Zagrowsky Tells" (originally called "Telling"), and "Listening" (*LSD*) are closely interrelated.

31. Mandel (90) says "unpredictably."

32. "No, it's just a common Jewish name," Paley has said (interview, 28 July 1988). But I would argue that a writer who chooses names like "Faith, Hope, and Charlie" must be watched at all times.

33. Adam J. Sorkin, "'What Are We, Animals?': Grace Paley's World of Talk and Laughter," *Studies in American Jewish Literature* 2 (1982): 144–54.

34. This story, which follows the two that introduce Faith, is the first to mention the name *Darwin*, Faith's maiden name.

35. Kathleen Hulley, "Interview with Grace Paley," *Delta*, no. 14 (1982): 24.

36. Again, "just a name," says Paley (interview, 28 July 1988).

37. William O'Rourke, ed., *On the Job* (New York: Vintage, 1977).

38. Kamel (48) thinks Edsel and Stubblefield are *two middle-aged* men.

39. *Atlantic*, May 1971, 66–67.

40. Interview, 28 July 1988.

41. Irving Howe and Ilana Wiener Howe, eds., *Short Shorts* (Boston: Godine, 1982), ix, xii.

42. Interview, 28 July 1988.

43. Blanche Gelfant, "Chronicles and Chroniclers," *Massachusetts Review* 16 (Winter 1975): 127.

44. *Noble Savage* 2 (1960): 67–82.

45. Marianne DeKoven, "Mrs. Hegel-Shtein's Tears," *Partisan Review* 48 (1981): 217–23. Minako Baba, in "Faith Darwin as Writer–Heroine: A Study of Grace Paley's Short Stories" *Studies in American Jewish Literature* 7 (1988): 40–54, finds an additional virtue in "unifying psychological imagery of the sea" (43).

46. Interview, 28 July 1988. Editor Lish was no doubt responding to what writer/writing teacher Lish regards most highly in narrative forms, the fully

articulated, idiosyncratic voice (see his *Peru* or, more enjoyably, his "For Jerome—with Love and Kisses," in *What I Know So Far*).

47. William Peden, "The Recent American Short Story," *Sewanee Review* 82 (Fall 1974): 722.

48. *Genesis West* 3 (1965): 12.

49. *New American Review* 1 (1967): 67.

50. Jacqueline Taylor calls this device a shift from "story time" to "narrative time," thus violating "the narrator-character duality and provid[ing] a corrective to the limitations on an accurate portrayal of events that exist any time a first-person narrator tells a story." See her "Documenting Performance Knowledge: Two Narrative Techniques in Grace Paley's Fiction," *Southern Speech Communication Journal* 53 (Fall 1987): 72. Commenting on this passage in conversation with me, 31 October 1988, Grace Paley said, "It's a story—the storyteller can have any character say anything she wants."

51. See Neil D. Isaacs, "Up a Tree: To See *The Fates of Men*," in *Anglo-Saxon Poetry: Essays in Appreciation*, ed. Lewis E. Nicholson and Dolores Warwick Frese, 363–75 (Notre Dame, Ind.: University of Notre Dame Press, 1975). Baba, who sees the story "structured by Faith's spatial movement from up in a tree down to the earth" (46), also finds "a series of nautical metaphors" (45).

52. Interview, 28 July 1988.

53. The situation is complicated—or the playfulness enriched—by a passing reference to Henry James and by references to others passing in the park, including Edward Roster, "a representational artist" (88). In conversation with me, 30 October 1988, Grace Paley confirmed that Gewirtz is real but that she was having fun with the other characters and their made-up names.

54. Interview, 28 July 1988.

55. Renee Winegarten, "Paley's Comet," *Midstream* 20 (December 1974): 67.

56. *Win* 4 (1968): 33. This "Urban Arts" issue of *Win* announces, "This is a special issue with its own special editor. Grace Paley is a writer, mother, peace worker, draft card burner, teacher and just plain good folk. We love her."

57. In this passage the phrase *little armored prick* replaces the *little armored peanut* of the version originally published in *Arafat* 8 (1967): 26. The only non-Armenian writer in that magazine, Paley was making a concession to her editor and audience (interview, 28 July 1988), another instance of the "politics of aesthetics."

58. See Hilda Morley, "Some Notes on Grace Paley While Reading Dante: The Voice of Others," *Delta*, no. 14 (1982), who calls this story "always the exception" to Paley's "wry sense of hopefulness" (67). While Peden speaks of its "stark hideousness' (722), Gelfant says that it gives "the story a last laugh"—*Women Writing in America* (Hanover, N.H.: University Press of

New England, 1984), 18. Audrey Roberts calls this Paley's "most powerful story . . . too painful to read." Roberts's 1974 MLA paper, "Grace Paley: Love and Death in the Afternoon," has unfortunately not been preserved (letter to me from Roberts, 2 October 1988).

59. *Paris Review* 14 (Spring 1974): 194.

60. Theodore Solotaroff, "Editor's Notes," *New American Review* 13 (1972): 10.

61. In her "Conversation with Ann Charters," Paley denied that one of the things the narrator doesn't want to look in the face is her father's death, which he is trying to prepare her for. Even in retrospect, Paley could not see that theme: "No. But maybe you're right. . . . That's not up to me to say. Maybe the reader of a particular story knows better than the writer what it means. But I know I wasn't thinking about that when I wrote it." She does say, however, that she put this story between "those two dark" ones, "The Little Girl" and "The Immigrant Story," "to show him I could look tragedy in the face": in *The Story and Its Writer*, 2d ed., ed. Ann Charters, 1316–17 (New York: St. Martin's, 1987).

62. Harry Blake, "Grace Paley, a Plea for English Writing," *Delta*, no. 14 (1982): 79.

63. See, e.g., Gelfant (1984), 17–18.

64. Nicholas Peter Humy, "A Different Responsibility: Form and Technique in Grace Paley's 'Conversation with my Father,'" *Delta*, no. 14 (1982): 87–95; D. S. Neff, "'Extraordinary Means': Healers and Healing in 'A Conversation with My Father,'" *Literature and Medicine* 2 (1983): 118–24.

65. See Part 2.

66. Ironically, Faith here is employing a psychoanalytic tool, what Frieda Fromm-Reichmann calls "therapeutic interpretation" of "parataxic distortion." See her *Principles of Intensive Psychotherapy* (Chicago: University of Chicago Press, 1950), 102ff. Fromm-Reichmann also stresses "Listening as a Basic Psychotherapeutic Instrumentality," 7–9. "Immigrant" provides a wealth of material for psychodynamic insight, especially those two fixed images Jack has of his childhood: (a) the boy peering out of the dark at his parents *holding hands* in the light and (b) the boy's shock at discovering his father *in the crib* one morning.

67. Jacqueline Taylor (1987), 70–72 discusses how "chamber theatre" explicates this story and its narrator's ignoring of "the story-time/narrative-time distinction."

68. Julia Wolf Mazow, ed., *The Woman Who Lost Her Names* (New York: Harper & Row, 1980), xvii; John W. Crawford, "Archetypal Patterns in Grace Paley's 'Runner,'" *Notes on Contemporary Literature* 11, no. 4 (1981): 10–12. See also Kamel (41–42) and Mandel (93–95). Gelfant, incidentally, has Faith literally running "backwards" (1984, 16).

69. Crawford (11) mentions the latter connection.

70. *New Yorker,* 8 October 1979, 37.

71. "Dreamers in a Dead Language," *American Review* 26 (1977): 391–411.

72. Ironically, Grace Paley has said in conversation with me, 12 October 1988, "Dreamer" retains more of the originally discarded novel material than "Faith in a Tree."

73. That *American Review* published it as plural 'Dreamers" in 1977 was apparently a mistake at the time and was shocking to Paley to have it pointed out in 1988 (interview, 28 July 1988).

74. Judy Slawson, "Grace Paley: Changing Subject Matter with a Changing Passionate and Committed Life," *Villager,* 18 May 1978, 13.

75. See Part 2.

76. The original version, *Mother Jones,* December 1983, 13, has the additional word "everything" in that sentence and begins the next with "For instance"—the only substantial change in the revision.

77. *Delta,* no. 14 (1982): 41; *Harbinger* 2 (1983): 39.

78. See Part 2.

79. Walker Percy's *The Second Coming* (1980) goes on at great length about the role of the Jews in history, so that part of the "joke" in this story (1981) could be directed good-naturedly thereat.

80. *Esquire,* December 1975, 85.

81. *Ms.,* May 1980, 100.

82. See Part 2.

83. "Anxiety," *New England Review/Bread Loaf Quarterly* 4 (1983): 607.

84. Interview, 28 July 1988.

85. John Barth, *Lost in the Funhouse* (New York: Bantam, 1969), xi.

86. The gardening metaphor reminds us of Paley's fondness for Miró's *I Work Like a Gardener* as a model or analogue for her own method; see Part 2.

87. William Kennedy, "Excerpts from the Speech by William Kennedy on the Occasion of Grace Paley Receiving the First New York State Edith Wharton Award," in *Climbing Fences* (commemorative journal honoring Grace Paley on her sixty-fifth birthday), ed. Sybil Claiborne, 18–19 (New York: War Resisters League, 14 December 1987).

88. One such subtlety has been lost in the book's version. In *Mother Jones,* the last word in Zagrowsky's performance is "Stories"; from title to end, the performance is framed by its subject, "Telling . . . Stories." "Telling," *Mother Jones,* May 1985, 34–42.

89. Interview, 28 July 1988.

90. David Remnick, "Grace Paley, Voice from the Village," *Washington Post,* Style, 14 April 1985, C14.

91. *TriQuarterly* 65 (1986): 151–53.

92. Paley often says she went to school on poetry. She must have been a fine student: In a single sentence here are echoes of Donne, Yeats, Hopkins, and Keats (with Milton very probably behind the last).

93. Paley has explained, in conversation with me (31 October 1988), what she was doing here: "I wanted to write some specifically, overtly, clearly political pieces, and I thought I'd like to use the characters to do it."

Part 2

THE WRITER

Introduction

Despite the many demands on her time and energy, Grace Paley has always been generously accessible for interviews, conferences, symposia, and compendia. The following remarks are assembled, under six general topics, from the remarkably open, frank, consistent statements she has made about writing, her own writing, and herself over two decades. The sources are indicated by date according to the key that follows. I have imposed a strict chronology only in the rare cases when doing so actually facilitates understanding. And, when necessary, I have interpolated (in brackets) the language of the question being asked. In some cases I have (in consultation with Grace Paley) edited or amplified the published text of the interview for the sake of coherence, consistency, continuity, or accuracy.

1969   Grace Paley, "Some Notes on Teaching: Probably Spoken," in *Writers as Teachers/Teachers as Writers*, ed. Jonathan Baumbach, 202–6 (New York: Holt, Rinehart & Winston, 1970).

1970   Barton Midwood, "Short Visits with Five Writers and One Friend," *Esquire*, November 1970, 150–52 (other writers were Russell Edson, James Purdy, I. B. Singer, and Frank Conroy).

1973   Grace Paley, "Conversations in Moscow," *Win* 10 (23 May 1974): 7–12 (Paley was a delegate of the War Resisters League to the 1973 World Peace Congress).

1974   Harriet Shapiro, "Grace Paley: 'Art Is on the Side of the Underdog,'" *Ms.*, May 1974, 43–45.

1976   Donald Barthelme, William Gass, Grace Paley, and Walker Percy, "A Symposium on Fiction," *Shenandoah* 27 (1976): 1976.

1979   Frieda Gardner, "The Habit of Digression: An Interview with Grace Paley," *Wordsworth* (literary supplement of the University of Minnesota *Daily*), 28 October 1979, 13.

1980H   Kathleen Hulley, "Interview with Grace Paley," *Delta*

1980G   Blanche H. Gelfant, "A Portrait in Collage," in her *Women Writing in America: Voices in Collage*, 11–29 (Hanover, N.H.: University Press of New England, 1984).

Part 2

1980 Leonard Michaels, "Conversation with Grace Paley," *Threepenny Review*, no. 3 (Fall 1980): 4–6 (stories by Michaels and Paley were grouped together by editor Theodore Solotaroff in *New American Review*).

1981 Joan Lidoff, "Clearing Her Throat: An Interview with Grace Paley," *Shenandoah* 32 (1981): 3–26.

1981Q Maya Friedler, "An Interview with Grace Paley," *Story Quarterly* 13 (1981): 32–39 (transcription of dialogue broadcast on WBEZ).

1982 Ruth Perry, "Grace Paley" (interview), in *Women Writers Talking*, ed. Janet Todd, 35–56 (New York: Holmes & Meier, 1983).

1983 Sara Poli, "Grace Paley" (interview), in *Vinduet* 37 (1983): 42–47 (*Window* is Norway's prominent literary magazine; translation for use here, from the Norwegian, by Eva Maria Fleck).

1985 Wendy Smith, "PW Interviews: Grace Paley," *Publishers Weekly*, 5 April 1985, 71–72.

1985C Barry Silesky, Robin Hemley, and Sharon Solwitz, "Grace Paley: A Conversation," *Another Chicago Magazine*, no. 14 (1985): 100–14.

1985P David Remnick, "Grace Paley, Voice from the Village," *Washington Post*, Style, 14 April 1985, C1, 14.

1986 "Grace Paley: A Conversation with Ann Charters," in *The Story and Its Writer*, 2nd ed., by Ann Charters, 1313–17 (New York: St. Martin's, 1987).

1986T Martha Satz, "Looking at Disparities: An Interview with Grace Paley," *Southwest Review* 72 (1987): 478–89.

1987 Jacqueline Taylor, "Grace Paley on Storytelling and Story Hearing," *Literature in Performance* 7 (April 1987): 46–58.

1988 Grace Paley in conversation with Neil D. Isaacs, Thetford, Vermont, 28 July 1988.

1988S Grace Paley in "Afterwords" to *Sudden Fictions*, ed. Robert Shepard and James Thomas (Salt Lake City: Gibbs M. Smith, 1986).

Other Writers: Influences,
Affinities, Tastes, Distastes

1983: When I was little I devoured everything I came across. Books I mean. I still do that, during the summer mostly, but I don't think that the books I read last year or last week mean so much to me. What really influences you, as far as literature is concerned, are the people you live with, and the books you read when you were a child and adolescent. I read enormous amounts of poetry, and the literary language which left its imprint and was used then in our every-day language within the family was enough to make a difference.

Many of my friends read a great deal, but I was even more interested in poetry than most of them. I had a big brother and especially a sister who encouraged me, and I am happy about that. But we all read Joyce's short stories . . . and we also read Chekhov. When I was a teenager Gertrude Stein was very important to me. I thought *Mrs. Dalloway* was fantastic! And *Ulysses*. We grew up with all that.

1981Q: People talk a lot about who influenced you. Well, as a kid, I was a big reader, like a lot of us. We read a lot: all the nice books and the good books and all the rotten books, too . . . all the trash that we could.

But we don't talk enough about the other influences that are really enormous literary influences. And that's the influence of your family's language, the way people speak in your house, the language they speak, the language of your street and of your time. Where you are. Where's your longitude and latitude and what's spoken around you. In that way, people from different countries can sometimes sound alike. Not because they're under the same literary influences but because they've the same parents . . . or the same *kind* of parents or grandparents.

Some have said that sometimes I'm a little like the Russian writers. . . . The fact is that I did read them a lot. But I loved *Dubliners*, too, and I think it had a strong influence on me. Irish. Yeats. I read all the Russian writers, and they all spoke to me in some way. Which of them was most important is really hard to know. The writer herself can say one thing and the rest of the world can say, "Ho-ho! *That's* what *you* think!" I'm just right in the middle of my own time, that's all.

[Chekhov?] That's sort of the influence of my family as much as Chekhov. It's not that my family was not despairing. As a matter of fact, very often I would say to my Aunt Mira, "What is it? What happened? How are you today? How are you?" And she'd say, "Ah-h-h, read Dostoevsky."

1986T: I was very much a small person among many large ones . . . really entranced most of the time by what was being talked about, by my father and his medical friends talking sometimes about cases, by the loud political arguments going on sometimes because my aunt who lived with us had very different politics from my family.

1979: That period was very important to me. I was lucky to be the youngest child and I was left alone a great deal. My parents weren't that old, but still they were tired, so that outside of having to wear very long stockings into April, I was let alone a great deal. I spent a lot of time on the street; you could hardly get me in. And the women talking on the street were important and exciting. I could hardly breathe. It was a whole life being discussed, an almost unknowable life.

1986: I paid attention to all [the poets I read] and listened to all of them. Some of them must have gotten into my ear. That's not up to me to say. That's for the reader to say. The reader of my stories will tell me, "This is whom you're influenced by," but I can't say that.

1980H: Everybody you read influences you. But I still think most of your influences are made early. When my first book was written, I'd never heard of most of these people [Coover, Barthelme, Barth].

1988: [Flannery O'Connor?] Yes, I know she had a copy of *Little Disturbances of Man* before she died. Cecil Dawkins gave it to her, but I don't know if she read it. I loved her use of language, but I couldn't accept her ideas about social work, that any good work had to come from inside the Church, from faith.

Yes, I was aware of the connection [people were making with J. D.

Salinger, that Faith was becoming like his Buddy Glass, who had to end up writing all his stories]. I think it's too bad what happened. He's holed up over here in New Hampshire.

1980G: People ask, "Who are your influences?" In my early thirties, I really became involved in the lives of the women around me. I had this subject matter really pummeling me, but I thought, "Aah, who'd be interested?" Most of the literature of the time came out of the Second World War, and it seemed to me that what I had to say was not really interesting; and so it sat in my head for a long, long time. I was reading Joyce, Proust, Virginia Woolf, Gertrude Stein. Oh, I loved *Three Lives.* Those stories had a very strong sound for my ear.

1982: Sometimes you come to literature that seems related to your own in some ways, but after you've been writing for a while. And then you feel terribly corroborated. Like Paul [Goodman]'s stories, the ones I really love the most, I read them much later, but they made me feel good about certain things I was doing. The other writer doesn't so much influence you as have the same historical life that you have, that you come from, the same language structures, talks English the same way—or Russian.

1985C: I never read [Babel] before my first book. Someone said that he had gotten a certain Yiddishness into Russian and I had gotten a certain Yiddishness into English. And I've had many people ask me that. But I didn't know him. I mean I knew him, I loved him, but I didn't know him. But when you're talking about influences, you're talking about who talked to you when you were little. And I would say we had the same grandfather. So it's an influence that's linguistic and social more than anything else.

1980H: The classical things are really quite marvelous, you know. It's just they have degenerated into a kind of "well-made story" of our time. But you could learn forever from them. Look at Maupassant's very short stories. Those wonderful short stories about soldiers. They are just beautiful. He could do everything in three pages. And academics, of course, were scared to use those to teach kids to write, because they'd never learn how to make the "well-made story," how to *develop* it. Development, ugh!

1981: When I began to think of short stories, all those forms were interesting to me. But apart from that, I read everything a big reader reads, a nice middle-class big reader. I had read [Joyce and Stein] when I was writing poetry; I read them when I was in my teens. They were useful. I read a lot of poetry, and the poetry I read had a bad influence on my poetry. It had to have had, because my poems weren't very good. They were literary. Poetry was very literary in that period in a way that Joyce's *Dubliners* really isn't and maybe those other stories, those short ones of Stein's. And novels are often not literary in that sense. I got to love a lot of the writers who may have had something to do with my thinking about form. Like Ivy Compton-Burnett, but I never wrote like her. On the other hand, every now and then, just some snip or something comes. . . . So my poems were written with my reading ear. For a year, I wrote like Auden, with an English accent. In stories, I started listening to other voices than my own, and I began to be able to clear my own throat.

1982: I loved Robinson Jeffers. I loved Auden. I loved H. D. . . . There was Christina Rossetti and Edna St. Vincent Millay, too. I was in love a lot, so I really read what they had to say.

1969: Something to read: Cocteau's journals.

> Two good books to read: *A Life Full of Holes*, Charhadi [and]
> *I Work Like a Gardener*, Joan Miro.
> Don't go through life without reading the autobiographies of
> Maxim Gorki, Prince Kropotkin, Malcolm X.
> The stories of Isaac Babel and the conversation with him
> reported by Konstantin Paustovsky in *Years of Hope*. Also,
> Paustovsky's *The Story of a Life*, a collection of stories
> incorrectly called autobiography.

1976: [Bob and I] read aloud often and certainly I think Henry James is much improved by being read three, four pages at a time aloud. In fact, he becomes quite bearable to me that way.

1985C: I do try to read [current American fiction], but I'm behind, mostly because of school. And it kills me. Not only do I want to read certain books, but I have others sent to me. Right by the bed, the pile looks like that. And it's very hard for me to get to it. [Milan Kundera?]

He writes about his prick too much. Excuse me, boys. I happen to like *The Book of Laughter and Forgetting* very much. But this last book [*The Unbearable Lightness of Being*], it's as though he's been consumed by Western concerns. I think it's a corrupt book. I mean I read it with great hopes because I really liked *Laughter and Forgetting*, I thought it was great. But I'm so disgusted. I mean who the fuck does he think he is? It's not that I don't think that a person can write about sexual obsession. I think there's not much more interesting than that, in a way. I'm all for it. But it's so egocentrical and false, admiring her so much for this idiotic loyalty . . . so obviously [using sex as a political metaphor]. But I still like the other book.

1988: I'm a woman and that makes a big difference. It separates me a lot from Bellow and Roth and all those guys. There's such distortion in their writing sometimes, the kind of stuff that gives men a bad name. It really louses them up. I think there's a lot of contempt for their fathers coming out and it doesn't do the books, or them, a lot of good. I'm lucky to be a woman.

1986T: You know you go through a period where you're very annoyed with all these male writers. They were your ideal intellectuals simply because they were the literary people of your youth. And then you go through a period where you just can't stand them. I just began to read Saul Bellow's short stories. I hadn't read Saul Bellow in a long time. But I saw how good the writing was. I liked his stories, they were so beautiful. And there were no women in it. The guys had a woman, or they didn't have a woman or there was an aunt that everybody loved or an aunt that everybody hated. Whatever. But the wives were terrible. But I thought to myself, "Well, it doesn't matter so much maybe as long as we women have a voice." But unless *we* tell about *our* lives, those stories can't be listened to. You can't bear half the truth. But as long as we *women* are being read, then I can accept *them*.

1981: It's not so much that I looked for women writers, but I had sense enough to know that, like Henry Miller, he wasn't writing for me. That's as far as I went. I knew that these guys, even the Beats— I thought they were nice, nice to see all those boys, and nice to see all the sexual feelings, but I knew it wasn't written for me at all. It's not so much that I looked for women writers, as that I understood certain much admired writers, like Burroughs, weren't talking to me. There was nothing to get from them. Though at the same time I did get stuff from Proust. That talked to me, but all those ballsy American heroes had nothing to say to me, though my friends thought they were just hot shit, excuse me.

1982:   I don't think the success of *The Women's Room* or *Fear of Flying* was just hype. I think maybe things they did after that could have been. I don't know but there could have been big advances which the publishers had to cover with a lot of hype. That's possible. But those books, those two books, really were very important for lots of women.

   . . . The women's movement . . . has supported every woman, not just me. I mean it's brought Meridel Le Sueur back to life and literature where she belonged, made her old age joyful even.

1983:   All of us who write about women—Tillie and I, Marge Piercy, all of us—are tremendously in debt to the women's liberation movement. It was a wave that came and carried us upwards and gave us a chance to be seen and heard. Women had written books before, too, but they lacked the support of the women's liberation movement. If the time is not right, then you stand completely alone. Ruth Herschberger wrote a book called *Adam's Rib;* it came out in 1948. Even today, there are not many feminists who are familiar with this book. But there is not a single thing contained in any of the books which were published later that Ruth Herschberger was not already aware of in 1948. It was just that she lacked the right wave to carry her upwards. At that time, what she wrote about women's sexuality was revolutionary. I remember that when I read her book I was thinking, "What is she talking about?" And then I thought, "She knows what she is talking about, but there are no others who say such things."

1981:   Joyce Carol Oates? Well . . . there's that woman [who] does an awful lot of work—from a person who doesn't accomplish as much— I have to have a lot of regard for that. I do.

   I love E. M. Broner . . . she's really interesting. She wrote a book called *Her Mothers* and another called *Weave of Women*. And she's pretty gutsy.

   I do like Doris Lessing.

   Susan Sontag has two stories that are absolutely magnificent. I just love her story about China. . . . There's the other story, the one that says goodbye to everything. That's very beautiful. They're wonderful stories.

Black women are really talking now because they're illuminating what's been hidden. For instance, Alice Walker, Toni Morrison, and Toni Cade Bambara are fine writers.

There's a very great book called *History* by Elsa Morante, which apparently the Italians look down on. I mean, she's Moravia's wife, how could she write a great book? But it is a great, wonderful book.

1985C: There's this East German writer, this woman who really should be read by everybody. And if she were a man and from the West—West German—she would be. That's Christa Wolf. . . . She's written half a dozen books. Some of them are so inventive and so imaginative. Her last book, called *Cassandra*, is such a strong feminist book. She does great things. With the novel are four essays on how she thought about the novel. Imagine that—giving us her thoughts and her method and the pathways she took. I had read her . . . *Quest for Christa T.* and another one called *Model Childhood* [also called *Patterns of Childhood*]. What she does in each book is really look for the book. She makes this great search.

1982: I'm always interested in what Marge [Piercy] does. I mean we have our differences about several things, and approaches to writing— what and who and how—but she's an amazing woman and a true writer, and she does a tremendous amount of work and is very particular about what she's doing. She's doing a certain kind of chronicling of our time. She has a book called *The High Cost of Living*. I think it's really a wonderful book. It's not well known. And it's one of her shortest things. I think she thinks she just tossed it off.

[Friends with other writers?] I had always shunned literary life. Just the same way that I was afraid of academic life and tried to stay away from it. But now I seem to know many writers. I've been active in PEN and I feel that community. There are people on my block who are writers I'm very fond of, and I'm very close to, friends like [Don] Barthelme. But I didn't want my everyday life to have anything to do with writers unless *they* were willing to have everyday lives.

1976: I think one of the things about Don's work is that he is a kind of cross between a poet and a journalist. I mean in his work and not in his job experience.

The new journalism? I think it's just an invention of publishing and the media. That kind of prose writing always existed, more or less, and it just got itself a fancy name and a way of publicizing itself. I don't see any difference between that and what went on when I was a girl.

1970: [Donald Barthelme] is giving us the news in his own way. . . . Yes, his art is nonobjective. The news too is a nonobjective art.

1981: [Tillie Olsen and I are] good friends. We just somehow got to know each other, I can't even remember the first time.

1982: When I go to California I spend time with Tillie. I mean time, like hours and hours; I stay at her house, we have taken long walks, you know. And I don't have really literary discussions with her. I don't have the knack, though I think she does. I mean we talk a little bit about it, but mostly we talk about women's lives, about different ideas.

1983: *Silences* is a great book and goes beyond dealing with the silences of women. It has a much wider scope than it seems to have and concerns many writers. [Olsen writes] about how we repress our identities. I believe there is hardly a woman to be found without a similar strict inner censor to be overcome.

1981: I do write with an accent. I did have three languages spoken around me when I was a kid: English and Russian and Yiddish. Those were my languages. That's what's in my ear, so it got through my Eustachian tubes or whatever into my throat, with several diseases that also came along.

1986T: Well, my family was atheist, all of them, except my grandmother. And my father and my mother really believed in their Socialist ideals. The Enlightenment crawled across Europe, and when it reached them, they were at home at last.

1981: My father was an atheist, but he really liked, felt related to the Old Testament. There were a lot of Bible stories around, as well as the Book itself; I loved reading them aloud. Sort of the way kids listen to the radio today, loud now. We used to listen to classical music just as loud. It's just what happens, I think; youngsters need to lie down in music, whatever the music is, even the music of words.

Nobody I know now and love, no writer, is an influence, much; let's put it that way, people I love, like Tillie or Don Barthelme, two people whose work is very different. But the *influences* on me happened long ago.

The Stories and Her Own Story

1985P: When I was little I loved to listen to my parents' stories, all the talk that went on. I loved to listen and soon I loved to talk and tell.

1980H: I always wrote, since I was a little kid. I was encouraged very much in verbal gift—don't call it gift, just call it "verbalosity." I had an older attentive sister and brother, so I'd do a song or a poem and she would write it down. Some writers are born by being made to shut up all the time, and others are born by having their sentences liked.

1983: I have written poems ever since I was a little girl. I have always thought of myself as a writer. It did not even occur to me that perhaps I was not a writer. But my poems were not all that terribly good. It was not till I was over thirty with small children of my own that I started to write short stories.

1985P: I really went to school on poetry. I learned whatever I know about language and craft from writing poems. I worked at it for years and years but I was never a great poet. I didn't know what to do about it, except keep at it. When I was in my early thirties and I wasn't doing my work, I was worried because what I was most interested in were the lives of the women around me and our various relationships. I just couldn't write about it in poems, and so I started trying a little prose.

1986: I would say that stories are closer to poetry than they are to the novel because first they are shorter, and second they are more concentrated, more economical, and that kind of economy, the pulling together of all the information and making leaps across the information, is really close to poetry. By leaps I mean thought leaps and feeling leaps. Also, when short stories are working right, you pay more attention to language than most novelists do.

1988S: [But] people are kind of scared by very very short stories—just as they are by long poems. A short story is closer to the poem than to the novel (I've said that a million times) and when it's very very short—one, two, two and a half pages—should be read like a poem. That is slowly. People who like to skip can't skip in a 3-page story.

1981: First of all, my husband [Jess] did encourage me, I have to say that. He did. But mostly, it was that I was really terribly upset and concerned about women, and men and kids and all of that. I became terribly interested in the life of women and children, how they were living apart from men. It just bugged me a lot. I had lived in Army camps with the guys during the Second World War. [My husband] was a soldier. Everybody's husband was a soldier. I mean, that was a big war. But that really troubled me. Not so much troubles between the two of us, but more troubles among my friends and also a sudden consciousness—I won't say feminist consciousness, because I didn't know enough, but a certain female or feminine or woman's consciousness . . . just feeling that I as part of this bunch of women, that our lives were common and important. A lot of that came from working with women in PTAs and organizations like that, groups that the early women's movement mocked and laughed at, but now know as important.

1980H: It's the park that brings all the people [and my characters] together. Our house was a decent house, but it was really a tenement right at the Port Authority, full of giant trucks going in and out, a hard neighborhood, a Cuban brothel on the same street. It was a very mixed neighborhood, but it has a very strong street life that my kids still remember with pleasure. That was where Ginny and Mrs. Raftery are from.

1981Q: When I first began to write about women and children, people really weren't [doing that]. That came after that long period of heavy masculine writing which followed the Second World War . . . so that I'm not speaking for myself or by myself alone. Lots of other women really felt that their lives were not interesting. And I certainly felt like that. I mean I felt that I was a writer and what was I going to write about? These ladies in these kitchens and these kids? Who'd be interested in that stuff? And, then, at a certain point, I just *had* to write out of feeling for the life of women around me. And then I thought, well, maybe it's trivial, maybe it's nothing; but that's what I have to do, I thought, and it's what I *will* do. So nobody'll read it—what can I do? So that's a political imperative, in a way.

Everybody is a *storyteller.* We all tell stories all the time. Every storyteller is a story *hearer* first. . . . I wrote a lot of poetry . . . but I couldn't write stories, really, until I really heard—*listened*—to enough other voices, until I began to pay great attention to other voices and tried to make that *stretch* to other voices. Then I really found my own.

1985: I'd been writing poetry until about 1956, and then I just made up my mind that I had to write stories. I loved the whole tradition of poetry, but I couldn't figure out a way to use my own Bronx English tongue in poems. I can now, better, but those early poems were all very literary; they picked up after whatever poet I was reading. They used what I think of as only one ear. You have two ears: one is for the sound of literature and the other is for your neighborhood, for your mother and father's house.

1982: I really had been living my life and writing poems with a kind of literary ear. But the ear was far too literary. . . . But somehow or other in fiction I was able to really hear with this other ear—to use both. I mean the kind of traditional educated literary knowledge of this ear and *then* the ear that really had been just listening to people all the time, and used the language of place and time.

When you write poetry—this is a false definition, but you'll see what I mean when I say it—it's really talking to the world . . . and fiction is getting the world to talk to you. When I was able to get into somebody else's voice, when I was able to speak in other people's voices, I found my own. Until then I did not have a voice that could tell a story.

1982: One of the things that made me write was that I was terribly upset about men. "The Contest" was the first thing I wrote. I was trying to think about what was going on between men and women, and the only way I could think about it was to write from [a man's] point of view. So I tried to get into this guy's head, and I wrote the story from his point of view, with him telling the story. I remember writing the first line—really it was the first line I wrote: "Up early or late, it never matters, the day gets away from me."

1981: The first story I wrote . . . was "The Contest." Because I was trying to figure out what made all these guys tick—this guy who was upstairs was the one really; I did my best, I got into his head and I just sorta sat there and I said, "I've gotta write this story." And then the second one was "Goodbye and Good Luck."

1982: There's a line in "Goodbye and Good Luck" . . . where [Aunt Rose] tries to talk to [Vlashkin] and she says to him, "A man's life is something I don't truly see." She says, in other words, "What do you want? What do you want here? What do you want to do? What do you have in mind?" She's asking him, you know, and she says, "A man's life is something I don't truly see."

And at the same time I was getting closer and closer to women's lives through the kids. Specifically women without men. So those two things were happening.

1981: I had a friend on the block whose kids used to look at television with my kids, and her husband was an editor and they were divorced. She was always trying to give him hard tasks. She said to him very angrily one day, "Well, the least you could do is read Grace's stories." He used to come around on Sunday; it was his Sunday to pick up his kids. He'd sit there like that, waiting for them to finish the program. So he read them ["The Contest," "Goodbye and Good Luck," and "A Woman Young and Old"] and he liked them and he said, write seven more and we'll publish them. He [Ken McCormick] was a senior editor at Doubleday. It was pure luck, really. But what was very interesting was that as I wrote them I would send them to magazines and they were returned, all the time. So if it hadn't been for him, I really might have stopped.

1980H: And that's how it happened. I sat down and wrote seven more over the next two years.

1980: I have used [lines from life] . . . as a matter of fact, in one of the first stories I ever wrote. . . . This old aunt says, "I was popular in certain circles." I have to tell you the truth: my husband's aunt said that. I was about twenty-five years younger then, and I looked at her, amazed, you know, that that was true. And then I just invented a circle for her to be popular in. I thought about that a good deal—but really, that is an example of a story which began with an absolute true sentence spoken to me by a person. But mostly I don't remember well enough, really. You have to really understand how people speak, and you have to reconstruct it, but you may not, at the same time, have it right. Most pleasure in writing, you know, is in inventing.

1981: I do somewhat [identify with Faith], but when I first used her she was absolutely not me at all. She really is my friend, up to whose house I went. I went to see my friend Sybil, and I saw she was sitting there, and there were "two husbands disappointed by eggs." I mean that really was true, a present husband and a former husband and they were both sitting there complaining about the breakfast. And that was the first line of the story I wrote: "There were two husbands disappointed by eggs" ["The Used-Boy Raisers"]. And that was really the beginning of Faith too. Actually, from then on, it wasn't Sybil either. She began to take on characteristics of at least four friends. She's somewhat different from me, but she's all of us, she's a collective of us really, but she began with my friend Syb. . . . Faith sort of became my women friends more than anything else—not a composite really, because you can't take four people and make a person. It's very hard to do. She became an invented person who lived in circumstances similar to most of the women I knew—which were not my circumstances, but which were the lives of women I knew pretty well during those years when my kids were small, and when I was very close mostly to lots of women with little kids.

1987: [Faith's] life is totally different from mine. I lived with my first husband, my children's father, for about twenty-two, twenty-three years. And I've lived with my present husband already about fourteen, fifteen years, at least, and I probably will for the rest of my life. I'm just a long-term person, and Faith is not particularly that. Nor are my children quite like them. I deliberately made them different from my kids. But I really knew a lot of children. I had all these kids around the house.

1982: I have worked alone almost all of my writing life. I always tell people that it takes too long that way. There has to be privacy but there ought to be community.

Relationship of Writing to
Other Aspects of Her Life

1982: The three things in my life have been writing, politics, and family. At different times each one has taken over, has been more strong. And when the kids were little, it was really family. I didn't do a lot of politics or stuff. Family of course means children, but it didn't mean my little nuclear family. It meant the life of families, schools, parks, the day-care centers. And that was the point at which I was most interested in those women and what was going on in the park. That was when I really began to think about our lives.

. . . I don't like giving anything up for anything. I have a terrible greed. I don't like giving up writing for family. I don't like giving up family for writing. I don't like giving up politics to go to my family parties, and I don't like missing my granddaughter just because I have to finish a piece of some kind. I do it all by push; I don't work it out.

1980H: Everything gets in the way of everything else. I'm not a careerist in any way. I mean I view life as a whole, and that's what interests me. And I'm interested in being as good a writer as I can. I can't live without writing, but I couldn't live without my children. And I couldn't bear not to respond to the awful things that are. I regret that I haven't written more, but I don't know how—with my view of how to live in this really hopeless world—I could have done more.

1979: Sure, [other activities keep me from writing enough], and so do the habits of digression I developed early, when I was raising kids. But the political stuff is equally important. There's nothing holy about writing. It's wonderful. It's a great gift to be given, to be able to carry through from your early years things that you imagined you might do. But it's only part of life.

1983: I think it's a shame that it has become almost a fashion not to have children. The question of the right time once again. Young women who nowadays choose to remain childless might perhaps have chosen differently if they had been born five years earlier or five years later. And they are missing out on a fantastic experience, a totally unique experience. [Can it work the other way?] Well, it is certainly true that one has to give up many things. Children are a lot of work— the entire day is spent on them. But we don't live for just five or seven years. We live, after all, through an entire lifetime. I think I'll put it this way: have children first, because you'll manage better while you're young and strong [but not so that you can spend all your energy later on on other things]—after all, we don't do just one thing at a time and just once during the course of a day. The day is long. You write, you love, you work.

1985P: I was dumb to try [a novel]. I had a lot of pages but it just wasn't any good. Thank God I was smart enough to throw them out. I didn't stay away from the novel—it stayed away from me. It probably has something to do with how I've chosen to use my time in this world. I've allowed all the distractions.

There have been long periods of my life when I was bringing up my two kids and playing with them at the playground or working on political things and the stories had to wait. I've let all that happen. No regrets. The stories come when they come.

1974: Maybe it's the way I've been living. Maybe I'll never write a novel.

1981: It's hard for me to say, really, if [my politics and my fiction fit together] or not. You know, people take areas to write about. Marge Piercy chronicles for us a really specific world of young and getting-older political activists. That's not ordinary everyday life, and yet it's essential. I don't say that what I write about is the only important thing. I know a lot of political people and I work a lot with them. But I just don't seem to write about them.

1985C: What I'm trying to write about is ordinary life as I know it, which involves politics. But it also involves ordinary life. So I tend to show politics as part of ordinary life. I tend to show it in arguments between the son and the mother . . . or among the women in the way they talk about that while they're also talking about the kids.

1981Q: The reason I'm interested in the political life of this world is that I'm interested in the people. The politics and literature come from the same impetus, really. It isn't that it's the same thing, but it comes from the same concern: how ordinary life can be lived in our cities—countrysides too.

1982: The act of illumination is a political act. That is, the act of saying, "See, this has been in darkness. This life has been unseen, and unknown." Now to make that decision and say, "I want to illuminate this life"—which is the act of bringing justice into the world a little bit, that's a decision you make. But if you say, "Here's a life that's lying there; now I'd like to take a rock and slowly cover it"—that's a political decision. I think people do that with language all the time. Sentimental language is a lie because it blurs or hides the truth.

1976: I would go a little further [than Walker Percy: "I think there are two things involved: there's a cultural decline and a cultural refreshment, and it is the vocation of the artist, the fiction writer, the playwright and the poet, to create new language"] and say that being American and living in the United States we really have a much better opportunity to do that than people in other countries. This language of ours, here in this country, is always being refreshed and scrambled up and knocked around. It's always coming up from the bottom, again and again, and I don't think that's a problem in a sense. It's just an event.

1973: As I live my talky, asking and answering life in the United States, I often remember the first amendment, how pleasant it's been to me and how useful to my country. I was taught to love it and wonder at its beauty by my parents, prisoners once of the Czar. And I do love it, though I also love literature, and it has made our literature one of the most lively and useless in the world. Of course, it's been good to write letters to the newspapers. Some are published. It *has* been pleasing to stand on the corner of Eighth Street and Sixth Avenue and hand out informational pamphlets, leaflets of protest, to assemble in rage a couple of times a year with tens of thousands of others.

The elected or appointed leaders of our country have often applauded our enactment of these freedoms. They were then able (with clear consciences) to undertake and sustain the awful wars we spoke and assembled against for ten years.

1982:   Right now, the problems with this political action of which I'm very much a part are complex, and require imagination. I have anxiety about that. Not guilt, but anxiety, because I really feel the world's in the balance. I don't feel essential to the world, to the solution, but I just feel my normal citizenship in this—and the pity of it all. So I just find myself using my mind in a different way. . . .

The whole point about teaching is to keep [students] from following false gods of all kinds and so on, and to be honorable, and to love the language. I think all teaching is moral. I mean, where it's not, we really have—in the sciences where it's not moral, or in the social sciences where it's not moral—we have the great economists of the corporate-loving right and the inventors of the neutron bomb and things like that. And also in literature you have a cold, conventional prose. It's only where you really feel a moral obligation towards literature and language that there's any hope. Part of what you do as a teacher of writing is to weed out the kids who think they want to be writers but really aren't interested in subject matter or language or aren't bugged by anything. You know, nobody needs them, nobody needs them to keep working.

1981:   [Feminist writer?] I'm a feminist *and* a writer. Whatever is in here comes from the facts of my life. To leave them out would be false. I do write a lot about women and the men they know. That's who the people are and what they think about.

1983:   No, rather I would say that my own experiences are like those of most other women. In a personal sense I see myself as a feminist, but as an author? I write about women's lives, whether they themselves are feminists or not. I talk to them and they answer, "You bet, yes, I've been through that myself too." It probably is the beginning of a growing political awareness to be able to say about other women's lives, "Sure, yes, I know exactly how you're feeling."

1974:   When women are treated badly in a book, it never passed me by. I always knew that when Henry Miller was fucking around and freeing us all sexually, he was only freeing himself. I always knew this great freedom those male writers were enjoying, if it didn't have me, unfortunately, as an object, really had nothing to do with me at all. As a woman I'm trying to restore something to the scales, so that the woman can be seen—not as she has been.

See, I think art also does another thing, and it may come from my political feelings, but I think art, literature, fiction, poetry, whatever it is, makes justice in the world. That's why it almost always has to be on the side of the underdog. It doesn't know it's on the side of the underdog. And I didn't know it. I'm saying it after the fact. You see it in all the Russian writers. They bring this guy, this person, this woman, this man, out of some shadows someplace, and they shine a light on him—this is a person, too.

1985: I feel I haven't written about certain things yet that I probably will at some point. I've written about the personal lives of these people; I haven't really seen them in political action, and I don't know if I need to, especially, for what I'm trying to do. There has to be a way of writing about it that's right and interesting, but I haven't figured it out. I've mainly been interested in this personal political life, but I refer peripherally to things: in "Living" . . . she remembers praying for peace on Eighth Street with her friend; in "Zagrowsky Tells" . . . he's furious because they picketed his drugstore. That's the way a lot of politics gets in, as part of ordinary people's lives, and that's really the way I want to show it, it seems to me now. What I want is for these political people to really be *seen*.

What Her Writing Is All About

1981: A story is for me—the word "conflict" is often used, and I don't really like that word. Maybe it's because I'm a pacifist or whatever reason. I think it's just a more simple dialectic than that. I think it's two events or two characters or two winds or two different weathers or two ideas or whatever, bumping into each other, and what you hear, that's the story. And that can happen in two pages.

1974: Look, a short story comes because it's about all of life at any moment. A short story, to be good, has to be about the whole of life. It can't be a slice of life. It's got to be about everything, even if it's two pages long. And when it isn't, it doesn't work.

1976: I can't say that I'm presenting a truth when I write. I'm trying to understand something which I don't understand to begin with. I begin by not understanding, and the tension and the excitement for me and the tension and excitement that the reader may get also is in that not understanding and that pull away from not knowing to knowing. . . . What happens is the reader will come into your book, and he isn't a total dummy. That reader has been alive and has been reading the papers and books, or if they're as old as me, they've lived through that whole period and they know a good deal about it. The whole business is joined and more knowledge occurs in your work, or more truth if you want to put it that way, than you know, or than you planned, or than you even wished.

1974: What you really write about is energy. It's what makes any work of art work. If you read something and say, "Oh, gee," it's because there's enough tension between that bare page and the writer that you can feel the energy of the writer's experience.

1980: I don't really intend to be funny. I don't, and there are certain stories I've done where I see that there are very easy laughs, and if there ever is some edition of some kind, I would take them out. I really don't like that at all. On the other hand, you really can't, if that's how you see it, you know. . . .

1982: I think what happens is humor sometimes takes the place of anger, and it may even subvert it. You know, in a way, sometimes there should be more anger, and there's humor instead.

1980H: I invent people, and they speak. And if they're speaking wrong, you know it. You read it aloud to yourself, and you know nobody ever spoke like that, or ever said that, or ever felt that. You know when you are forcing things. You don't know in the beginning. Sometimes you really want your people to fall in love, or to be happy, or to commit suicide. A lot of writers are crazy about having people commit suicide to end their books. But people don't usually commit suicide. It spoils it for me that in Chopin's *The Awakening* the woman kills herself. And it's bad that Anna Karenina kills herself. . . . Both of them have the wrong idea, the wrong idea of how much terrible life people can bear, how much women have borne and still continued to live. . . .

Stories illuminate. That's the purpose of a story for me. To shine a light on what's dark and give it light. And the balance is something else—it's justice. The dark lives of women . . . is what made me write to begin with. And at the time I thought no one would be interested in seeing it, but that I had to illuminate it anyway, if for nobody else for myself and my friends. . . . I write for my friends, to tell the stories of their lives.

1981: I went to some meetings at MLA last year, to try to see what's going on. I think a lot of that [the theoretical speculations the French like] is interesting, but, see, first of all, for me the story exists really off the page in a way that, for them, it's all lying around there on the table. And for a lot of Americans too it does. And I don't think that's the direction for literature to go. I see it getting deeper and deeper into the page, until it disappears out the back end of the book. So that's the direction it's going to take. It's not that I don't love the page. I mean I love the books. But we really have to think of the throat it comes out of. I feel it's too great a movement away from the people, if you want to put it that way, and certainly away from female life.

1980H: In a way, now, I feel much freer to deal with lots of different things. Women's lives are just as interesting later on, after they have kids, maybe more so. Life is just continuously interesting, but if something's been written, and I've already read it, I tend not to need to write about it myself. I write stories that I need to hear. There are things I want to know about and I don't know about. Once I read a story by someone else, I find out all about it. It's not very interesting for me to investigate the same thing.

. . . I don't write about anything but what I'm writing about. . . . I don't feel mystical. What I think is mysterious is life. What I'm trying to do is show how mysterious ordinary life is. But . . . if you're at all surrealistic when you write, you do go beyond just telling. . . . You do mean more than you say, which I suppose is better than saying more than you mean. . . .

I *am* interested in form, despite [saying] that the real experiments were in subject matter. That really is a class idea, a Marxist idea. But I do agree . . . that language and subject matter must come together. Still, you have whole periods when Blacks are not written about, or they're written about as slaves. And if you're a Black person, you'll say, "Where the hell are all the Black people? Why aren't they writing about my life?" And then some Black people will start to do it. And they'll pay attention and suddenly realize that they have a speech and that language is part of the story. Language is what the American language is about. What I write about is a coming together of all sorts of other languages.

1976: When you talk about new forms or different forms, it seems to me this non-linearity has really run its course, played its game out. I understand it, it has been my way of working too. I haven't moved dead ahead except once in a while in that sense, and I wonder about our need for storytelling in its most simple linear sense of *what happened then, and then what happened, and what came next.* I wonder to what extent that isn't going to make a very vigorous comeback and if it isn't necessary. I think a lot of it has to do with speaking aloud and with the word as a said thing, not as a written word but as a spoken word. I am simply interested in it, you have to come at things not knowing. I come at that too, in a sense, not knowing, and yet understanding that I probably know more than I think. I've heard lots of stories and I've told lots of stories, and it seems to me to be a very honorable business to be a storyteller and to tell stories to people. Just as language rises again and again from new voices, from Black people, as Walker [Percy] said, and in my own world, from foreigners of all kinds. So do new forms come or old forms turn round on that wheel, come again and again as new people tell stories. I think particularly at this point of women. I might say that this is the first place that I've been in for five years where women haven't been mentioned until this moment, and I'm nervous about it. Different people, new people, are telling stories, and women haven't told stories yet, not really. I think of myself as a woman who has been a writer and who has been in a tradition which is largely male.

1980H: Writing does not help me deal with anything. I don't look at the facts of life as something that you have to be "helped to deal with." Unless you just can't deal with life. If you're a person who can't deal with life, you're not going to be able to deal with death. So I don't have that therapeutical attitude towards the things one does. I mean, if I wrote a poem, it doesn't help me to *deal with* it, it helps me to *think about* it. If I'm going to write something about a kid dying, I'm really doing a couple of things. I'm knocking wood about such an event, 'cause it's totally invented and yet could happen every day and probably has happened several times in the New York subways. And I'm investigating something. I'm trying to understand what that event is, and what it is to the people around it—what it is to the other little boys, what it is to the motorman, what it is to the women, and what it is mostly to the mother. So I'm trying to understand. Not to deal with it. I'm not soothing myself. I'm as unsoothed at those deaths right this minute as I was when I began to write about them.

1987:   I think we worry too much about what form is which.

1980:   I don't like . . . the word "fiction." I think it's a false word, and it's led to "non-fiction." I mean, you're either a storyteller, an inventor in language or event or whatever, or a poet of storytelling—or you're not. I guess I'd use the example of Maxine Hong Kingston, who for *The Woman Warrior* got a nonfiction award. Well, that really got me sore, because that really was a great work of storytelling. But see, non-fiction is supposed to sell better than fiction, and novels are supposed to sell better than short stories, and so on down the line.

A person telling her own story is also storytelling, and the truth of the matter is that telling your own story is great, for once. . . . You

want to tell it, tell it. But the fact is that the job of the storyteller—
you know, the task, as an imposed task—that task is the task of the
story hearer. It's wonderful to tell what happened to you at this and
this time, and at a certain point, like when you're ninety, you should
do that—you know, you've probably by then amassed so much experience and so many interesting events, and you have such a view of the
world, you should absolutely do it. But the job—I keep using that
word, maybe you should change it—but the interest is really to tell the
story of the people, of the life of your time. I mean, you have to keep
saying how it was. And even if you're writing a story about the history
of the past, like Maxine did—almost all of it, and even in her new
book, is just telling, "This is how it is now because of how it was then."

A lot of people cannot begin to speak out of their own throats until
they have listened enough, and heard enough the stories of others.
Again, nothing wrong with telling your own story—tell it! . . . But if
you speak for others—if you really perform that great social task (I have
a lot of useless sentences like that)—you'll really begin to be able to
tell your own story better.

1987: I use "storytelling" because I hate the word "fiction." . . . It
just divides from nonfiction, and yet they're somebody's true stories.
A lot of oral histories. Those are stories. What makes a piece of fiction?
What makes fiction is a person telling it, to me. And what makes a
story is . . . bringing together two stories in some ways. So it really
exists on a lot of levels. I mean a kid comes home from school and tells
a story, says "Ma! I gotta tell you something!" And that's the first im-
pulse of a little storyteller. "I gotta tell you something. I want to tell
you something." And proceeds to tell the story. Now the mother receives it in two ways. First, she knows the kid, and then she listens to
the story. If it's true or false, it doesn't really matter. But the life of
this little child and the voice of this little child coming together with
the story tone, becomes the story.

1976: I don't think [storytelling] is a dead art form at all. I think that
women do tell lots of stories and I think they're probably among the
last of a great oral tradition, and it's called gossip. When men do it it's
telling stories and when women do it it's gossip. Except that men don't
tell stories anymore, they talk shop. But I think that's where it's going
to come from, the great oral tradition that women have of handing

down stories from grandmother to granddaughter and speaking together wherever they are.

We all live in a society in which everybody says the word "alienated" (that's only the second time I've used that word in my life, by the way, and I feel sheepish about it), but people do live alone and are competitive from a very early age, brothers and sisters are, and it's supposed to be natural but I think that's the bunk. What happens to them is that they're supposed to fulfill themselves and develop themselves; and not one of us, really, can labor to refine and cultivate and develop ourselves, our single self, without being hurtful to others. This kind of life is extremely painful to people. I think it hurts everybody that this is how they were brought up. Every person here feels a little sick about it and I think that people, even if you don't know it, really are moving now more and more towards real experiments with different ways of life, and many of them I can't imagine because I don't have a very good imagination. But I think that storytelling and people telling stories to other people and the experience of paying attention and listening in some way relate to that former loss of community.

. . . When I talk about telling stories I assume that the language is beautiful and I don't care who tells the story. I don't mean it has to be a fantastic writer. It can be my aunt or someone like that who doesn't like to write at all and doesn't. But storytelling has more to it than that narrative drive. It does have that, but it ought to speak beautifully. I would not be interested in a writer that I couldn't read aloud. But the real point that I wanted to make is this: I consider that as a writer I have several obligations and one of them is to write as damn well as I can. I take that very seriously and responsibly and write as truthfully as I can, as well, and I do really feel responsible for the future of literature. So that I'm saying a funny kind of thing. The moral word is "ought to be," which people don't like to use too much these days. Something ought to be. What ought to be? People ought to live in mutual aid and concern, listening to one another's stories. That's what they ought to do. I'm not doing that. I'm very much a person in my time, but I'm saying that that's the next thing that interests me. The next thing that interests me is the last thing to have interested anyone. I want to find out a way. Is there a way for people to tell stories to one another again and to bring one another into that kind of speaking and listening and attending community?

. . . I've really been thinking about what it means for writers not to make large statements or to make large statements. We haven't liked to say we like to make truthful statements since Bill [Gass] has scared us on that a little bit. . . . But I think I look at this stuff a little more politically maybe, and it seems to me that large statements *are* made and we don't notice they're being made. There's a large statement being made right around the corner from you and you don't know it.

About Individual Stories

1981: Sometimes they're really invented, like "Goodbye and Good Luck." She's very much invented, although she comes from people of that generation.

1980H: People *do* talk like that. They speak beautifully. That kind of language is common to me. I could think of any one of my aunts talking like that. The speech of people is very beautiful, and that's what I think is missing in the god-damned novel. Especially when an old person is telling their story. It's almost always beautiful because they don't fuck around. They really are telling you something. Rosie's telling all her feelings to her niece. She's justifying her life. She's saying, "I lived for love." It's very romantic and yet she's a very independent woman. For her time. She's from my parents' time, and she worked in the garment industry, like all of them did. Got theater crazy and worked in the theater and then went back to the garment industry. And she had this big love affair with this guy. But the story is invented. Rose is a cross between my aunts and other people. And the actor is a typical actor, Jewish. You bring it all together so that you hear it for the first time. For that kind of speech. We *all* hear a lot and say a lot, more than you would think. A lot of us, we're cut off from our language, the language of place.

1980H: ["The Contest" was] the first story I wrote. I was thinking about women and what was wrong between men and women, and I thought, "Why not see how a man thinks on this issue?" So I let him do the talking. I sure was [rough on him]. I let him talk his own language and let him say exactly what he wanted to say. And I've had men come up to me and say, "That was really great! You really understand him. He really let that bitch have it!"

1982: I had a wonderful discussion at City College where a young Black girl got up and said, "You know that woman you had in that story, that 'Interest in Life,' you know her?" I said, "Yeah." She said, "She

135

didn't seem to learn. I mean the way she was waiting for that guy all the time. Did you think she was a hero or something?" I said, "No, I didn't think she was a hero, but she was a woman." The kid says, "Well, I think she was a dope." I said, "That's good. That means your life will be better."

1980H: You write about two things: you write about what is like you and you write about what is totally unlike you. Both are equally fascinating. You say, this is like me, this is unlike me. This is another world in which many things can happen. Mrs. Raftery, for example, is totally different, a different generation, and she has a totally different way. Whereas Ginny was really just another woman in a different apartment in the same building, and not unlike Faith. Not like me, but less unlike Faith because Faith is also alone with kids.

1980H: I like [the guy in "An Irrevocable Diameter"]. He's nice. That's . . . the other. Why should *I* always tell the story? I like the other to tell the story. I was trying to think of a guy who wasn't a bad guy in this situation. You know, with one of those little girls who aren't bad little girls, but who are powerful.

1983: "A Subject of Childhood" . . . ends with the little boy putting his hands over his mother's heart. I had forgotten this story, but then I read it again not long ago, and I believe that I expressed what I really felt when I wrote it.

1980H: Some [women] are better off without the men. If the men were there, *then* they'd be victims. In the story, when Clifford leaves, she ceases to be a victim. While he is there, she is. But everybody's a victim. We're more victims of our society. And men are much more victims than women, I think. I think my women characters are very strong. Their children strengthen them a lot. I don't even think Ginny's a victim. She really likes the guy, and she refuses to be a victim. I feel that the women are very remarkable. That's what interested me in these women in the first place. How strong they were. Having a hard time is not being a victim. It's how you deal with it.

1980H: There were kids like [Eddie in "In Time Which Made a Monkey of Us All"]. Kids who "dropped out" of sanity even then. Even in my generation.

1980H: It's interesting about that story ["The Floating Truth"]. I'd written the first page and I had no intention of going on with it. I read it to Jess, my former husband, and he said, "You'd better finish that. That's funny. You finish it now." That story is really about work, about doing work in this world.

1974: I work on my own until I can't do any more with a story. ["Faith in the Afternoon" started out as a novel.] I wrote seventy or eighty pages. Wrong. The wrongest thing I ever did and if I'd gone on in that direction, I would have been in hot water. It didn't explore any new territories—it wasn't mysterious. I did it because people said I should.

1980H: I don't like plot, it's true. It's too much of a line. It just goes a different way. It moves by pictures. Certainly "The Burdened Man" is pure plot.

1980H: I like that story ["Politics"] a lot. One of the editors wanted me to leave it out of the book, but I really liked it. . . . Don [Barthelme] also loved it and stuck by me on that.

1981Q: ["The Little Girl"] was, of course, a terribly hard story to write. But I was very close to one of those guys. He was an old friend and we had done a lot of political work and tenant organizing. . . . That's what interested me when I was young. He was a good friend of mine and he was the one who told me the story. He told me the story of the killing of this little girl about four times. I mean, he would grab me, sort of, by the wrists and just stop me on Macdougal Street or on Sixth Avenue, or wherever, and just tell me the story again and again. So that I had to tell it for *him*. I had to tell that story for this guy, Bill, who is dead now. . . . And so, he was what I knew and the story I told was what I had to go after, to *stretch*, for what I didn't know about that. It began with him, but the other people were invented because I didn't really know them. But I did know fourteen/fifteen-year-old kids. I did know runaways. I know the park. But it was hard.

1980H: The little girl being killed is not about her being killed. It's about the guy who tells the story.

1981: I think by writing ["A Conversation with My Father"] I sort of screwed myself up, because people really don't read. I mean, a great deal happens in almost any one of those stories, really sometimes more than in lots of other people's, enough to make a novel or something. When people say, "Well, she really doesn't care much about plot," all they're doing is repeating what I said in my story. Plot is nothing. Plot is only movement in time. If you move in time you have a plot; if you don't move in time, you don't have a plot, you just have a stand-still, a painting maybe, or you have something else. But if you move in time you have a plot.

. . . Actually the story's about a couple of things. It's about story-telling, but it's also really about generational attitudes towards life, and it's about history. I tend not to look at things psychologically so much, but historically, I think. And for him, he was quite right, from his point of view. He came from a world where there *was* no choice, where you couldn't really decide to change careers when you were forty-one years old, you know. You couldn't decide to do things like that. Once you were a junkie, that was the end of everything. Once you were anything, that was it. Who you were was what you were.

And she was speaking really from her own particular historical moment, and in another country besides, where things were more open. So it wasn't that she was giving some philosophical attitude, or some attitude close to her own optimistic disposition, although both of those things were true. That's also true, but she was also really (although neither of them knew it, only the writer knew this), they were really speaking from their own latitude and longitude, and from their own time in history when they spoke about these things.

So that's really, I think, what was happening there. And her feeling which she talked about in terms of stories was pretty much exactly the same. I mean she really lives at a time when things have more open possibility, and for a group or a class that had more possibilities and a generation in that line, because he was an immigrant and he just about got here and did all right by the skin of his teeth. So she was really speaking for people who had more opportunities. And so she brought that into literature, because we just don't hop out of our time so easy.

1980: [In that story], my father keeps telling me, "All you do is tell jokes." And it was true—talking about family reactions, this was one of the things that he would always kind of bug me about. He'd say,

"Okay, yeah, more jokes, you think that's funny, right?" And I'd say, "No, I didn't say it was funny. If people laugh, I can't help it—I didn't say it was funny."

1982: [And the incident where he says to you, "Can't you write stories like you used to? Like Chekhov?" That's all made up?] Yeah, the specific occasion is invented.

1981Q: That story, in which I say that I'm opposed to plot because it takes away the open destiny of life and literature, has been interpreted that I'm against plot. But you can't be against plot. Plot is something that happens, whether you *do* it or not. Plot is only the movement of a thread through time. It's what happens after something else happens. You can't stop plot like you can't stop time.

1980: I have a story called "The Immigrant Story," and I had that— the specific story of that story, the specific tale of that story—in mind for about twenty-five, thirty years, and I never could figure out how to tell the story. I knew what the story was about, I knew it, and I couldn't deal with it. And it wasn't until one day I was simply going through these papers . . . these beginnings of stories, that I found two pages of dialogue, rather abstract dialogue, really ideas mostly, and I understood how to tell that story. It simply began with these two people speaking to each other. I knew the story, but I didn't know what a complicated way I would have to tell it. That was sort of the discovery of form—which the Lord gives you sometimes, and sometimes he don't.

1981: I had always wanted to tell that story because I had always thought about those old people and how awful my friend had been towards them. I had always wanted to speak for them in some way. It's what we call in art what's dark; what's hidden is what we want to illuminate. When we say, "This is what happened. If I didn't tell you, you'd never know it." Of course that's not true. Someone else would tell.

1980H: In "The Long-Distance Runner" I'm writing about a woman going back, but I'm also writing about a place and a time and a specific relation to it.

1981Q: I did write a story about a visit to China ["Somewhere Else"] which dealt with just that problem [of not knowing what I don't know about certain people]. It was about taking pictures, about photographing, and it really was about dealing with another people. There's no telling what you can do in your life if you live long enough.

1982: I have two stories in a story that I wrote about China. One was about an event that happened in China where people didn't want to be photographed and the other was an event that happened in this country on the Lower East Side [moved, in the story, to the South Bronx] where people didn't want to be photographed. That story about what happened in China, it interested me as a story to tell, you know, to gab about, to tell everyone who said, "Tell us about China." But it didn't interest me as a real hard-written story until I thought about the other story and decided to tell them together. One just didn't seem enough. It could have been a little article, a small journalistic thing. But it didn't really interest me until I began to realize what it was about and how it needed the other one.

1980: But as for finding out what a story is about, that happens to me all the time. And it happened in a rather long story . . . called "Friends." Well, I began that story simply writing about the death of my friend, and it went on and on, and it just became more and more clear that it was really a story about all of these women that my children and their children had grown up with—and that I had grown up with, really. So that it was really a much more complicated story than I ever intended telling, and other characters took over entirely, and seemed to me more important, finally.

1981: In that story "Friends" those women, we *were* awfully close and we began by hanging out in the park together, but we did an awful lot of politics together. We really did have a collective existence in a way, you know. And in the anti-war movement, we were a different, older group of people. But we raised our kids a lot together, and that was the beginnings of a political period. There are a lot of people living like that now. I do want in some way to be able to speak for them, in a way that they've allowed me to. . . . That story "Friends" I really wrote for my friends. I hoped that they would read it. I wrote it toward them and also from them.

1980H: That story called "Friends" is really about grief for the children.

1980: And as for my friends, I try not to think about [their response to stories] too much. If they have something to say to me, they say it. [But] I cared about how my friends felt about that "Friends" story, especially the friend with whom I hadn't spoken for several years because of a great quarrel. And when she called me up and said, "That was okay, Grace". . .

1980H: I arrange [the stories in the collection] very carefully. But they're not in the order that they were written at all. The first thing is I try to start out with an interesting story, but then . . . it just seems to read right. I'd go over it and over it. And, you know, not have all the very long ones together . . . some long ones, some short ones, some heavy ones, then some lighter.

The Writer on Her Craft: Process, Technique, Credo

1980G: When I wrote my first couple of stories, because of the poetry, I worked aloud from the very beginning. I would read a paragraph to myself and then type it, and then I'd reread it and I'd take it apart. And every day I'd reread what I wrote the day before aloud. That became my method.

1985P: I'm always making little notes, false starts, beginnings. I wrote poetry for years before I ever wrote a story. I still work like a poet, real slow.

1974: I used to start simply from language, especially in the first book. I would write a couple of sentences and let them lay there. Not on purpose, but just because I couldn't figure out what was going to come next. I've always worked blind. Cocteau has a sentence: "My work is finished but I have to discover it." I don't know how I worked with this [second] book. I won't know for another few years. I would really like to get very simple. I think the language in my writing now may be simpler, but the stories are not so simple.

1980: Well, how do stories begin for me? In one of about four or five ways. One way is when I am walking down the street—it never happens, really, when I'm sitting at my desk. Taking a bath is very good too. But I simply—sentences occur to me, and those sentences are sometimes—sometimes I lose them because I'm not near any writing material, and that's the first thing you should all know, you should always be near a pencil and paper, your whole life.

Sometimes what it comes from is just pure language. I can't even tell you that I'm thinking specifically of any event of any kind, and I may simply write two or three sentences that seem to me beautiful or right or true for the day. And then what would happen would be that I might type up a page or so. I tend to work like that in general. I just

142

work in pieces, and I don't always know that I've begun a story. I just add that page to an infinite number of pages in a drawer in my desk. And very often they are beginnings, when I go back over it.

I have lots of pages that I'll never turn into a story. I'm sure all writers do. I have lots of pages that are just a paragraph of nice writing, or something like that, and don't seem to me—. It's not that they're not *worth* working with, but nothing in that paragraph gives me that feeling which is one of the impetuses of all storytelling: "I want to tell you a story, I want to tell you something." So those paragraphs may never enter into my I-want-to-tell-you-somethings. I may never want to tell you anything about that story. But actually, some of them become two pages, and what they really are are simply ways of taking stabs at that mystery, really.

Whenever I finish a story, I go back to that drawer. And as a matter of fact, when I'm in the middle of a story and stuck, I go back and look at these other pieces. There's this book by Joan Miró, the artist, called *I Work Like a Gardener.* It's a small book, it's very beautiful, and he says, "I work like a gardener. I'm never so happy as when I'm rich in canvases." He says, "Then I get up in the morning and I prune one, I water another." I had been working very much like that. It's such a nice corroboration from another art, that I'm grateful to it, and it's become a way that, with my bad habits and my natural disinclinations, I can work.

Another way I begin, often, is with a person speaking, because I have an awful lot of speaking in my ear, and an awful lot of words, ideas, persons having spoken to me, or persons whom I would like to speak through me, and other voices, and so I will often begin with a sentence, a couple of sentences of people speaking. I never have begun with a story, and that's caused some problems for me, but it's the way I've worked.

1986T: I have this idea that you should begin the story where the story begins, not two pages before with a lot of introduction and stuff like that. The fun of writing, because you know there's a lot of fun, is really getting it all to happen at once, if you can.

1981: Before I wrote ["The Contest" and "Goodbye and Good Luck"], I was just stuck in myself. Until I was able to use other people's voices, until I was able to hear other people's voices, that I'd been hearing all my life, you know, I was just talking me-me-me. While I was doing that I couldn't write these stories. And when I was able to get into other voices consciously, or use what I was hearing, and become the story-hearer—when I could do that, I just suddenly wrote them. It was a true breakthrough.

1969: Literature has something to do with language. There's probably a natural grammar at the tip of your tongue. You may not believe it, but if you say what's on your mind in the language that comes to you from your parents and your street and friends you'll probably say something beautiful. Still, if you weren't a tough recalcitrant kid, that language may have been destroyed by the tongues of schoolteachers who were ashamed of interesting homes, inflection, and language and left them all for correct usage.

1982: What happens with me and probably other writers as well—something really bugs me for a long, long time and I may write a page or two on it but I don't know what the hell to do next. That story . . . "Friends" . . . was after me a long, long time. I had written the first page maybe a year and a half before I wrote the rest of it. I wanted to write about this woman and I wanted to put it in terms of a visit. The visit is invented in the sense that I went to see her pretty much by myself, but I knew that groups of friends had gone to see her at different times. We were all pretty close. . . .

But I didn't know what to do with that beginning—it couldn't just be a story about her dying and our visit. I began with "To put us at our ease, to quiet our hearts as she lay dying, our dear friend Selena said, Life, after all, has not been an unrelieved horror—you know, I *did* have many wonderful years with her." I wrote that paragraph partly because she really said it, and I never forgot that language. After that, it was really a big problem. Maybe a year later, you know, I was really doing other things, finishing up some other stories. But I would write things, different parts, not so much about her but different conversations or different small sections. And when I really began to do Ann and her son and the conflicts among the women, I realized that it really wasn't just a story about Selena but it was a story about the end of relationships or the dying of long friendship. (I hate that word "relationship"—I thought I'd never use it but I did. Now I don't have to be mad at other people who do it.) Something about, you know, deep, deep friendships and what they're based on and what happens to them.

But, I mean, I didn't know that especially until—in a way I had to make two stories before I could make one.

That very often happens. You really don't have a story until you have two stories. It's those two stories working against each other and in connection with each other that make it happen. So I had to have those people visiting her and I had to figure out who they were, I had to make them up. They are pretty much, you know, based roughly on several women, but they're reinvented in different ways.

1980H: What I *am* against is *thinking* about plot. And it is not the way I write. . . . Plot does *not* move the story along. People pull you to the next event. Life pulls you. The story of the little girl getting murdered, I told it from five different points of view before I figured out the right way, the right voice. You see you do a lot of things you don't know how to do yet. You don't make a decision to do something so much as you . . . can't. You are totally unable. You don't know how. You can't teach yourself to do the other thing.

1983: I believe that women are in the process of changing their language. . . . Because women use language in a different way, because they are more revolutionary than men. . . . In this context the word "revolutionary" is often too easily applied to experiments in form only. The "Beats" created an experimental form, but in reality both the content and the message were completely different too. The whole thing was narcissistic and entirely masculine—and not only that, it was boyish, it was juvenile. But their form was revolutionary. . . .

The people I am thinking of are the ones who at each breakthrough in any art movement feel compelled to look into the darkest corners. Then they say, "We haven't really seen this life yet. Now I will shed light on it so that I can look at it." I believe that this is one of the most important facts in women's literature, and that's why the language is often different. Women illuminate realities that haven't been looked at for a long time—their own lives. For me revolutionary art is the way a new group of people becomes finally visible—Blacks, women, Native Americans—it *seems* that they were there all along but they were not in the limelight of their own or others' attentions.

. . . I worry about people, not art; my goal is not to create a new form within language. If some forms appear to be new, then that's a coincidence—I didn't do it on purpose, it was a necessity. The light you shed on things gives them new form. It's a sculptural and meta-phorical fact.

1981: I don't like the word "new" [as in "something new with form"] because I've lived through a time when everything was new every five minutes, and it's very easy to be new. I mean, you stand on your head and then you find that people have been standing on their heads for years, so it wasn't new anyway. What happens is that you try to tell the story and then the story is complicated. Everybody is a story-teller, but very often, even in telling, someone is going to say, "Sister, I don't know how to tell you this story; how am I going to tell it to you? I've got to drag in my dead uncle and then at the same time there are these people in Hoboken." You really are faced with a problem of how to tell the story so that the story is known. And not all stories are simple. So you try to tell certain stories, but you need the form, that's what it is. You look for the form, and until you have the form you can't tell the story. And the form, I don't know how it's gotten; I consider it received, like grace.

How to tell the story. I have a story . . . called "The Immigrant Story." Well, I knew that story for twenty-five years. I didn't know how to tell it, and I had to tell it not just in terms of the last paragraph which said his mother and father came from Poland, et cetera, but in terms of everything that came after that, which I had to put first. But I didn't understand that. It took me twenty years to figure out how to tell that story so that it could be understood for what it was. That is not "new." I just think of it as trying to tell a certain kind of story and not having the means. As far as I'm concerned, the means did not exist in my literary education or in my experience so I had to wait until I had enough writing experience to be able to tell it.

1988: If all you have is the story of a story, then you don't need to write it. You can tell it over and over again to your friends. It's only when you find the right form, or it's revealed to you, that you put it down.

1980H: [Use of time, "a whole life in a flash,"] comes from starting to write later in life. Time goes by so fast. And I think you *can* cover a lot in a short period of time. It's one of the gifts of the short story. I don't think you need transitions. You're taught about transitions, but you don't need them. People's imagination has been changed a lot by television. You sit and look at some TV shows, some of the worst, some of the cheapest, and you'll see them do technical tricks with time that Don [Barthelme], Coover, Barth, and everybody rolled into one would be terrified to do. Kids say that something they read is too hard for them, yet watching TV they are making jumps and assumptions and understanding things that none of those so-called post-modernists could *dare* to do. And yet these crappy hack-writers on TV know their audience and know that they really can pull off an awful lot of stuff.

1980H: I don't pretend to have the real Irish lingo. Whatever I say comes from what I hear. It comes from the speech of my city. But that has to go through my American-Jewish ear.

1983: English is a hospitable language; it says, "Come in, come in, bring your baggage with you, pronunciation and sentence structure, and let's see if we can't make room for all." . . . I did carry a little bit of foreign baggage with me [Russian, Yiddish], and particularly the language which the women in our family spoke—and the women out in the streets, our lives were part of the streets too—that language became part of my language. Most people have no idea that common people express themselves quite poetically, but people really have a wonderful language.

1981: I don't like to give up certain sayings. I was thinking of writing something about that, about hanging on to idioms and slangs of earlier times, not giving in to the moment, being faithful to your own seventeenth year or something.

1980H: You have to pay attention. Sometimes it's language and sometimes it's not language. Sometimes it's movement. With me it's a lot of listening. I write things down all the time. Sometimes the beginnings, sometimes it's the middle of a story that I've already written the beginning of. They really come to me in the voice of the teller. Sometimes I have a storyteller but I don't have a story.

1976: It's perfectly true I can't say *everything* about my block in the city. I never can, but I can say enough so that anybody who is anywhere out there, who lives or who understands or who guesses at it, can build up enough of the rest of it and recognize that block, maybe even in a better way than a kind of quantification of events and people and paving stones and rubble and pieces of brick. I think that is art, and I think it's been omitted from a lot of our talking. And it is *two* things: the reader and the writer, and that's the whole of the experience.

[William Gass responded by saying that he didn't want a "creative reader . . . filling in anything behind the language," and Grace Paley said:] Right, that's what's wrong with you. You don't leave him enough space to move around.

1969: It's possible to write about anything in the world, but the slightest story ought to contain the facts of money and blood in order to be interesting to adults. That is—everybody continues on this earth by courtesy of certain economic arrangements, people are rich or poor, make a living or don't have to, are useful to systems or superfluous. And blood—the way people live as families or outside families or in the creation of families, sisters, sons, fathers, the bloody ties. Trivial work ignores these two FACTS and is never comic or tragic.

1981Q: I guess I mean [by "facts of money and blood"] something very simple. It really means family, or the blood of ordinary life. . . . As for money, it's just that everybody makes a living. And that's one of the things that students forget entirely. . . . I mean it's not that they have to say what they do at their job. . . . It's just that they never go to work. The story takes place between eight in the morning and eight the next morning with nobody ever leaving the room. And those are the things that our life in this world and in this society and in every other society is really made up of. . . . It's made up of our relationships—our family relationships are of the utmost importance, and when they don't exist they're equally important—and how we live, how we make a living. The money in our lives, how we either have it or we don't. . . . If people live without working, that is very important. It's called "class," and that really is another way of saying that you really *do* write about classes—whether you know it or not.

1980H: You can't fall in love with your own work. I don't mean that you have to be humble. I mean when you have too much vanity, when you love yourself too much, it's evident in your work. And that self-love, that self-admiration, fights too much against the important factor of attention to what's outside. It's the quality of attention to what is outside, or even inside, that's flawed by vanity. Vanity is the destroyer of truth. But ego is what helps you think something is worth writing down. You have to have a certain sense of yourself.

For a long time I thought women's lives—I didn't really think *I* was shit, but I thought, "Who could be interested in this stuff, even other women?" I was very interested in it, but I didn't have enough social ego to write it down. I had to develop that to a point where I said, "I don't give a damn." Women who had thought their lives were boring found that they were interesting to one another, interesting in and to literature.

1969: What does it mean To Tell the Truth? It means—for me—to remove all lies. . . . I am, like most of you, a middle-class person of articulate origins. Like you I was considered verbal and talented and then improved upon by interested persons. These are some of the lies that have to be removed.

1. The lie of injustice to characters.
2. The lie of writing to an editor's taste, or a teacher's.
3. The lie of writing to your best friend's taste.
4. The lie of the approximate word.
5. The lie of unnecessary adjectives.
6. The lie of the brilliant sentence you love the most.

Part 3

THE CRITICS

"It is surprising that Grace Paley has not yet received any significant critical attention," goes the fatuous cliché at the start of an essay presuming to correct the situation.[1] Ironically, more than a quarter-century after that was written, the identical gambit could be fairly used.

From the start of Paley's career as a published writer, readers and reviewers have been full of praise, enthusiastic with affection, and lavish with superlatives for her stories. The first two, "Goodbye and Good Luck," and "The Contest," published in *Accent* in 1956 and 1958, attracted a great deal of attention and were passed around among readers and writers so eagerly that when *The Little Disturbances of Man* appeared there was already an audience, small but eloquent, a professional in-group, to embrace it. Grace Paley had emerged as an overnight cult figure, the proverbial writer's writer incarnate. As William Kennedy put it, in a speech honoring her as the first New York State Edith Wharton Award winner, this "means that other writers read her work and say, 'I wish I'd written that.' And this sort of thing does happen often when you read Grace Paley's fiction."[2]

The book suffered the usual fate of such work—not significantly reviewed, unsuccessful in hard cover, modestly successful in paper, out of sight and print in a matter of five years. Rollene Saal had hailed Paley in *Saturday Review* as one of the successful new faces in fiction,[3] and *The Little Disturbances of Man* was reissued with blurbs by Philip Roth, Herbert Gold, and Harvey Swados; though sales had flagged, the literary community was an unflagging claque, and in 1968 Ivan Gold exulted "On Having Grace Paley Once More among Us."[4]

The in-group grew, nurtured by the appearance of new stories in *Esquire*, *Atlantic*, *New American Review*, and elsewhere; by the frequent anthologizing of the old ones; and by reports of a novel taking shape. *Enormous Changes at the Last Minute*, then, fifteen years in the making after the publication of *The Little Disturbances of Man*, breezed into a climate of ready-made critical acclamation. There were brief raves from Lis Harris in the *New York Times Book Review*, Burton Bendow in the *Nation*, and Walter Clemons in *Newsweek;* there were more thoughtful paeans from Renee Winegarten in *Midstream*, Jonathan Baumbach in *Partisan Review*, Jerome Klinkowitz in *North American Review*, Blanche Gelfant in *Massachusetts Review*, and William Peden in *Sewanee Review*.[5]

Peden called Paley a "unique and wonderful writer" and said that "if I had the vote and if 1974 were ending tomorrow I would nominate *Enormous Changes* for whatever fiction honors this country can bestow, along with a gold medal for its author" (721–22). Gelfant, treating such writers as John Hawkes, Harry Crews, David Madden, and Tillie Olsen, frames her whole essay with a discussion of Paley. She says, in part,

> Grace Paley—marvelous, spunky, smart, funny writer—she too has had to conquer the forces of silence. . . . Her stories are charged with energy and wit, the language modern, sometimes cute, fresh, in both senses of the word, inventive and pleasurable; the spirit indominable. Indominability shapes both her characters . . . and her structure. Like Hawkes, an utterly different writer, elephant to butterfly, she too considers plot the enemy of fiction. Plots demand closure, and she is for open forms, in fiction and in life. . . . In Paley, plotlessness brings not menace, as in Hawkes, but hope and surprise, and the infinite pleasure both produce. Characters change in unexpected ways, defying the determinism seemingly inherent in time passing.
>
> . . . In a short book, Paley covers much territory in that world. She is a wonderfully economic and elliptical writer. . . . All the stories [imply change and continuation] as they show how children grow up, lovers meet, marry, separate, come together again, ex-marrieds chance upon each other, revive their past, suffer again, and go their ways, grandparents find new interests and styles in old-age condominiums. Neighborhoods change, Vietnam replaces McCarthyism as baby-carriage strolling conversation. Character changes. . . . Grace Paley . . . saves the short story form, from inanition. (1975, 141–43)

Klinkowitz's remarks occur in the context of addressing issues of women writing serious fiction that is at the same time seriously ideological. Taking Erica Jong's *Fear of Flying* as the "archetype," he places Paley at a higher level of accomplishment, on a par with Anais Nin:

> Today readers will create the popularity for aesthetically inventive fiction. Grace Paley's collection . . . works on both [the level of "social relevance" and that of "literary artistry"]. The book has a

unity—most of the characters in these stories live in the same apartment house, interacting with each other and reappearing in other stories—but there is a further range which Paley's art allows. The characters speak unique languages, and what they say is less important than how they say it.

. . . Unlike Jong, her characters are better at artistic self-reflection than real-life moralizing. As one of them admits, "My vocabulary is adequate for writing notes and keeping journals but absolutely useless for an active moral life. If I really knew this language, there would surely be in my head, as there is in Webster's or the *Dictionary of American Slang*, that unreducible verb designed to tell a person like me what to do next." (1975, 89)

Baumbach's praise included, in passing, a keen insight on critical responses: "Paley is a major writer working in what passes in our time as a minor form. Her short fiction has continually deceived media, that system of mirrors that tends to discover the very things it advertises to itself, into taking it for less than it is" (1975, 305). And Winegarten perceptively developed that point in the course of her analysis:

Grace Paley's early work was greeted with remarkable critical acclaim—particularly remarkable in that the object of the acclaim was not a novel. . . .

Certainly, here was an intelligent, individual, independent voice; a style cool on the outside, warm and sweet on the inside, like a dish of cherries jubilee. Here was a writer endowed with a zany though rather self-conscious charm. . . .

Grace Paley's voice sounded like that of a young person sorely tried by experience, a wryly sagacious, long-suffering innocent, a sort of remote urban female descendant of Huck Finn, or younger New York sister of Augie March. She shared the same casual attitude to plot as Huck's creator who, it will be remembered, gave notice that "persons attempting to find a plot . . . will be shot." This indifference to considerations of plot has become even more marked in her latest volume.

Moreover, she made no bones about female sexuality, and wrote about sex-crazed little girls or neglected, unsatisfied women, well before the advent of the bra-burning brigade, and unlike so many of its members she has revealed no compensatory interest in Lesbos. (65)

Short as it is, the Winegarten essay makes two important contributions. It touches on the issues that would occupy subsequent critics: the social-work perspective, the ethnic/regional dimension, the politics, the feminism, the humor, the achievements of voice, form, and style. And it suggests the inevitable demurrers, reactions, and attacks that were already starting to come—the reassessments and resentments that are properties of any cultural-cultic phenomenon.

For one thing, the "insider's writer's writer" label, worn with characteristic casualness by Grace Paley as she became more and more prominent as an activist, produced a kind of "Paley chic"; this, too, guaranteed a reactive backlash. Thus, in 1969, Stephanie Harrington was gushing over Paley for *Vogue* as one of "The Passionate Rebels" and Cathy Cevoli in *Mademoiselle* would group her with Helen Caldicott, Jane Alexander, and Randall Forsberg in "These Four Women Could Save Your Life." Perhaps it is no wonder that Kristin McMurran's brief piece in *People* is headlined "Even Admiring Peers Worry That Grace Paley Writes Too Little and Protests Too Much."[6]

Yet the chic persists. In 1985 the Style section of the *Washington Post* featured a profile that ran more than ninety column inches, including a seven-by-ten-inch photograph. Under the forty-two-point italic banner headline, reading "Grace Paley, Voice from the Village," the lead caricatures her in-ness: "Grace Paley hardly exists west of the Hudson or east of Fifth Avenue. Her short stories are a kind of New York chamber music in which the instruments are the voices of the city—more specifically Greenwich Village, more specifically Eleventh Street between Sixth and Seventh." Most remarkable about this piece is the absence of sensation; it was featured because it is a sensitive, perceptive portrait by David Remnick of a writer judged—for the Style readership at least—to be worthy of serious consideration.[7]

I suspect that the very existence of a chic—radical or otherwise—associated with Paley's name is at best a mixed blessing. While some reviewers will assume an iconoclastic attitude, others will feel compelled not only to assess the stories but to defuse gratuitous or spurious attacks on them. Thus Baumbach begins,

Enormous Changes at the Last Minute is not, as advertised by some reviewers, inferior to *The Little Disturbances of Man*. It is a different book by the same author (who, changed by life and time, is also a little different here), a continuation of the other, a further exploration. Where Grace Paley's first book, for all its originality and surprise, is a collection of by and large traditionally made stories, the second is made up of seeming fragments, an indication not of haste

. . . , but of a distillation of materials, a more daring openness of form. Paley's titles, *The* Little *Disturbances of Man* (emphasis mine) and Enormous *Changes at the Last Minute,* playing off the first, refer to size in an exaggerated, essentially ironic way. The author's characterization of what she's about, an occasion for the literal-minded to complain she has not given us the major (meaning large) work we've been led to expect, is a little like Cordelia's representation of her love to her father. Paley is at her best in *Enormous Changes*—her fiction at its most consequential—in the smallest space. (1975, 303)

Some reviewers, like Martha Duffy in *Time* and Isa Kapp in the *New Leader,* damned *Enormous Changes at the Last Minute* with extraliterary praise, and others, like Michele Murray in the *New Republic* and Michael Wood in *New York Review of Books,* tended to lament what the book was not.[8] Vivian Gornick assigned such exceptions to "academic" bias, countering them with these words:

> Paley when she is good is so good that she is worth ninety-nine "even" writers, and when one hears that unmistakable Paley voice one feels what can be felt only in the presence of a true writer: safe. The darkness is pushed back, solid warmth fills the gut, the universe is re-created in the company of a living intelligence; flesh and blood is on that page; it's good to be alive again. . . . In her extraordinary tone of voice and use of imagery, in the shape and rhythm of her language, is captured whole the incredible combination of shrewdness, naivete, appetite, and insight that is uniquely New York street life; and therein stands revealed in all its rich particularity the essence and emotional meaning of "idiom"; very few writers— and almost no New York writers—have ever managed it; and if that isn't an accomplishment to take one's hat off to, then I am hard put to know what the storyteller's art is all about.[9]

One may experience the blunt outlines, without nuance, of the whole anti-writer's-writer-chic backlash in a review essay by Roger Sale in the *Hudson Review.* He finds Paley's "tales . . . written within an inch of their lives. . . . The words tuned and fitted, every sentence carrying its exactly contrived weight of irony or surprise. . . . The individual tales meld and blur into each other, because Paley works too hard, I think, at the wrong things." And then Sale hastens, lamely, to cover his own tale or trail: "But she is good, no question, careful, aggressive, confident, in pain." It is only fair, however, to place Sale's remarks in context: The essay covers new books by Joseph Heller,

Richard Brautigan, David Wagoner, John Knowles, John le Carré, Anthony Burgess, Barry Malzberg, Herbert Gold, Paul Theroux, Frederick Buechner, and Thomas Savage, and it is an occasion for Sale to rise to a climactic cry of exultation when he says—having put Paley down for being "all New York . . . and mostly Jewish"—"the WASP novelist is not dead!"[10]

Fully fleshed, the backlash looks ugly indeed, as in the five-full-page screed by Carol Iannone in *Commentary*: "A Dissent on Grace Paley." Billed as comment on "fiction," this piece attacks Paley's stories by way of her politics, activism, life-style, and personal history, not excepting her person and her character. Iannone's resentment is manifold, directed first at the literary reputation: "Mrs. Paley is a writer with a large reputation built on a small output. Considered by many to be a master of the short-story form, she has to her credit just three slim volumes after nearly three decades of writing."[11] The reason for the "slimness" being the busy life of a mother, teacher, and political activist, Iannone condemns the life itself and, with a vengeance, Paley's politics. The phrase *character assassination* is then given new meaning by Iannone, who launches ad hominem attacks on the women who people Paley's stories, *their* lives and *their* behavior.

Iannone's stance might pass as new-right libertarianism, but her ideological posturing is betrayed by her sarcastic tone. "Paradoxically," she concludes, "this self-appointed champion of little people manages to make their lives even littler than they supposedly are. It is not life that is so limited, it is Mrs. Paley's imagination, an imagination formed and finally trapped by ideology and therefore entirely unable to make much of the world as it is, let alone suggest a means of transcending it" (58). But it is the critic's limitations that have been demonstrated. When politics impose limitations on appreciation or understanding of a story, the burden should properly be borne by the reader, not the writer.

It may be appropriate to observe, at this point, that Grace Paley is one of many writers for whom the FBI has kept ongoing files. As Natalie Robins's forthcoming book will document in detail, a 1969 review of Paley's case produced the following FBI comment: "Subject is not being recommended for interview in view of the fact that she is currently an English Professor at Sarah Lawrence College and does some writing."[12]

The appearance of *Later the Same Day* brought new rounds of encomia and exceptions, rejoicing and regret. In *Newsweek*, to take what seems to be an exemplary case, Laura Shapiro—whose byline had graced *Mother Jones* alongside Paley's in the early 1980s—scrupulously separates the person-as-"personality" ("A Woman of Principle" is boxed at the bottom of the page) from the person-as-writer-of-*Later the Same Day*. While the former testifies to an open integrity, the latter, the reviewer's subject proper, begins as a process of integrating separate elements: "Everything about Grace Paley is invigoratingly out of date. In an age of assembly-line fiction, her collections of stories are lovingly made by hand, appearing before the public at a pace that gives new meaning to the term 'long awaited.' While other writers forge ahead to the era of postfeminism (which looks suspiciously like the era of prefeminism), Paley keeps women and their concerns at the heart of her work. Finally and most remarkably, her politics have neither softened nor grown more accommodating in the quarter century that separates her first collection from this, her third."[13]

Anne Tyler, in the *New Republic*, praised Paley as "one of the toughest" of the tough breed of American short story writers: "She continues to speak in a voice so absolutely her own that a single line, one suspects, could be identified as hers among a hundred other lines. She is resolute, stalwart, vigorous." And Tyler closed by borrowing one of those lines, referring to Faith and her friends, to describe the stories "equally well: 'They were all . . . ideologically, spiritually, and on puritanical principle against despair.'"[14] Robert R. Harris, in the *New York Times Book Review*, said, "Miss Paley's work has an honesty and guilelessness about it, qualities made all the more luminous by an artfully intricate prose style full of surprises. Her (mostly) plotless narratives seem straightforward until a turn of phrase catches you off guard and, quietly but purposefully, breaks your heart. Irony is crucial in her stories, though she does not use it to sentimentalize or mock her characters but to delineate the offbeat ways in which they muddle through their lives, facing up to hurt without forfeiting their humanity."[15] Patricia Blake, in *Time*, echoes some of that satisfaction: "The familial tragedies are much the same [as in the earlier collections], and they are still leavened by the author's lively erotic imagination and her invincible ironies." And where Harris concludes, "This is fiction of consequence," Blake's conclusion is, "Fortunately for Paley and her readers, the little disturbances of women have a way of adding up to major work."[16]

A minor dissenting chord was struck by Adam Mars-Jones in the *Times Literary Supplement*. Vexed by the "slimness" of the Paley corpus and addressing "problems" apparently related to a perceived impracticality of its politics (defined as "going to meetings"), he says, "But the world which Grace Paley in most of these stories puts all her energy into saving is not a shared and vulnerable planet, but her private world of unified emotions and assumed politics, which she must perpetually repair without ever actually admitting that it has been exposed to damage."[17]

Clara Claiborne Park had no such problems in recognizing the world of Paley's stories; Park's problem, as she acknowledges in *Hudson Review*, is to limit her quotation of passages from the text: "For Paley writes no prose for prose's sake, still less for poetry's; the meanings that flood our heads with brainy light are human meanings, relational by their very nature, inextricably textured into our own most valuable, most threatened world. They cry out for context, for the web of fact which Paley's stories, like our lives, provide with random generosity." Paley, she concludes, "is better than anybody we've got," the stories both like a poem because "you can read [them] over and over until you know bits of them by heart" and like a novel because "you can absorb the characters into your life." They are "heirlooms of our moment, beautiful, permanently made things."[18]

With Grace Paley reviews abounding throughout the world of English-language arts and letters, the paucity of serious or sustained critical analysis up to now seems anomalous or at least curious. In 1982 Kathleen Hulley assembled a collection of pieces for a special issue of *Delta*, a semiannual review published by the Paul Valery University's *Centre d'Étude et de Recherches sur les Écrivains du Sud aux États-Unis* at Montpellier. She attributed the critical inattention to Paley's "resistant form," which includes a "resistance to criticism," and said that a number of critics who had originally agreed to contribute to the collection had subsequently withdrawn, saying, in one form or another, that Paley's writing leaves critics with nothing left to write.[19] Whatever the reasons, the eight pieces in *Delta* that can be called scholarly or critical treatments of Grace Paley's work compose nearly half of all the articles in print to date devoted to her, though there are several other studies that include Paley among multiple subjects.

Hulley's introduction suggests some ambivalence about the thrust of the collection as a whole. For example, she says, "there is hardly a piece . . . which does not refer to the problem of the father" (1982, 13), that is, reflect a feminist perspective. But she also says, "Most of the articles in this collection are specifically concerned with Paley's formal structures and strategies of resistance to traditional forms" (1982, 7). And again, "In one way or another, most of the contributions to this book will demonstrate Paley's emphasis on voice, her inscription of the subject in an *other* register and degree, and her decentering of the subject" (1982, 9). The reader, however, finds yet another unifying strain in the volume, that is, the language-at-play and play-at-language of deconstruction. Indeed, the names of Culler, de Man, Derrida, and Lacan recur frequently in frames of reference. That strain begins in Hulley's own critical observations: "This formal resistance has a metaphoric relationship to the subversive praxis on the one hand, and on the other, to the physical realities of her life: each is symptomatic of the other" (1982, 7).

One other attempt to provide an overview of Paley's work appeared in Catherine Rainwater and William J. Scheick's *Contemporary American Women Writers: Narrative Strategies*. Ronald Schleifer, in an essay called "Chaste Compactness," tries to integrate the issue of form, feminism, and voice in the language if not the ontology of deconstruction. Thus, he generalizes,

> [Paley's] stories aim . . . at reconceiving the form of storytelling by reconceiving their endings and at discovering a different authority of telling by articulating a new sense of their subject's relation to voice. At her best, Paley achieves the chaste compact spaciousness of short stories in which authority does not come from deathbed pronouncements and summings up, but can best be figured in terms of birthbeds, listening, and calling forth voices.
> . . . Both little disturbances and enormous changes are brought together at the close of her stories to create a sense of ordinary ongoingness that eschews that melodrama of closure.[20]

Unfortunately, Schleifer's ponderous critical machinery tends to obscure rather than illuminate Paley's stories.

It is Dena Mandel's special insight to make the connection between Paley's social-work perspective and her Jewishness. Mandel's essay, "Keeping Up with Faith: Grace Paley's Sturdy American Jewess," begins, "Unsuccessful daughter, twice-abandoned wife, struggling single mother, Faith Darwin embosses Grace Paley's fiction as an emblem of hope in a hopeless world. Despite hardships, both real and self-perpetuated, Faith Darwin, the protagonist of eight of Paley's short stories

. . . , has willfully chosen her crusty life and is sustained by a rosy, secular creed. Faith's averred bohemianism, her marginal existence, her commitment to urban life, her adoration of her children, her love of her family, her devotion to friends and neighbors, comprise the ever-expanding nucleus of her alternative faith."[21]

Mandel proceeds with an apparent assumption of Faith Darwin's identity with Grace Paley: "Faith Darwin, like her creator, is a product of a dual heritage and Faith's altruistic creed has been enriched by the plurality of her Jewish American upbringing" (86). Again, "Faith Darwin, like Paley herself, is the product of an urban environment and the offspring of Jewish immigrant parents, who raised their daughter upon the liberalism and Zionism of the 1920s, the inspirational socialism of the 1930s, and the dreams of American prosperity and happiness of the 1940s. Faith's sense of her Jewish American identity modulates her blithesome view of the world. Unlike her parents and grandparents, she identifies herself as an American and disavows any allegiance to the Jewish homeland" (86).

Yet Mandel is careful "to differentiate Faith from the Paley persona who narrates several [other] stories" (89). Isolating several Faith stories for examination, Mandel presents a coherent account of Paley's development of a major character (or persona):

> In *The Little Disturbances of Man* Faith is depicted primarily as a woman in search of a self-awareness which will grant her some satisfaction for the unpaid work she performs—raising children, keeping house, and caring for the men in her life. The issues of Paley's first volume revolve around what has been derogatively designated as the themes of "women's fiction." But in Paley's second collection . . . , Faith's quest for self-assertion is no longer the motivating force behind her actions. In this second collection of stories Faith displays a surer sense of herself and her values. She appears to know both what she is as well as what she might have been. She concedes her mistakes, and given her idealism, will probably have to concede a few more. But in *Enormous Changes at the Last Minute* Faith is not preoccupied with who she is, but with how to live. . . .
>
> Personal maturity precedes social and political activism in *Enormous Changes at the Last Minute*. (91)

Mandel follows readings of "Faith in a Tree," "The Long-Distance Runner," and "Friends" with remarks on "The Immigrant Story" that reaffirm that Faith Darwin has "inherited" her "optimism" from Grace

Paley. The closing paragraph underscores the association of secular, humanistic, social-work values with at least one strong strain of American-Jewish heritage:

> Like the title of Paley's first book, Faith Darwin comes to regard her personal disappointments as nothing more than the "little disturbances of man." Because this sturdy American Jewess with her staunch set of values remains adamantly optimistic, she can always envision the possibility of "enormous changes at the last minute." Faith believes in the simple, yet seldom respected, and less seldomly extolled values of motherhood, childhood, and social good. In the course of those stories in which Faith figures prominently, she graduates from rosy optimist to committed activist. If some are disturbed by the optimism and spunk of this sturdy woman, then perhaps Faith should be regarded metaphorically as the Jewess who endures because her "capacity for survival has not been overwhelmed by her susceptibility to abuse." (97)

Too often, however, it seems to me, the assignment of Grace Paley to the category "Jewish American" is done by default, in the daunting face of an "original" who defies categorizing. Nor is her place in that category universally accepted. Allen Guttmann includes her, but Mark Shechner does not, and Louis Harap gives brief, tangential acknowledgment.[22] Perhaps the best argument for the label is that of Theodore Gross, editor of *The Literature of American Jews*, who includes "The Loudest Voice" in a section called "After the War: A Creative Awakening." Having charted the passage from the anti-Semitism of the 1920s and 1930s through the "movement to urban sensibilities," Gross, writing in 1973, succinctly poses the question, "What are the essential qualities of Jews, at least in the writing of Jewish-American authors?" His answer includes criteria that many readers may readily associate with Paley's work:

> Suffering, certainly, attended by pathos, humor, and compassion; a feeling for ambiguity and irony, controlled by reason and expressed usually from an alienated point of view; a self-conscious, highly intellectualized morality that carries a burden of individual righteousness, responsibility, guilt, and social concern.
>
> Clearly these qualities are present in all literature of consequence, but, when grouped together, they serve to distinguish Jewish-American writing from that of other ethnic groups and particularly from

the mainstream of American literature. Jewish-American writing is rooted in the specific human being who is suffering or pathetic, humorous or compassionate, ambiguous or righteous or guilt-ridden—there is a strong element of naturalistic detail in this work, the smell and taste and feel of human life. . . . Jewish-American writing, with its constant return to the reason, analyzes the disparate emotional experiences on the human level before applying to them universal referents. Emotion is everywhere—emotion in excess—but it is framed by a recurrent reference to the intellect and by a quixotic sense of humor that humanizes an emotion before it can become an abstraction.

. . . Jewish-American writing . . . has been the most important literary expression in our time, American in its broadest contours, but Jewish in its silent, intimate furrows, in its buried places and hidden, half-forgotten echoes of immigration, childhood, family, and religion. American, certainly, but somewhere in its tangled roots, Jewish. Stubbornly Jewish.[23]

A caveat must be appended here, lest the reader fall prey to the dangers of confusing the Jewish American milieu of Grace Paley the writer/activist/person with the elements of a Jewish American milieu in her created world. Thus, in "Imagining Jews," Philip Roth took Christopher Lehmann-Haupt to task:

By 1974, Lehmann-Haupt could actually disapprove of Grace Paley's personal-*seeming* (and, in fact, highly stylized) short stories . . . for precisely the reasons he had given to praise such a book five years earlier—and without the slightest understanding that for a writer like Grace Paley (or Mark Twain or Henry Miller), as for an actor like Marlon Brando, creating the illusion of intimacy and spontaneity is not just a matter of letting your hair down and being yourself, but of inventing a whole new idea of what "being yourself" sounds like and looks like; "naturalness" happens not to grow on trees.

"You can see Mrs. Paley getting closer and closer to autobiography . . . leaning increasingly on a fictional self she calls Faith, and revealing more and more the sources of her imagination. In short, it now seems as if she no longer had the strength or the will to transmute life into art. . . . What has gone wrong, then? What has sapped the author of her will to turn experience into fiction—if that in fact is the trouble?" The trouble? Wrong? Well, mindlessness marches on. Still, by keeping track of the "thoughts" of a Lehmann-Haupt, one can over the years see just which hand-me-down, uncompre-hended literary dogma is at work, in a given cultural moment, mak-ing fiction accessible and "important" to basically insensate readers like himself.[24]

Rose Kamel, in "To Aggravate the Conscience: Grace Paley's Loud Voice," does more than assume the identity of Faith with Paley. Using such constructions as "Faith-Grace," "Paley-Asbury," and "Faith Asbury–Grace Paley," Kamel goes so far as to identify the narrator of "A Conversation with My Father" as "Faith" (totally unjustified in text and controverted by Paley's insistence that the father, unima-gined, is Dr. Isaac Goodside—not Mr. Gersh Darwin) and to treat the short story "Somewhere Else" as a piece of occasional reportage. Nevertheless, Kamel's reading of the stories frames a worthwhile at-tempt to classify Paley's narrative voice:

> Grace Paley's narrators . . . exhilarate us, if not with tales of gender success, then with a jaunty confidence that they have something vital to say about women, Jews, the city streets, and authority. . . .
> Paley's narrator-personae are one generation removed from East European mass migration to overcrowded American cities that began in 1881. Hers is the need to shape language of a dominant and often antagonistic WASP culture contemptuous of manual workers, mi-norities, women; to reflect the ethnic experience of her parents and to reject the East European puritanism relegating Jewish women to wife and mother roles, limiting their sexual experience. Paley's women narrators refuse to conform to both old and new world puri-tanism that excludes their gender experience. Hence Paley's lan-guage is an amalgam both ethnic and women centered: inverted syntax, Yiddishisms, New York slang echoing Italian, Irish, Black and Hispanic rhythms of speech; her images are clearly sensual and celebrate femaleness.[25]

Kamel finds "style, plot, and theme . . . seamlessly interwoven" but isolates elements of "Jewish heritage, male-female relationships, polit-ical issues, bonding to other women, and a no-nonsense authoritative voice." And "onto all the bits and pieces she has sprinkled the balm of maternal eros" (30–31). The critical strategy is to examine themes one at a time, moving freely among the stories, but its effectiveness is mit-igated by blurrings among the writer as person, the writer as revealed in the stories, and the writer's characters as *porte-paroles* for the writer.

Along the way, even the most insightful of Kamel's observations reveal that the "loud voice" of her own title is the one shouting feminism. From "the bonding-bondage encompassing single parenthood," she moves to this: "Interestingly enough the bondage inherent in one's relationship with men and children seems entirely absent when the narrator bonds with other women. Story after story attests this sisterly fidelity transcending generational boundaries." And yet, "Paley never sentimentalizes women" (38–40). Building toward her perorational reading of "Conversation" (in which she invents a feminist reply that Paley never makes in the story), Kamel says, "Secular and socialist though Grace Paley's heritage was, even progressive humanitarian ideas tend to reject the quirky, the eccentric, the 'Other' personified by a woman authoring a life story. And when Paley-Asbury willingly sustains an undying love for her father, himself an artist and storyteller opinionated about craft, she must fight harder for the freedom to write unconditionally in a loud voice she must finally use" (44–5).

The narrowing of focus exemplified by such treatment of Paley in a *Journal of Ethnic Studies* is in strong contrast with the rather playful openness of Melissa Bruce in her contribution to *Delta*. Bruce calls *Enormous Changes at the Last Minute* a "subversive song book," which contains varieties of speech acts—expressive, suppressive, explosive— in "primarily discursive narratives."[26]

Taking as her purview the broadest political parameters of Paley's work, Bruce identifies narrative strategies that effectively envelop rhetorical structures of song (and poetry). The critic thus performs a creative act herself, translating politics into the language of technique, just as the writer has transformed politics into the language of art:

> Language as written or spoken expression of inner desire (in the
> form of poem or song) is countered by language as written or spoken
> suppression of this expression of desire (in the narrative or one of its
> many forms); this act of suppression is either accepted, whether willingly [or not,] or countered in its turn either by language as written
> or spoken explosion, a generally abortive act (usually in the form of
> dirty words), or, more effectively, by another linguistic act . . . that
> of language as written or spoken subversion (in the form of political
> or narrative song), which for Paley is the most important mode of
> discourse, a new language in the process of finding its voice. (98)

Bruce's taxonomy comprises six categories: song as expression, poetry as expression, narrative as suppression, song as subversion, political song as subversion, and song narrative as subversion. While admiring the playing out of her creative scheme, I take issue with one of Bruce's examples. She calls Dennis's improvised lyric about "the ophidian garden" in "Enormous Changes at the Last Minute" *apolitical* (101), but the lyric itself is not only explicitly antifeminist but also a parody of Bruce Phillips's antifeminist song, "Rocksalt and Nails." Ironically, however, Phillips's song was best known at the time in Joan Baez's gender-appropriate, feminist version.[27]

Though much of Paley's political concerns, premises, protests, activities, and commitments have centered on issues of peace and the supremacy of community over nation (what she calls "anarchism"), the proponderant political preoccupation of her commentators has been feminist. Increasingly a curricular staple of "women's studies," Paley's work has a rich vein of material (theme, tone, character, situation, event) that may be mined to fuel feminist positions of almost any stripe.

In her contribution to *Delta*, Diane Cousineau, for instance, uses several examples from the stories to describe a generalized answer that Paley makes to the riddle/question of "The Wife of Bath's Tale": What is it that women really want/most desire? Cousineau credits the question to Freud, perhaps to introduce her own Lacanian frame of reference. She lets the Paley material speak for her, so that the result is more illuminative of regard for the writer's accomplishment than presentative of a set of values shared with the critic:

> The consciousness of difference, the recognition of the inaccessible otherness that each sex holds for the other and the division which woman finds within her own body, is the distinguishing mark of Paley's fiction. In the stories this awareness issues in a generosity of vision, an openness towards other human beings and the other within the self. The stories are thus free to delight in the unexpectedness of human response and the contradictions and inconsistencies that abound in personal relations. . . . The voice of Paley's fiction luxuriates in the irreconcilable and illogical and assumes its freedom to create its own laws and logic through play. . . .
>
> Paley's refusal to dwell within the restraints of a narrow logic is an aspect of her desire to give speech to the voice of the other which hovers at the edge of thought. . . . If woman submits to the laws and desires of men, she does it laughingly, with a sense of irony that never allows man's vision to eradicate her own. When she speaks in her own voice, she refuses to be bound by the laws of men or con-

vention. . . . Paley's humour, her lightness and sureness of tone enable her to deal with the most crucial of human matters without undue solemnity or sentimentality. Through this mastery of tone, she can suggest the implicit incompatibility of the desires of women and the presence of men at the same time that she affirms the enigmatic dance of difference at the center of being.[28]

Joyce Meier's essay in *Delta*, by contrast, makes of Paley's stories a rallying cry in the war of the sexes. Setting up gender polarities in aesthetic terms, Meier exults in the patent superiority of Paley's aesthetic and its contribution to the process of change:

> Some women writers—such as Mary Wollstonecraft and more recently, Kate Millett—reacted to this [male] aesthetic with anger, with a form of logic paradoxically masking much bitterness beneath the very persistence of argument. Others, such as Jane Austen and Virginia Woolf, responded in more subtle ways. Ostensibly assuming control, like their male contemporaries, of a naturalistic and presumably realistic universe, these women writers nonetheless subverted the Father-figure in their fiction. Within this second group, the tales of the twentieth-century American author Grace Paley must be placed. Given the context of the Father-artist aesthetic, and the various responses to it, Paley's works reverberate with possibilities. For subversively, Paley uses the culturally imposed mythos of women as child-raisers to reaffirm her own creative voice; she uses the voice of her mother-characters to undermine the "Father," and the mythos of the Father-artist as it exists in Western culture.[29]

Though thesis ridden, Meier's essay is nicely supported by its many references to the stories of the first two collections; she makes no effort to mask the stridency of her feminist critical stance. Somewhat muted is the feminist criticism of Anne Z. Mickelson's *Reaching Out: Sensitivity and Order in Recent American Fiction by Women*. As the excerpts below demonstrate, Mickelson's method is descriptive, neutral, even nonjudgmental in the sense that the bitterness and anguish of her subjects are simply reported without either the rhetoric of a cultural cynicism or the smarminess of empathic embrace. Thus, her summary of Paley's narrative treatment of women's status, in a section called "Piecemeal Liberation," eschews commentary on rhetorical *effects*, focusing instead on concise accounts of rhetorical *devices* and the themes they serve:

[Paley] illuminates a segment of experience in language which reflects a tragi-comic view of life. . . . Even the old in Paley's stories
. . . manage to summon up some jaunty courage. . . . So too with
Paley's younger women, who huddle together for psychological
warmth and comfort with other solitary women in parks and playgrounds, while their children play; the writer has only admiration for
the way these women ride the stormy currents of their lives without
being swamped.

[Paley is] concerned with a moral imperative. . . . The ways
women manage to cope . . . compel her respect. . . .

Paley's language, with its sensitivity to nuances of dialect, offers
an assortment of stories in these two books, mixing yarn, monologue, dialogue with very little comment, allegory, anecdote, the
tale of pointless garrulity, the character Faith as wife/mother/de-
serted woman, the comedy of the man/woman encounter, the de-
lusions and illusions of women about men, and the love of women
for children. Surprise, coincidence, burlesque, hyperbole, understatement, flippancy, and certain liberties with language combine to
give her stories a variegated texture which seldom fails to hold the
reader's attention. The language is always portrayed in its function
within the people's lives: as solace, as defense against what so often
threatens to be intolerable. Yet, at her best, Paley—so keen and
firmly concrete is her realism—does not let the language blur for us
the genuine stresses of her characters' lives.

. . . Grace Paley may write of age, adultery, going back to the
past, men, sex, immigrants—but her great theme is motherhood. . . .

The precise imagery of Grace Paley's language tells us that motherhood imprisons with its demands. . . . The constraints of motherhood simply belong to the various constraints of the world which
have to be encountered. A number of the author's stories, however,
imply that the women, like women everywhere, wish that some of
these constraints would be shared by men. . . .

Mothers and children are bound together by love, kinship, and
proximity. Yet mothers are women in their own right, with a cumulative courage that is impressive. Faced with so many swirling head-
waters—separation from husbands, the wanderings of their own
children, the withdrawal of parents' approval—they keep their own
often eccentric, fairly erratic, but flexible and intuitively-right
course. They try to avoid drifting by holding on to certain values,
remnants of habits which give life some order. Their will to survive
is not opposed to these values, but takes life from them. . . . In fact,
it is the communication and help between women which sustains
them. . . .

Part 3

The lives of Paley's women are limited to motherhood, desertion of husband, and a procession of transient lovers. Lovers are taken out of a preoccupation with the necessity of keeping an illusion of the centrality of marriage and family. They also testify to the human need for intimacy, love, some commitment, emotional and other kinds of support. Written mostly in the last two decades, Paley's stories bear witness to the upheaval in society caused by war, social and economic conditions, and the way men, unable to make adjustments and yearning for simplification of their lives, just leave. On a lower economic and less sophisticated level, they go back to the line of Hemingway heroes who, chafing at domesticity and responsibility, take off to ski, travel, fight, pick up a new woman, a new life. In contemporary fiction we perceive something of the same in the works of Brautigan and others, though the sporting life men desire is presented in different terms.

Beneath the banter, the jokes, the jocularity of tone, Grace Paley is concerned with the breakup of family, and the ways women try to hold the family together. In the struggle to do so, those who have hidden talents have little time to do something with them. After a while, the urge to create becomes like the scratchings of an old record—and nothing more. Granted all this, Paley's stories are conditioned by her eye on bankrupting American families and her conviction that there is some hope of solvency—in children and in some men.[30]

To read Paley's stories as polemic or bitter social commentary (frequent modes of feminist discourse) is of course to miss their humor if not their artistry. E. M. Broner, herself a comic novelist of some distinction, discusses Paley, along with Erica Jong, Linda Schor, and Rhoda Lerman, in an essay called "The Dirty Ladies: Earthy Writings of Contemporary American Women." "Writing humor is a serious business," Broner says. "Writing dirty is a cleansing one. Why do we do it, we who write earthy humor? Perhaps it is a holdover from those preadolescent years of etymological research. We would go to the dictionary as one went to the candy store, in search of goodies, for the meaning of those words that so embarrassed us." And she concludes, "Paley's character, Virginia, thinks about the world but doesn't know how to tell her young children the hard facts about right and wrong, goodness and meanness, men and women. Dirty ladies can tell about men and women—that sexual, that original battle. Paley's women look for the right language. The others insist on using language that is labeled wrong to make it right for them, for women everywhere, in bed, in the kitchen, in playgrounds, in joy and in sorrow, demand speech and words that fit their women's experiences."[31]

Broner's approach to the language of humor seems, if not more insightful, at least more accessible than the generic machinery employed by Catherine Vieilledent in "Le comique dans *Enormous Changes at the Last Minute*" in *Delta*. Warning against any pretense of generalization for a collection of stories with infinite variety in tone and voice, with wholesale shattering of form, Vieilledent nevertheless suggests that the book has an internal cohesion that gives *"l'illusion de la multiplicité du réel"*[32] (the illusion of the multiplicity of reality).

Vieilledent pursues the comic in Paley from the ridiculous to the sublime. She finds virtues in the use of stereotypes and the lack of transcendence, praises the conciseness and economy of the *"aplatissement"* (flattening) of characters' personality, and approves the reduction of *"l'être"* (being) to a pure phenomenality, to a stereotyped and caricatural identity *"vidée de toute intériorité et de tout contenu vécu"* (emptied of all interiority and any experienced content, 131). All this leads to a satiric function.

But there is much more. Beyond its picaresque aspects, in its polyphony, where different voices, *"consciences en situation"* (situational consciousnesses), speak successively in the first person and the present tense, Paley's work approaches the comic novel form of Sterne and Fielding, with one important improvement: that each voice or consciousness establishes itself as storyteller, without there being any privileged narrator or hierarchy.

Irony, parody, and self-reflexivity are all comic forms and elements Vieilledent sees in Paley, who according to Vieilledent extends her comic field to the poles of the absurd and of the tragic in order to subject both poles to ironic treatment. But Vieilledent warns us not to see Paley's *"retrait"* (withdrawal) as aloofness or ironic distancing; rather, by cutting off the mechanisms of catharsis and comic resolution, Paley is issuing a call to freedom, freedom from the restraints of imposed ways of thinking *"qui dégradent la vie"* (which devalue life, 144).

Our culture, according to Vieilledent, has assigned to art the function of representing reality. Paley's radical irony subverts that function; the *"qualité hybride"* (hybrid quality) of her comic mode creates a malaise in the reader; and by being manipulated, the reader may be brought to an ironic consciousness of his or her own manipulations. Paley thus offers a *"véritable débat sur la 'Modernité'"* (true debate on "Modernity"), rather than what is traditional or familiar—*"complicité rassurante entre l'auteur et son lecteur aux dépens des personnages"* (a reassuring complicity between author and reader at the expense of characters, 145).

In 1977, *Revue Française d'Études Américaines* devoted an entire issue to humor. A section on women's humor, subtitled "A Game of Himages," was edited by Nancy Blake. Kathleen Hulley's contribution was "Women's Humor: An Anatomy," in which she says that "at its best, feminine humor merits serious consideration" and then names Grace Paley "first and foremost among contemporary humorists."[33] Blake's "Introduction" places Paley in lofty company indeed:

> The women we have chosen to study would seem, at first glance, or even at second, to have little in common apart from their sex and nationality. Some seem genuinely feminine and are often labeled as such, like Emily Dickinson and Grace Paley. Mary McCarthy, on the other hand, has often written works which could easily be the products of a masculine pen. Other artists studied here like Gertrude Stein and Mae West have often been perceived as non-women and critics have seen their use of humor as proof of an absence of femininity.[34]

Blake's own contribution to the volume is "Grace Paley's Quiet Laughter," in which she says, "In a world where only happiness has a statutory existence and where misery is a rather shameful mistake, one needs a weapon to protect oneself against the consequences of expression. For Grace Paley, that weapon, that shield is humor." And as for Paley's character Faith, "her humor comes, not from a sure mastery of the language but from an embarrassed insecurity faced with the power of the code."[35]

One of Blake's major points is to remove the label of realism from Paley's products (Hulley, too, calls them "oddly surrealistic," 62): "Humor is like a slipping of gears in an otherwise well-running machine. All of a sudden you are somewhere else. The rug is pulled out from under your feet. It is not an escape from the law, but rather a temporary annihilation of the law through disregard for its rigors." And this point relates as well to the author's voice: "Paley's humor is carried by a disembodied voice for the author refuses to let her characters be tied down to life. At any moment the sense of the passage can dissolve and reassemble other possibilities" ("Quiet," 57).

Blanche Gelfant has also made that connection. In her *Women Writing in America: Voices in Collage*, she begins with a piece on Paley, who "may be the emblematic figure" with her "inimitable voice": "Paley's joking seems a way of searching within life's inevitabilities for a loophole— some surprise opening in the concatenation of events that seem to se- rious and acquiescent observers inexorably linked. Refusing to follow the absolute straight line of causality, which she sees as the tyranny of plot, Paley traces loops and twists and unexpected turnings that cir- cumvent doom. These curlicues seem comic, jokes that Paley plays on life."[36]

Critics who make any serious effort to deal with techniques in Grace Paley's stories inevitably confront the issue of her fictional voice. But having pointed out that it is distinctive, they are often frustrated in attempts to analyze it, to account for its distinctiveness. Even the effort of identifying what it *is not* can be frustrating.

Peden summarizes the matter thus:

> Whatever her ethnic background, Grace Paley's voice, her style, her view of the world are uniquely hers and hers alone. A Paley story could not be taken for someone else's, any more than Hemingway's or Faulkner's or Sherwood Anderson's or Joyce's could be mistaken for someone else's: this is something to be cherished in the so-often imitative and conforming world of large-circulation periodical fic- tion. . . . It's frequently a harsh and strident voice. . . . Yet there is considerable emotional range. (722)

But Peter Ackroyd says, "Everything which Grace Paley writes, in her bland and dead-pan way, depends upon the particular tone of voice which she adopts—whether it be pleading, cajoling, whining."[37]

Where the narrative voice once sounded to Winegarten "like that of a young person sorely tried by experience, a wryly sagacious, long- suffering innocent, a sort of remote urban female descendant of Huck Finn, or younger New York sister of Augie March" (65), Jane Larkin Crain found it in *Enormous Changes at the Last Minute* to have "become somewhat more cryptic than it used to be."[38] With the publication of *Later the Same Day*, Laura Shapiro recognized one key to "the voice": "Paley's distinctive voice is many voices: her favorite setting is a poly- glot New York neighborhood, and she has raised the quintessential New York pleasure of eavesdropping to a high art. The stories in *Later the Same Day*, as in her other books, gather together thoughts and con- versations and soliloquies; then, in a miracle of compression, the whole is reduced to a startling intensity" (91). Sandra Gilbert and Susan

Gubar hear the voice as echoing not only the sounds around Paley but the substance of those sounds as well: "Paley captures the everyday cadences and causes of the immigrant Jews, impoverished blacks, and displaced Irish Catholics who inhabit neighborhood playgrounds and P.T.A.s, Brooklyn's Coney Island, and Manhattan's subways."[39]

Clara Claiborne Park's analysis relates voice to several other aspects of the stories, thus bringing them together for considerable praise:

> Paley has the gift of tongues which all-refusing Zeus so seldom vouchsafes to fiction writers. It is a gift, not an acquisition. Henry James and Virginia Woolf didn't have it and didn't want it. Chaucer had it, Forster had it, Joyce had it; so did Flannery O'Connor. Where it exists it is the manifest of a consciousness that thrives on human difference. Paley's ear is unerring for the speech of children, women, and men. She knows a three-year-old doesn't talk like a five-year-old or a fresh nine-year-old like a fresh adolescent. She won't pretend that social classes don't exist in America, or that they sound the same. Her city is loud with voices—Irish, Puerto Rican, black, Jewish. of all degrees of generationality, intellectuality, and education, a continuing festival of difference. Paley's New York is as wide as the world, but it is unshakeable in the specificity of its peopled streets and parks and schools, stores and subways and play-grounds. Not since Dublin has there been such a city. Reinhabiting these stories, I realize at length the uniqueness of this gradually accreting body of work, a uniqueness much more than stylistic. For years now, while our most sophisticated literary voices have spoken for isolation, Paley, second to none in narrative sophistication, has been establishing a subject-matter of neighborhood, of affirmed community, the mingled James Joyce and Jane Jacobs of our time and place. (484)

Kathleen A. Coppula had heard the characters of *The Little Disturbances of Man* as "loud, energetic, quirky voices full of Paley's humor" and also locates the power of the stories in those voices. Although there is a "pattern of eccentricity and energy in her style," Paley seems to Coppula "nearly absent" in the early stories, limiting herself to a role of "story-hearer."[40]

Coppula charts Paley's development as a writer attempting "to unite story and form with writer and culture" (63). Though she mentions Paley's "own unique personality and social perspective" (63) and focuses on issues of "language," these matters are treated essentially as themes, rather than ways of understanding or appreciating aspects of form, style, or structure. That is, Coppula's concern is with meaning— and not meaning as it emerges from the stories but the "traditional meaning" it is the purpose of Paley's "work to renew" (72).

Coppula's essay begins by citing Marianne DeKoven's description of Paley's fiction as reconciling "the demands of avant-garde or post- modern form for structural openness and the primacy of surface with the seemingly incompatible demands of traditional realist material for orchestrated meaning and cathartic emotion" (63). But to Coppula, that makes Paley sound like a "hybrid, self-consciously balanced be- tween the demands of two audiences" (63). Accepting the possibility that Paley may indeed be bridging two opposing literary forces, Coppula urges that the "reconciliation" comes from a "less critically self-conscious motivation" (63). Hence Coppula's title: "Not for Lit- erary Reasons: The Fiction of Grace Paley." The essay itself, however, is not a direct response to DeKoven's analysis; rather it uses DeKoven as a point of departure to pursue Coppula's own valid line of argument.

For analysis of technique, then, one may look to DeKoven for a start, to various remarks in the several contributions to *Delta*, and in vain for much else in the critical commentary so far. A few early re- viewers, such as Gelfant, pointed to paths not yet taken, and Gelfant later added at least one significant matter in her comments on self- reflexivity in "A Portrait in Collage": "[Paley's] stories are clearly conscious of their purposes and processes as art; and like much contem- porary fiction, they call attention to this art by self-reference: by stories within stories that are invented before our eyes, and by comments on stories that define the nature of fiction and its relationship to truth" (1984, 18).

Baumbach's review of *Enormous Changes at the Last Minute* accounted for the analytical reticence: "Grace Paley's stories resist the intrusion of critical language about them, make it seem, no matter what, irrele- vant and excessive. The stories are hard to write about because what they translate into has little relation, less than most explication, to what they are: themselves, transformed events of the imagination. The voice of Paley's fiction—quirky, tough, wise-ass, vulnerable, bruised into wisdom by the knocks of experience—is the triumph and defining characteristic of her art" (1975, 303).[41]

Yet even while calling commentary intrusive, Baumbach sets up some potentially valuable guideposts for analysis. For example, after urging the primacy of style in Paley's work, he says this about the combination of major themes: "The stories . . . deal on the one hand with their own invention and, on the other, profoundly (and comically) with felt experience. In this sense, and in a wholly unschematic way, Paley combines what has been called the 'tradition of new fiction' in America with the abiding concerns of the old" (1975, 303).

Again, developing his perception of "improvisatory casualness" as a "disguise" of Paley's fiction, Baumbach says, "A high degree of technical sophistication is its true condition. Paley's stories rarely insist on their own achievement, deny their own audacity, her craft to cover its own traces. To say that Paley is knowing as a writer is not to imply that her work relies in any way, obvious or subtle, on formula" (1975, 304). Perhaps the most important of Baumbach's recommendations to critics is that they treat each story on its own: "Each of Paley's stories is a separate discovery, as if she begins again each time out to learn what it is to make a story" (1975, 304).

One of the twin treasures of the *Delta* collection finds Jerome Klinkowitz fashioning a bridge improbably linking the isle of metafiction ("I wander the island, inventing it," says a Robert Coover narrator)[42] with the mainland of social function. Winegarten had likened some stories in *Enormous Changes in the Last Minute* to "imaginative elaborations of notes from a social worker's experience" (66), and Klinkowitz develops that perspective. Paley's "sociological concerns," as he calls them, integrate her writing with her life, in that her treatment of the "stuff of realism" in the lives of her characters reports, implies, or demands the kinds of activism that have weighted the writer's agenda for nearly four decades.

In Paley's stories, says Klinkowitz,

> the traditionally moral role for the fictionist . . . becomes a metafictional concern. But for all her friendships and stylistic allegiances with innovators such as Donald Barthelme, Mark Mirsky, and others of this manner, Paley holds fast to several older, sociological concerns. For one, she is a woman writing; and secondly, of even more importance, she is an older woman, divorced, mothering two nearly-raised children while coping with the economic and social difficulties of life in a not-too-fancy neighborhood of New York City. Thirdly, she is a writer concerned with the viability of her occupation, particularly from the posture of the woman that she is. Hence for Grace Paley metafiction—fiction which explores the conditions of its own making—is a peculiarly social matter, filled with the stuff of realism

other metafictionists have discarded. For them, realistic conventions have been obstacles to or distractions from self-consciously artistic expression. Only Grace Paley finds them to be the materials of metafiction itself.[43]

In *Delta*'s other gem, Hilda Morley responds to the stories with an engaging immediacy: The techniques that transmute Paley's experience into the language of art are placed in a broader context of a reader's own literary experience.[44] Making some startling comparisons of Paley's rhythms with those of Dante's *Commedia,* Morley identifies "a resilient enjoyment of the unexpected" (71). Some of the stories thus become "mythic and poetic," the style "no longer an echo of the voices of the world received by the writer's meticulously receptive ear" (66)— a persistent "undercurrent of . . . poetry" (66).

In this context it is worth citing, from Paley's collection of poems, *Leaning Forward,* Jane Cooper's afterword, which begins, "Before, during, and after writing her stories, Grace Paley has always been a poet" and goes on to celebrate that "unique voice . . . discovered in sentences and paragraphs" in the early stories and in the later "extended to the whole story form." Cooper thinks more attention should be paid to the very brief tales, to which "the poems are most nearly related, having the same abrupt, often brilliant transitions and apparently candid speech."[45]

DeKoven's essay, standing virtually alone as a distinguished piece of work on Paley in a major journal and thus appropriately a standard point of reference for subsequent critics, also opens ways to richer illumination and enlightenment of the stories by delightedly identifying techniques.[46] She speaks both of Paley's "deep empathy with her characters" (222) and of her "innovative activism" (223), and she draws particular attention to a passage in "Faith in the Afternoon":

> The image of Mrs. Hegel-Shtein's tears swerving along deep tracks, formed by seventy-seven years of peculiar smiling, to hang from her ear lobes like crystals, is so striking that it appropriates most of our attention as we read, preventing us from noticing particularly the pathos which we nonetheless feel. The fate of Mrs. Hegel-Shtein's tears is exactly the fate of our own. They fall, but they are "wildly" diverted along literally comic tracks to become something other than tears, something not at all commonplace; in fact, something transcendental: they crystallize into literary epiphany. (221)

Finally, in an important essay called "Women on Women: The Looking Glass Novel," Marianna da Vinci Nichols asks not whether the fiction by women that fills the bookstalls is a significant "socio/literary phenomenon" (patently it is) but whether it is art (mostly not, she thinks). "The most skillful among them," Nichols says, including Paley, "suggest that our climate of feminism may have created new aesthetic dilemmas out of the old aesthetic formulae; the most socially conscious among them stir the suspicion that exorcising ancient images of the self may be infinitely more difficult than learning a new rhetoric."[47]

Nichols's argument builds persuasively through a wealth of examples in a broad frame of reference to Grace Paley's work, placing it at a level of the highest achievement, alongside that of Margaret Atwood, Margaret Drabble, and Doris Lessing. What is noteworthy is the way Nichols's observations of technique are made to serve the larger contexts of thematic, sociocultural significance:

> Two criteria for the novel . . . have to do, ultimately, with the division between good books and great ones. No matter how removed we may be today from traditional novels, we expect plot, subject or theme to observe context and dimension; we require the build-up of a texture—whether historical, cultural or intellectual—that situates the central characters *in* a world, accurately observed and acutely felt, even if it is not our world. We want the narrative voice to describe the breadth of its perceptions, its insights into complex beings, by themselves and in relation to others. We want perspective to shift and accumulate evidence of the secret anguish, pleasure, folly and grandeur that make characters live, while their creators, like James Joyce's god, retire under a tree to pare their fingernails. Novelists do not accomplish such feats merely by cloaking their identities. Their eyes must be trained outward on a universe larger than that of any single character . . . patiently detail[ing] the minutiae of routine events so that the inner life is mirrored and made significant by its external conditions.
>
> This difference, between mere subject or theme and a novel with texture and substance, is diagrammed for us with gentle wit by Grace Paley in "A Conversation with My Father." (11)

In Nichols's view of this story, the narrator's two versions of a story designed to satisfy her father's criteria dramatize Paley coping with the problem of texture—of what her father calls "interest"—and is quite successful. Her cast of city characters is usual: whores, junkies, workers, street children; they are unusual in that they have been domesticated, so to speak, by realism. We see them in apathetic attitudes, with bawling babies and tiresome parents. All the sex, violence and stupidity of the best-seller formula are there, not sensationalized but documented in that dry voice of inconsequence such things so often have in life. As the heroine's father says, this writer can make us hear "people sitting in trees, talking senselessly."

Still, the effectiveness of Paley's style is somewhat beside my point; her experiments with form make a more important one. Not condemned to realism in the narrow sense that Jong, [Lois] Gould and [Sue] Kaufman are, she can give free range to her inventiveness and thereby attempt to satisfy a major demand of all high fiction—to create allegorical universes that limit and delimit our real but incomprehensible one. Innovations with form and convention in novelistic worlds respond to our powerlessness over actuality, just as all artistic games extend our boundaries in life. If great novelists have anything at all in common, it may be the assumption that the world around them can be manipulated: it is raw material to be played with, adapted, re-molded, or rejected at will by an autonomous artist free to make art that is also free. Men have always had this option, for the free world has always been theirs. Women have had to claim the world and some have done so through art. (12–13)

Grace Paley has authoritatively staked her claim to the world through the hearts and minds of her readers. Her stories may be resistant to criticism, as Hulley, Baumbach, and others say, but as these pieces overcome that resistance they persuasively argue that there is much yet to be accomplished.

Notes to Part 3

1. Irving Malin, "The Verve of Grace Paley," *Genesis West 2* (Fall 1963): 73.

2. William Kennedy, "Excerpts from the Speech by William Kennedy on the Occasion of Grace Paley Receiving the First New York State Edith Wharton Award," *Climbing Fences* (commemorative journal honoring Grace Paley on her sixty-fifth birthday), ed. Sybil Claiborne, 17 (New York: War Resisters League, 14 December 1987).

3. Rollene Saal, "Four New Faces in Fiction," *Saturday Review*, 11 April 1959, 38.

4. Ivan Gold, "On Having Grace Paley Once More among Us," *Commonweal* 89 (1968): 111.

5. Lis Harris, *New York Times Book Review*, 17 March 1974, 3; Burton Bendow, *Nation*, 11 May 1974, 597; Walter Clemons, *Newsweek*, 11 March 1974, 78; Renee Winegarten, "Paley's Comet," *Midstream* 20 (December 1974): 65–67; Jonathan Baumbach, "Life-Size," *Partisan Review* 42 (1975): 303–6; Jerome Klinkowitz, "Ideology or Art: Women Novelists in the 1970s," *North American Review* 260 (Summer 1975): 88–90; Blanche Gelfant, "Chronicles and Chroniclers," *Massachusetts Review* 16 (Winter 1975): 127–43; William Peden, "The Recent American Short Story," *Sewanee Review* 81 (1974): 712–29. Further references to these and subsequent sources will be made parenthetically, by page number, in the text.

6. Stephanie Harrington, "The Passionate Rebels," *Vogue*, May 1969, 150; Cathy Cevoli, "These Four Women Could Save Your Life," *Mademoiselle*, January 1983, 104; Kristin McMurran, "Even Admiring Peers Worry That Grace Paley Writes Too Little and Protests Too Much," *People*, 26 February 1979, 22. Another price to pay for chic is *Inquirer*-level notoriety. When Harriet Shapiro mistakenly reported in *Ms.* (May 1974, 43) that Paley's "first marriage . . . ended emotionally after about three years, but the actual divorce didn't come for over twenty years," it came as a shock to Grace and Jess Paley and their children, Nora and Danny, all of whom believed they had lived together as an intact, fully functional family for more than twenty years.

7. David Remnick, "Grace Paley, Voice from the Village," *Washington Post*, Style, 14 April 1985, C1. Remnick currently sits at the Moscow desk of the Washington Post Foreign Service. Less than eight months before the Paley feature, in his "Appreciation" following the death of Truman Capote, he wrote, "Capote returned to New York [from the execution of Jack Hickock and Perry Smith in Kansas] and to nearly 20 years of celebrity. He befriended a coterie of wealthy socialites who confided in him. Grace Paley, Gloria Vanderbilt, C. Z. Guest, Lee Radziwill and a ballroom full of others." What a colossal joke for Grace to lead that cotillion (instead, of course, of "Babe," the late Mrs. William B. Paley). Remnick either already had Grace on his mind then or later decided to atone for the gaffe with his respectful tribute.

8. Martha Duffy, *Time*, 29 April 1974, 108; Isa Kapp, *New Leader*, 24 June 1974, 17–18; Michele Murray, *New Republic*, 16 March 1974, 27; Michael Wood, *New York Review of Books*, 21 March 1974, 21–22.

9. Vivian Gornick, *Village Voice*, 14 March 1974, 25, 28.

10. Roger Sale, "Fooling Around and Serious Business," *Hudson Review* 28 (Winter 1974–75): 629–30, 635.

11. Carol Iannone, "A Dissent on Grace Paley," *Commentary*, August 1985, 54.

12. Natalie Robins read this notation to me over the telephone, 5 May 1988.

13. Laura Shapiro, "Handcrafted Fictions," *Newsweek*, 15 April 1985, 91.

14. Anne Tyler, "Mothers in the City," *New Republic*, 29 April 1985, 38–39.
15. Robert R. Harris, "Pacifists with Their Dukes Up," *New York Times Book Review*, 14 April 1985, 7.
16. Patricia Blake, "Little Disturbances of Woman," *Time*, 15 April 1985, 98.
17. Adam Mars-Jones, "From Red-Diaper Baby to Mother of the Planet," *Times Literary Supplement*, 22 November 1985, 1311.
18. Clara Claiborne Park, "Faith, Grace, and Love," *Hudson Review* 38 (Autumn 1985): 482, 488.
19. Kathleen Hulley, "Introduction: Grace Paley's Resistant Form," *Delta*, no. 14 (May 1982): 9.
20. Ronald Schleifer, "Grace Paley: Chaste Compactness," in *Contemporary American Women Writers: Narrative Strategies*, ed. Catherine Rainwater and William J. Scheick, 33, 37 (Lexington: University Press of Kentucky, 1985).
21. Dena Mandel, "Keeping Up with Faith: Grace Paley's Sturdy American Jewess," *Studies in American Jewish Literature* 3 (1983): 85. The issue of Paley's Jewishness has been convincingly articulated in John Clayton, "Grace Paley and Tillie Olsen: Radical Jewish Humanists," *Response* 46 (1984): 37–52.
22. Allen Guttmann, *The Jewish Writer in America: Assimilation and the Crisis of Identity* (New York: Oxford, 1971); Mark Schechner, *After the Revolution: Studies in the Contemporary Jewish American Imagination* (Bloomington: Indiana University Press, 1987); Louis Harap, *In the Mainstream: The Jewish Presence in Twentieth-Century American Literature, 1950s–1980s* (New York: Greenwood, 1987).
23. Theodore Gross, ed., *The Literature of American Jews* (New York: Free Press, 1973), 179–80.
24. Philip Roth, "Imagining Jews," *New York Review of Books*, 3 October 1974, 22.
25. Rose Kamel, "To Aggravate the Conscience: Grace Paley's Loud Voice," *Journal of Ethnic Studies* 11 (1983): 21–22. To err in the opposite direction, by failing to see Faith in all her roles, is the flaw in the otherwise excellent Minako Baba, "Faith Darwin as Writer-Heroine: A Study of Grace Paley's Short Stories," *Studies in American Jewish Literature* 7 (1988): 40–54.
26. Melissa Bruce, "*Enormous Changes at the Last Minute:* A Subversive Song Book," *Delta*, no. 14 (May 1982): 98.
27. Asked about this, Paley said she wasn't aware of making deliberate reference to that song, but that very probably it (Baez's version) was one of those things "in the air" that often find their way into stories (interview, 28 July 1988).
28. Diane Cousineau, "The Desires of Women, the Presence of Men," *Delta*, no. 14 (May 1982): 59–65.
29. Joyce Meier, "The Subversion of the Father in the Tales of Grace Paley," *Delta*, no. 14 (May 1982): 116.

30. Anne Z. Mickelson, *Reaching Out: Sensitivity and Order in Recent American Fiction by Women* (Metuchen, N.J.: Scarecrow, 1979): 206–7, 224–25, 228–29, 233–34.

31. E. M. Broner, "The Dirty Ladies: Earthy Writings of Contemporary American Women—Paley, Jong, Schor, and Lerman," *Regionalism and the Female Imagination* 4 (Winter 1979): 34, 41.

32. Catherine Vieilledent, "Le comique dans *Enormous Changes at the Last Minute*," *Delta*, no. 14 (May 1982): 130.

33. Kathleen Hulley, "Women's Humor: An Anatomy," *Revue Francaise d'Études Américaines* 4 (November 1977): 62.

34. Nancy Blake, "Introduction: Women's Humor: a game of Him-ages," *Revue Francaise d'Études Américaines* 4 (November 1977): 42.

35. Nancy Blake, "Grace Paley's Quiet Laughter," *Revue Francaise d'Études Américaines* 4 (November 1977): 56.

36. Blanche Gelfant, *Women Writing in America: Voices in Collage* (Hanover, N.H.: University Press of New England, 1984), 18.

37. Peter Ackroyd, *Spectator*, 22 February 1975, 215.

38. Jane Larkin Crain, "'Ordinary' Lives," *Commentary*, July 1974, 92.

39. Sandra M. Gilbert and Susan Gubar, *Norton Anthology of Literature by Women: The Tradition in English* (New York: Norton, 1985), 1919.

40. Kathleen A. Coppula, "Not for Literary Reasons: The Fiction of Grace Paley," *Mid-American Review* 7 (1986): 63–64.

41. Another way of looking at—or listening to—the voice of Paley in her stories is presented by Jacqueline Taylor, "Documenting Performance Knowledge: Two Narrative Techniques in Grace Paley's Fiction," *Southern Speech Communication Journal* 53 (Fall 1987): 65–79.

42. Robert Coover, "The Magic Poker," in *Pricksongs and Descants* (New York: New American Library, 1969), 20.

43. Jerome Klinkowitz, "The Sociology of Metafiction," *Delta*, no. 14 (May 1982): 290.

44. Hilda Morley, "Some Notes on Grace Paley While Reading Dante: The Voice of Others," *Delta*, no. 14 (May 1982): 67–71.

45. Jane Cooper, Afterword to *Leaning Forward*, by Grace Paley, 87–88 (Penobscot, Maine: Granite Press, 1985). Stuart Friebert, too, reviewing *Leaning Forward* along with Laura Jensen's *Shelter* (and praising Cooper's afterword along with the poets' work), relates Paley's "fresh and sturdy forms" and the ability of her poems to "catch us off guard" to her work as "one of the finest prose writers of our time." See "Kinswomen," *Field* 34 (Spring 1986): 93–102, esp. p. 93.

46. Marianne DeKoven, "Mrs. Hegel-Shtein's Tears," *Partisan Review* 48 (1981): 217–23.

47. Marianna da Vinci Nichols, "Women on Women: The Looking Glass Novel," *Denver Quarterly* 11 (Autumn 1976): 1.

Chronology

1922	Born 11 December in the Bronx, New York, youngest child of Isaac and Manya Goodside—brother Vic (later an ophthalmologist) is sixteen, sister Jeannie (later a teacher) is fourteen.
1938	Graduates from Evander Childs High School.
1938–1944	Attends classes at Hunter College, City College, New York University, and—for practical reasons—Merchants and Bankers Business and Secretarial School.
1942	Marries Jess Paley, cameraman and filmmaker.
1942–44	Lives in U.S. Army camps.
1949	Daughter Nora born.
1951	Son Danny born.
1952	Helps close Washington Square Park to traffic.
1956	"Goodbye and Good Luck" published in *Accent*.
1959	*Little Disturbances of Man*.
1961	Helps found Greenwich Village Peace Center; receives Guggenheim Fellowship.
1965	Begins teaching at Sarah Lawrence College (has also taught at City College, and Columbia and Syracuse universities).
1966	First arrest in demonstration at Armed Forces Day parade.
1968	Guest editor, *Win*, urban arts issue; separates from Jess Paley.
1969	"Distance" selected for O. Henry Prize Stories; visits North Vietnam.
1970	Receives American Academy and Institute of Arts and Letters Award in Literature.
1971	Divorces Jess Paley.

1972   Marries Bob Nichols, writer, poet, landscape architect; spends two months in Chile during Allende government.

1973   Delegate of War Resisters League to World Peace Congress in Moscow.

1974   *Enormous Changes at the Last Minute.*

1977   Alternates with Noam Chomsky as columnist in *Seven Days.*

1978   Arrested demonstrating against nuclear bombs on White House lawn.

1980   Granddaughter Laura born; "Friends" chosen for *Best American Short Stories;* elected member of American Academy and Institute of Arts and Letters.

1980–81   Helps organize Women's Pentagon Action.

1984   "The Story Hearer" included in O. Henry Prize Stories.

1985   *Later the Same Day; Leaning Forward* (poems).

1986   "Midrash for Happiness" chosen for O. Henry Prize Stories.

1987   National Endowment for the Arts Senior Fellow; named first New York State Author and first winner of Edith Wharton Citation of Merit for Fiction Writers.

Bibliography

Primary Works

Short Story Collections

The Little Disturbances of Man. New York: Doubleday, 1959; Meridian, 1960; Viking, 1968; Penguin, 1985. (*LDM* was also published in the United Kingdom by Andre Deutsch and, in translation, in Germany by Suhrkamp Verlag of Frankfurt, in Spain by Editorial Anagrama, in France by Editions Recherches and in paperback by Rivages, and in Sweden by Trevi.)

"Goodbye and Good Luck." *Accent* 16 (1956): 158–66. Reprints: Hornblow, Leonora, and Bennett Cerf, eds. *Bennett Cerf's Take Along Treasury*. Garden City, N.Y.: Doubleday, 1963. Bellow, Saul, ed. *Great Jewish Short Stories*. New York: Dell, 1963. Ribalow, H. U., ed. *My Name Aloud*. Altshuler, Thelma, ed. *Interactions: Themes for Thoughtful Writing*. Beverly Hills, Calif.: Glencoe Press, 1972. Roberts, Edgar V., and Henry E. Jacobs, eds. *Literature: An Introduction to Reading and Writing*, 2d ed. Englewood Cliffs, N.J.: Prentice Hall, 1989.

"A Woman Young and Old." Reprint: Carter, Angela, ed. *Wayward Girls and Wicked Women*. London: Virago, 1986.

"The Pale Pink Roast."

"The Loudest Voice." Reprints: Malin, Irving, and Irwin Stark, eds. *Breakthrough: A Treasury of Contemporary American Jewish Literature*. New York: McGraw-Hill, 1964. Lewis, Jerry D., ed. *Tales of Our People: Great Stories of the Jew in America*. New York: Bernard Geis, 1969. Gross, Theodore, ed. *The Literature of American Jews*. New York: Free Press, 1973. Smith, Elliott L., and Wanda V. Smith, eds. *Access to Literature*. New York: St. Martin's, 1981. Davis, Robert Gorham, ed. *Ten Modern Masters: An Anthology of the Short Story*, 3d ed. New York: Harcourt, 1972. *Hoyaku No Sekai* (Japan), 1980. *Tales for Travelers*. Napa, Calif.: Gabrielle P. Swabey & James H. Schmidt, 1987.

"The Contest." *Accent* 18 (1958): 137–44. Reprint: Halpern, Daniel, ed. *The Art of the Tale*. New York: Viking Penguin, 1987.

"An Interest in Life." Reprints: Marcus, Steven, ed. *The World of Modern Fiction*. New York: Simon & Schuster, 1966. Smart, William, ed. *Women and Men, Men and Women*. New York: St. Martin's, 1975. Howe, Irving, ed. *Fiction as Experience*. New York: Harcourt, 1978. Cahill, Susan, ed. *Women and Fiction: Short Stories by and about Women.* New York: New American Library, 1975.

"An Irrevocable Diameter."

"Two Short Sad Stories from a Long and Happy Life."

    1. "The Used-Boy Raisers." Reprints: Hills, Penney Chapin, and L. Rust Hills, eds. *How We Live.* New York: Macmillan, 1968. Kraus, Richard, and William Wiegand, eds. *Student's Choice.* Columbus, Ohio: Merrill, 1970. Cassill, R. V., ed. *Norton Anthology of Short Fiction.* New York: Norton, 1977. Carver, Raymond, and Tom Jenks, eds. *American Short Story Masterpieces.* New York: Delacorte, 1987.

    2. "A Subject of Childhood." Reprints: Lish, Gordon, ed. *New Sounds in American Fiction.* Menlo Park, Calif.: Cummings, 1969. Hills, Penney Chapin, and L. Rust Hills, eds. *How We Live.* New York: Macmillan, 1968. Kraus, Richard, and William Wiegand, eds. *Student's Choice.* Columbus, Ohio: Merrill, 1970. Prescott, Peter, ed. *Norton Book of American Short Stories.* New York: Norton, 1988.

"In Time Which Made a Monkey of Us All." Reprint: Charyn, Jerome, ed. *The Single Voice.* New York: Collier, 1969.

"The Floating Truth." Reprint: O'Rourke, William, ed. *On the Job.* New York: Vintage, 1977.

Enormous Changes at the Last Minute. New York: Farrar Straus & Giroux, 1974. (*ECLM* was also published in the United Kingdom by Andre Deutsch and, in translation, in Germany by Suhrkamp Verlag, in Spain by Editorial Anagrama, in France by Editions Recherches, in Italy by La Tartaruga, in Norway by Pax Forlag, and in Israel by Givat Share.)

"Wants." *Atlantic,* May 1971, 67. Reprint: Howe, Irving, and Ilana Wiener Howe, eds. *Short Shorts.* Boston: Godine, 1982.

"Debts." *Atlantic,* May 1971, 66.

"Distance." *Atlantic,* December 1967, 111–15. Reprints: Abraham, William, ed. *Prize Stories 1969: The O. Henry Awards.* Garden City, N.Y.: Doubleday, 1969. Richter, David H., ed. *The Borzoi Book of Short Fiction.* New York: Knopf, 1983.

"Faith in the Afternoon." *Noble Savage* 2 (1960): 67–82. Reprint: *Bas de Casse* (Paris), no. 2 (1981): ("Faith l'apres-midi").

"Gloomy Tune." *Genesis West* 1 (1962): 53–55; reprinted in 3 (1965): 13–15.

"Living." *Genesis West* 3 (1965): 11–12.

"Come On, Ye Sons of Art." *Sarah Lawrence Journal* (Winter 1968): 49–54.

"Faith in a Tree." *New American Review* 1 (1967): 51–67. Reprint: Solotaroff, Theodore, ed. *Many Windows.* New York: Harper & Row, 1982.

"Samuel." *Esquire,* 1968, 88 (under "Two Stories from the Five Boroughs"). Reprint: Current-Garcia, Eugene, and Walton R. Patrick, eds. *American Short Stories,* 4th ed. Glenview, Ill.: Scott, Foresman, 1981.

"The Burdened Man." *Esquire,* 1968, 89, 151–52 (under "Two Stories from the Five Boroughs").

"Enormous Changes at the Last Minute." *Atlantic,* May 1972, 70–75. Reprints: Greenberg, Martin H., and Charles G. Waugh, eds. *Arbor House Celebrity Book of Greatest Stories Ever Told.* New York: Arbor House, 1983. Gilbert, Sandra M., and Susan Gubar, eds. *Norton Anthology of Literature by Women: The Tradition in English.* New York: Norton, 1985. Howard, Daniel F., and John Ribar, eds. *The Modern Tradition.* Boston: Little, Brown, 1979.

"Politics." *Win* 4 (1968): 32–33.

"Northeast Playground." *Ararat* 8 (1967): 25–26.

"The Little Girl." *Paris Review* 14 (1974): 194–200.

"A Conversation with My Father." *New American Review* 13 (1972): 146–51. Reprints: Sullivan, Nancy, ed. *Treasury of American Short Stories.* Garden City, N.Y.: Doubleday, 1981. Howard, Daniel F., and John Ribar, eds. *The Modern Tradition.* Boston: Little, Brown, 1979. Charters, Ann, ed. *The Story and Its Writer.* New York: St. Martin's, 1987. Bergman, David, Joseph de Roche, and Daniel M. Epstein, eds. *The Story.* New York: Macmillan, 1988. Bohner, Charles H., ed. *Classic Short Fiction.* Englewood Cliffs, N.J.: Prentice Hall, 1980. Berg, Stephen, ed. *In Praise of What Persists.* New York: Harper & Row, 1983. Taube, Eva, ed. *Seasons of Life.* Toronto: McClelland & Stewart, 1986.

"The Immigrant Story." *Fiction* 1, no. 3 (1972): 10.

"The Long Distance Runner." *Esquire,* 1974, 102–4, 108, 182. Reprints: Rotter, Pat, ed. *Bitches and Sad Ladies.* New York: Harper's Magazine Press, 1975. Faderman, Lillian, ed. *Speaking for Ourselves.* Glenview, Ill.: Scott, Foresman, 1975. Litz, A. W., ed. *Major American Short Stories.* New York: Oxford, 1975. Lish, Gordon, ed. *All Our Secrets Are the Same.* New York: Norton, 1976. Hall, James B., ed. *The Realm of Fiction.* New York: McGraw-Hill, 1977. Mazow, Julia Wolf, ed. *The Woman Who Lost Her Names.* New York: Harper & Row, 1980. Scholes, Robert, ed. *Elements of Fiction.* New York: Oxford, 1981. *Great Esquire Fiction: The Finest Stories from the First Fifty Years.* New York: Viking, 1983.

Later the Same Day. New York: Farrar Straus & Giroux, 1985; Penguin, 1986. (*LSD* was also published in the United Kingdom by Virago Books and, in translation, in Spain by Editorial Anagrama, in France by Rivages, in Germany by Suhrkamp Verlag, in Norway by Pax Forlag, in the Netherlands by Contact Publishers of Amsterdam, and in Brazil by Paz e Terra.)

"Love." *New Yorker,* 8 October 1979, 37.

"Dreamer in a Dead Language." *American Review* 26 (1977): 391–411 (called "Dreamers . . ."). Reprint: Sennett, Dorothy, ed. *Full Measure: Modern Short Stories about Aging.* St. Paul, Minn.: Graywolf Press, 1988.

"In the Garden." *Fiction* 4, no. 2 (1976): 8–9.

"Somewhere Else." *New Yorker,* 23 October 1978, 34–37.

"Lavinia: An Old Story." *Delta* 14 (1982): 41–45 (called "Lavinia"); *Harbinger* 2 (1983): 39–41 (called "Lavinia").

"Friends." *New Yorker,* 18 June 1979, 32–38. Reprints: Elkin, Stanley, ed. *Best American Short Stories 1980.* Boston: Houghton Mifflin, 1980. Stone, Wilfred, Nancy Huddleston Packer, and Robert Hoopes, eds. *The Short Story,* 2d, ed. New York: McGraw-Hill, 1983. *Nuovi Argomenti* (Rome), no. 22 (July-September 1987): 21–29 ("Amiche," trans. Giovanni Zucconi).

"At That Time, or The History of a Joke." *Iowa Review* 12 (1981): 266–67.

"Anxiety." *New England Review/Bread Loaf Quarterly* 4 (1983): 605–9.

"In This Country, but in Another Language, My Aunt Refuses to Marry the Man Everyone Wants Her To." *Threepenny Review* (1983): 3 (called "In This Country but in Another Language My Aunt Refuses to Marry the Men Everybody Wants Her To").

"Mother." *Ms.,* May 1980, 100 (called "My Mother" with the subhead "The Times She Stood in the Doorway . . ."). Reprint: Shapard, Robert, and James Thomas, eds. *Sudden Fiction.* Salt Lake City: Gibbs M. Smith, 1986.

"Ruthy and Edie." *Heresies* 3 (1980): 8–9 (called "Edie and Ruthy"). Reprint: *New Statesman,* 1 November 1985, 28–30.

"A Man Told Me the Story of His Life." *Poets and Writers.* New York: Poets & Writers, 1980 (also called "The Roseland Book," published privately as a program for the tenth birthday party of Poets and Writers). Reprints: Burroway, Janet, ed. *Writing Fiction.* Boston: Little, Brown, 1986. *Harper's and Queen* (London), December 1985, 72.

"The Story Hearer." *Mother Jones,* December 1982, 32–36. Reprint: Abraham, William, ed. *Prize Stories 1984: The O. Henry Awards.* Garden City, N.Y.: Doubleday, 1984.

"This Is a Story about My Friend George, the Toy Inventor." *Transatlantic* 58/59 (1977): 5–6.

"Zagrowsky Tells." *Mother Jones,* May 1985, 34–42 (called "Telling"). Reprint: *Short Story International* 60 (International Cultural Exchange, 1986–87).

"The Expensive Moment." *Mother Jones,* December 1983, 13–17 (called "Unknown Parts of Far, Imaginable Places").

"Listening."

Uncollected Stories, Miscellaneous Writings

"Report from the DRV." *Win* 5 (15 September 1969): 4–10.

"Some Notes on Teaching: Probably Spoken." In *Writers as Teachers/Teachers as Writers,* ed. Jonathan Baumbach, 202–6. New York: Holt, Rinehart & Winston, 1970.

"I Guess It Must Have Been Someone Else." *Win* 7 (15 May 1971): 30–33.

"The Man in the Sky Is a Killer." *New York Times,* 23 March 1972, 43.

"Introduction" to *Peacemeal* (cookbook, Greenwich Village Peace Center). New York: 1973.

"Chilean Diary" (with Robert Nichols), *Win* 9 (17 May–7 June 1973): 6–8, 10–12, 9–10, 12–13, respectively.

"Conversations in Moscow." *Win* 10 (23 May 1974): 7–12.

"Peace Movement Meets with PRG in Paris." *Win* 11 (24 April 1975): 4–5.

"Other People's Children." *Ms.,* September 1975, 68–70, 95–96 (follow-up response to letter, *Ms.,* February 1976, 10).

"Mom." *Esquire,* December 1975, 85–86. Reprints: *Feminist Studies* 4 (1978): 166–69 (under original title "Other Mothers" in issue subtitled "Toward a Feminist Theory of Motherhood"). *New Directions for Women* 14 (May/June 1985).

"Preface: Notes in Which Answers Are Questioned." *What Did You Learn in School Today?* (*1977 Peace Calendar*). New York: War Resisters League, 1976.

"Demystified Zone" (under column head "Conversations"). *Seven Days* 1 (28 February 1977): 15. Reprint: *1989 Peace Calendar.* New York: War Resisters League, 1988.

"The Lion and the Ox" ("Conversations"). *Seven Days* 1 (26 March 1977): 36.

"In a Vermont Jury Room" ("Conversations"). *Seven Days* 1 (9 May 1977): 51. Reprint: *1989 Peace Calendar.* New York: War Resisters League, 1988.

"Living on Karen Silkwood Drive" ("Conversations"). *Seven Days* 1 (6 June 1977): 11–12. Reprint: *1989 Peace Calendar* (called "Conversation: Some History"). New York: War Resisters League, 1988.

"Essay on Dogs." *Win* 16 (17 January 1980): 21.

"Cop Tales." *Seven Days* 4 (April 1980): 24. Reprint: *1989 Peace Calendar.* New York: War Resisters League, 1988.

"Feelings in the Presence of the Sight and Sound of the Bread and Puppet Theater." *Where You Put Fire to the World* (*1981 Peace Calendar*). New York: War Resisters League, 1980.

"Child-Molesting—Why Parents Won't Listen" (review of *The Best Kept Secret* by Florence Rush). *Ms.,* January 1981, 39–40.

"The Seneca Stories: Tales from the Women's Peace Encampment." *Ms.,* December 1983, 54–62, 108.

Preface to *The Shalom Seders: Three Haggadahs.* New York: Adama Books, 1984.

Leaning Forward (poems). Penobscot, Maine: Granite Press, 1985.

"Introduction" to *How Shall We Live Together?* (*1985 Peace Calendar*). New York: War Resisters League, 1984.

"Introduction: Thinking about Barbara Deming." In *Prisons That Could Not Hold,* by Barbara Deming. San Francisco: Spinsters Ink, 1985.

"Of Poets and Women and the World." *TriQuarterly* 65 (1986): 247–53.

"Midrash on Happiness." *TriQuarterly* 65 (1986): 151–53. Reprints: Abraham,

William, ed. *Prize Stories 1987: The O. Henry Awards.* Garden City, N.Y.:
Doubleday, 1987. Claiborne, Sybil, ed. *Climbing Fences* (commemorative
journal honoring Grace Paley on her sixty-fifth birthday). New York: War
Resisters League, 14 December 1987. *1989 Peace Calendar.* New York:
War Resisters League, 1988.
Introduction to *Coat upon a Stick,* by Norman Fruchter. Philadelphia: Jewish
Publication Society, 1987.
365 Reasons Not to Have another War (1989 Peace Calendar with paintings by Vera
B. Williams). Paley's text includes nineteen poems, many of them pub-
lished here for the first time, and eleven prose pieces. Of the latter, five
are reprints, the four previously noted plus a passage excerpted from
"The Long-Distance Runner," here called "Devastation." Among the
original pieces, two ("Across the River," and "POW") are derived from
earlier material, and another is a new addition to the "Conversations"
series ("My husband's mother . . ."). "Life in the Country/A City Friend
Asks 'Is It Boring?'" is a new personal essay, and the two other pieces,
"Answers I" and "Answers II," are in a new form for brief storytelling.
New York: War Resisters League, 1988.
Introduction to *Soulstorm* by Clarice Lispector, translated by Alexis Levitin.
New York: New Directions, 1989.

Secondary Works

Interviews

Berg, Beatrice. "Grace Paley: Writer's Writer." *Washington Post,* 29 December
1968, D2.
Charters, Ann. "Grace Paley: A Conversation with Ann Charters." In *The Story
and Its Writer,* 2d ed., by Ann Charters, 1313–17. New York: St. Martin's,
1987.
Doyle, Charlotte L. "Honesty and the Creative Process." *Journal of Aesthetic
Education* 7 (July 1973): 43–50.
Friedler, Maya. "An Interview with Grace Paley." *Story Quarterly* 13 (1981):
32–39.
Gardner, Frieda. "The Habit of Digression: An Interview with Grace Paley."
Wordsworth (literary supplement of the University of Minnesota *Daily*), 28
October 1979, 13.
Gelfant, Blanche. "Grace Paley: Fragments for a Portrait in Collage." In *Women
Writing in America,* by Blanche Gelfant, 11–29. Hanover, N.H.: University
Press of New England, 1984.

Hulley, Kathleen. "Interview with Grace Paley." *Delta*, no. 14 (May 1982): 19–40.

Lidoff, Joan. "Clearing Her Throat: An Interview with Grace Paley." *Shenandoah* 32 (1981): 3–26.

Marchant, Peter, and Mary Elsie Robertson. "A Conversation with Grace Paley" (Peter Marchant and Earl Ingersoll, eds.). *Massachusetts Review* 26 (Winter 1985): 606–14.

Mehren, Elizabeth. "For Paley, It's Simply Not All That Simple." *Los Angeles Times*, 22 May 1985, sec. 6, pp. 1, 6.

Michaels, Leonard. "Conversation with Grace Paley." *Threepenny Review*, no. 3 (Fall 1980): 4–6.

Midwood, Barton. "Short Visits with Five Writers and One Friend." *Esquire*, November 1970, 150–52. (The other writers are Russell Edson, James Purdy, I. B. Singer, and Frank Conroy.)

Perry, Ruth. "Grace Paley." In *Women Writers Talking*, ed. Janet Todd, 35–56. New York: Holmes & Meier, 1983.

Poli, Sara. "Grace Paley." *Vinduet* 37 (1983): 42–47.

Pool, Gail, and Shirley Roses. "An Interview with Grace Paley." *New Boston Review* 2 (Fall 1976): 3–4, 6.

Remnick, David. "Grace Paley, Voice from the Village." *Washington Post*, Style, 14 April 1985, C1, 14.

Satz, Martha. "Looking at Disparities: An Interview with Grace Paley." *Southwest Review* 72 (1987): 478–89.

Shapiro, Harriet. "Grace Paley: 'Art Is on the Side of the Underdog,'" *Ms.*, May 1974, 43–45.

Shapiro, Laura. "A Woman of Principle." *Newsweek*, 15 April 1985, 91.

Silesky, Barry, Robin Hemley, and Sharon Solwitz. "Grace Paley: A Conversation." *Another Chicago Magazine*, no. 14 (March 1985): 100–14.

Slawson, Judy. "Grace Paley: Changing Subject Matter with a Changing Passionate and Committed Life." *Villager*, 18 May 1978, 13.

Smith, Wendy. "PW Interviews: Grace Paley." *Publishers Weekly*, 5 April 1985, 71–72.

Stevens, Andrea. *New York Times Book Review*, 14 April 1985, 7.

Taylor, Jacqueline. "Grace Paley on Storytelling and Story Hearing." *Literature in Performance* 7 (April 1987): 46–58.

Symposia

Barthelme, Donald, William Gass, Grace Paley, and Walker Percy. "A Symposium on Fiction." *Shenandoah* 27 (1976): 3–31.

Baranczak, Stanislaw, Terrence Des Pres, Gloria Emerson, Leslie Epstein, Carolyn Forché, Michael S. Harper, Ward Just, Grace Paley, Mary Lee Settle, Robert Stone, Derek Walcott, and C. K. Williams. "The Writer in Our World." *TriQuarterly* 65 (Winter 1986): entire issue.

Selected Reviews

Little Disturbances of Man

Healey, Robert C. *New York Herald Tribune Book Review*, 26 April 1959, 8.

Hicks, Granville. *Saturday Review*, 27 April 1968, 29–30.

Hollinghurst, Alan. *New Statesman*, 14 March 1980, 402–3.

McManus, Patricia. *New York Times Book Review*, 19 April 1959, 28–29.

Enormous Changes at the Last Minute

Ackroyd, Peter. *Spectator,* 22 February 1975, 215.

Baumbach, Jonathan. *Partisan Review* 42 (1975): 303–6.

Bendow, Burton. *Nation,* 11 May 1974, 597–98.

Clemons, Walter. *Newsweek,* 11 March 1974, 78.

Crain, Jane Larkin. *Commentary,* July 1974, 92–93.

Duffy, Martha. *Time,* 29 April 1974, 108.

Gornick, Vivian. *Village Voice,* 14 March 1974, 25, 28.

Harris, Lis. *New York Times Book Review,* 17 March 1974, 3.

Kapp, Isa. *New Leader,* 24 June 1974, 17–18.

Murray, Michele. *New Republic,* 16 March 1974, 27.

Novak, William. *America,* 8 June 1974, 459–60.

Winegarten, Renee. *Midstream* 20 (December 1974): 65–67.

Wood, Michael. *New York Review of Books,* 21 March 1974, 21–22.

Later the Same Day

Blake, Patricia. *Time,* 15 April 1985, 98.

Broner, E. M. *The Women's Review of Books,* September 1985, 7–8.

DeKoven, Marianne. *Partisan Review* 53 (1986): 315–18.

Harris, Robert R. *New York Times Book Review,* 14 April 1985, 7.

Mars–Jones, Adam. *Times Literary Supplement,* 22 November 1985, 1311.

Park, Clara Claiborne. *Hudson Review* 38 (1985): 481–88.

Rushdie, Salman. *Guardian* (London), 14 November 1985, 20.

Shapiro, Laura. *Newsweek,* 15 April 1985, 91.

Tyler, Anne. *New Republic,* 29 April 1985, 38–39.

General

Davidon, Ann Morrissett. "Women Writing." *Nation,* 10 September 1973, 213–14.

Gelfant, Blanche. "Chronicles and Chroniclers." *Massachusetts Review* 16 (Winter 1975): 127–43.

Klinkowitz, Jerome. "Ideology or Art: Women Novelists in the 1970s." *North American Review* 260 (Summer 1975): 88–90.

Peden, William. "The Recent American Short Story." *Sewanee Review* 82 (1974): 712–29.

Saal, Rollene. "Four New Faces in Fiction." *Saturday Review*, 11 April 1959, 38. (The other "faces" are Philip Alston Stone, Joan Vatsek, and Philip Roth.)

Sale, Roger. "Fooling Around and Serious Business." *Hudson Review* 27 (Winter 1974–75): 623–35.

Swados, Harvey. "Good and Short." *Hudson Review* 12 (1959–60): 454–59.

Criticism

Baba, Minako. "Faith Darwin as Writer-Heroine: A Study of Grace Paley's Short Stories." *Studies in American Jewish Literature* 7 (Spring 1988): 40–54.

Barthelme, Donald. "As Grace Paley Faces Jail with 3 Other Writers." *New York Times*, 2 February 1979, A25.

Barthelme, Frederick. "On Being Wrong: Convicted Minimalist Spills Bean." *New York Times Book Review* (3 April 1988): 1, 25–26.

Blake, Harry. "Grace Paley, A Plea for English Writing." *Delta*, no. 14 (May 1982): 73–80.

Blake, Nancy. "Grace Paley's Quiet Laughter." *Revue Francaise d'Études Américaines* 4 (November 1977): 55–58.

———. "Introduction: Women's Humor: a Game of Him-ages." *Revue Francaise d'Études Américaines* 4 (November 1977): 39–42.

Broner, E. M. "The Dirty Ladies: Earthy Writings of Contemporary American Women—Paley, Jong, Schor, and Lerman." *Regionalism and the Female Imagination* 4 (Winter 1979): 34–43.

Bruce, Melissa. "*Enormous Changes at the Last Minute:* A Subversive Song Book." *Delta*, no. 14 (May 1982): 97–113.

Byatt, A. S. Introduction to *Enormous Changes at the Last Minute* by Grace Paley. London: Virago (Modern Classics), 1979.

———. Introduction to *Little Disturbances of Man* by Grace Paley. London: Virago (Modern Classics), 1980.

Cevoli, Cathy. "These Four Women Could Save Your Life," *Mademoiselle* 89 (January 1983): 104–7. (The other three are Randall Forsberg, Jane Alexander, and Dr. Helen Caldicott.)

Claiborne, Sybil. Tribute to Grace Paley in *Climbing Fences* (commemorative journal honoring Grace Paley on her sixty-fifth birthday), ed. Sybil Claiborne, 3–15. New York: War Resisters League, 14 December 1987.

Clayton, John. "Grace Paley and Tillie Olsen: Radical Jewish Humanists." *Response* 46 (1984): 37–52.

Cooper, Jane. "Afterword to *Leaning Forward*, by Grace Paley, 87–90. Penobscot, Maine: Granite Press, 1985.

Coppula, Kathleen A. "Not for Literary Reasons: The Fiction of Grace Paley." *Mid-American Review* 7 (1986): 63–72.

Cousineau, Diane. "The Desires of Women, the Presence of Men." *Delta*, no. 14 (May 1982): 55–65.

Crawford, John W. "Archetypal Patterns in Grace Paley's 'Runner.'" *Notes on Contemporary Literature* 11, no. 4 (1981): 10–12.

Darnton, Nina. "Taking Risks: The Writer as Effective Teacher." *New York Times*, 13 April 1986, sec. 12 ("Education Life"), 65–67.

DeKoven, Marianne. "Mrs. Hegel–Shtein's Tears." *Partisan Review* 48 (1981): 217–23.

Friebert, Stuart. "Kinswomen." *Field* 34 (Spring 1986): 93–102.

Gelfant, Blanche. "Grace Paley: Fragments for a Portrait in Collage." *New England Review* 3 (1981): 276–93. Reprinted in her *Women Writing in America: Voices in Collage*, 11–29. Hanover, N.H.: University Press of New England, 1984.

Gold, Ivan. "On Having Grace Paley Once More among Us." *Commonweal* 89 (1968): 111–12.

Gross, Theodore. *The Literature of American Jews*. New York: Free Press, 1973.

Guttmann, Allen. *The Jewish Writer in America: Assimilation and the Crisis of Identity*. New York: Oxford, 1971.

Harap, Louis. *In the Mainstream: The Jewish Presence in Twentieth-Century American Literature, 1950s–1980s*. New York: Greenwood, 1987.

Harrington, Stephanie. "The Passionate Rebels," *Vogue*, May 1969, 150–51, 248.

Hulley, Kathleen. "Introduction: Grace Paley's Resistant Form." *Delta*, no. 14 (May 1982): 3–18.

———. "Women's Humor: An Anatomy." *Revue Francaise d'Études Américaines* 4 (November 1977): 59–63.

Humy, Nicholas Peter. "A Different Responsibility: Form and Technique in Grace Paley's 'Conversation with my Father.'" *Delta*, no. 14 (May 1982): 87–95.

Iannone, Carol. "A Dissent on Grace Paley." *Commentary*, August 1985, 54–8.

Isaacs, Neil D. "Fiction Night at the Comedy Club." *New England Review/Bread Loaf Quarterly* 11 (Spring 1989): 305–19.

Kamel, Rose. "To Aggravate the Conscience: Grace Paley's Loud Voice." *Journal of Ethnic Studies* 11 (1983): 29–49.

Kennedy, William. "Excerpts from the Speech by William Kennedy on the Occasion of Grace Paley Receiving the First New York State Edith Wharton Award." In *Climbing Fences* (commemorative journal honoring Grace Paley on her sixty-fifth birthday), ed. Sybil Claiborne, 17–19. New York: War Resisters League, 14 December 1987.

Klinkowitz, Jerome. "Grace Paley: The Sociology of Metafiction," *Delta*, no. 14 (May 1982): 81–85.

McMurran, Kristin. "Even Admiring Peers Worry That Grace Paley Writes Too Little and Protests Too Much." *People*, 26 February 1979, 22–23.

Malin, Irving. "The Verve of Grace Paley." *Genesis West* 2 (Fall 1963): 73–78.

———— and Irwin Stark. *Breakthrough: A Treasury of Contemporary American-Jewish Literature.* New York: McGraw-Hill, 1964.

Mandel, Dena. "Keeping Up with Faith: Grace Paley's Sturdy American Jewess." *Studies in American Jewish Literature* 3 (1983): 85–98.

Meier, Joyce. "The Subversion of the Father in the Tales of Grace Paley." *Delta*, no. 14 (May 1982): 115–27.

Mickelson, Anne Z. *Reaching Out: Sensitivity and Order in Recent American Fiction by Women.* Metuchen, N.J.: Scarecrow, 1979.

Morley, Hilda. "Some Notes on Grace Paley While Reading Dante: The Voice of Others." *Delta*, no. 14 (May 1982): 67–71.

Neff, D. S. "'Extraordinary Means': Healers and Healing in 'A Conversation with My Father.'" *Literature and Medicine* 2 (1983): 118–24.

Nichols, Marianna da Vinci. "Women on Women: The Looking Glass Novel." *Denver Quarterly* 11 (Autumn 1976): 1–13.

Remnick, David. "Grace Paley, Voice from the Village." *Washington Post*, Style, 14 April 1985, C1, 14.

Robins, Natalie. "The Defiling of Writers." *Nation*, 10 October 1987, 367–72.

Roth, Philip. "Imagining Jews." *New York Review of Books*, 3 October 1974, 21–22.

————. "Writing American Fiction." *Commentary* 31 (March 1961): 223–33. Reprinted in *The Sense of The Sixties*, by Edward Quinn and Paul Dolan, 445–61. New York: Free Press, 1968.

Schleifer, Ronald. "Grace Paley: Chaste Compactness." In *Contemporary American Women Writers: Narrative Strategies*, ed. Catherine Rainwater and William J. Scheick, 30–49. Lexington: University Press of Kentucky, 1985.

Shinn, Thelma. *Radiant Daughters: Fictional American Women.* New York: Greenwood, 1986.

Sorkin, Adam. "'What Are We, Animals?': Grace Paley's World of Talk and Laughter." *Studies in American Jewish Literature* 2 (1982): 144–54.

Taylor, Jacqueline. "Documenting Performance Knowledge: Two Narrative Techniques in Grace Paley's Fiction." *Southern Speech Communication Journal* 53 (Fall 1987): 65–79.

————. "Paley on Screen: Enormous Changes." *Literature in Performance* 7 (April 1987): 81–83.

Vieilledent, Catherine. "Le comique dans *Enormous Changes at the Last Minute*." *Delta*, no. 14 (May 1982): 129–45.

Wisse, Ruth. *The Schlemiel as Modern Hero.* Chicago: University of Chicago, 1971.

Index

196

The Author

Neil D. Isaacs is professor of English at the University of Maryland, College Park, and a clinical social worker. His books include *Structural Principles in Old English Poetry, Fiction into Film: A Walk in the Spring Rain, Eudora Welty, All the Moves: A History of College Basketball, Jock Culture, U.S.A.*, two collections of essays on J. R. R. Tolkien (edited with Rose Zimbardo), and *The Sporting Spirit: Athletes in Literature and Life* (edited with Jack Higgs). Isaacs's essays, short stories, poems, reviews, and newspaper columns have appeared in scores of publications on five continents.

The Editor

Gordon Weaver earned his Ph.D. in English and creative writing at the University of Denver in 1970, and is currently professor of English at Oklahoma State University. He is the author of several novels, including *Count a Lonely Cadence, Give Him a Stone, Circling Byzantium*, and most recently *The Eight Corners of the World*. His short stories are collected in *The Entombed Man of Thule, Such Waltzing Was Not Easy, Getting Serious, Morality Play*, and *A World Quite Round*. Recognition of his fiction includes the St. Lawrence Award for Fiction (1973), two National Endowment for the Arts fellowships (1974 and 1989), and the O. Henry First Prize (1979). He edited *The American Short Story, 1945–1980: A Critical History* and is currently editor of the *Cimarron Review*. Married and the father of three daughters, he lives in Stillwater, Oklahoma.